WHAT YOUR COLLEAGUES ARE SAYING . . .

"Students and teachers need accessible ways to talk about and use grammar. In Gretchen's trademark style, she gets these ever-important conversations started and keeps them going. This book is a keeper."

—JEFF ANDERSON, author of
Revision Decisions and *Everyday Editing*

"Gretchen Bernabei is a force as a teacher and an important mentor for using grammar instruction to help students become better writers. Gretchen has always bridged teaching the mechanics of language with authentic reading and writing because, as she says in this practical, straightforward book, 'We have time only for the best authors, the best poetry, the best ways of living, the best ways to learn the most valuable things.' . . . This is a smart book to add to your collection of professional resources."

—PENNY KITTLE, author of
Write Beside Them and *Book Love*

"*Grammar Keepers* is designed for the master teacher who wants to take students to the limits of grammatical knowledge. Thanks to the variety of excellent materials that take the reader and student beyond the simple 'labels' of grammar, you'll be fully equipped to help students make the subtle power of detail possible."

—HARRY NODEN,
author of *Image Grammar*

"Gretchen Bernabei presents teachers with a buffet of concrete strategies to help student tackle grammar within the context of their own writing. *Grammar Keepers* provides teachers and their students with easy-to-follow, step-by-step recipes ranging from the simple concepts of grammar to more advanced structural understanding of writer's craft."

—TIM MARTINDELL, EdD, president,
Texas Council of Teachers of English Language Arts

GRAMMAR KEEPERS

For Sue

My first instructor when we were small,
my first ears ever since.

GRAMMAR KEEPERS

Lessons That Tackle Students' Most Persistent Problems **Once and for All**
Grades 4–12

GRETCHEN BERNABEI

www.resources.corwin.com/bernabeigrammar

CORWIN LITERACY

FOR INFORMATION:

Corwin

A SAGE Company

2455 Teller Road

Thousand Oaks, California 91320

(800) 233-9936

www.corwin.com

SAGE Publications Ltd.

1 Oliver's Yard

55 City Road

London EC1Y 1SP

United Kingdom

SAGE Publications India Pvt. Ltd.

B 1/I 1 Mohan Cooperative Industrial Area

Mathura Road, New Delhi 110 044

India

SAGE Publications Asia-Pacific Pte. Ltd.

3 Church Street

#10-04 Samsung Hub

Singapore 049483

Publisher: Lisa Luedeke

Editorial Development Manager: Julie Nemer

Editorial Assistant: Emeli Warren

Production Editor: Melanie Birdsall

Copy Editor: Patrice Sutton

Typesetter: C&M Digitals (P) Ltd.

Proofreader: Caryne Brown

Interior Designer: Leonardo March

Cover Designer: Rose Storey

Director of Marketing Strategy: Maura Sullivan

Copyright © 2015 by Corwin

Face drawings for "Practice the Conversation" in Lessons 1, 8, 12, 18, 25, 35, 41, 48, 57, 63, 73, 79, 85, 93, and 101 and in Lessons 2, 11, 15, 20, 24, 34, 38, 43, 47, 56, 60, 65, 69, 78, 82, 87, 91, and 100 by Talia Delambre

Face drawings for "Practice the Conversation" in Lessons 6, 10, 17, 22, 29, 33, 40, 45, 51, 55, 62, 67, 77, 84, 89, 95, and 99 by Anael Ashkenazi

Face drawings for "Practice the Conversation" in Lessons 5, 14, 21, 28, 32, 37, 44, 50, 54, 59, 66, 72, 76, 81, 88, 94, and 98 and Lessons 4, 9, 16, 23, 27, 31, 39, 46, 49, 53, 61, 68, 71, 75, 83, 90, and 97 by Tori Shiver

Face drawings for "Practice the Conversation" in Lessons 3, 7, 13, 19, 26, 30, 36, 42, 52, 58, 64, 70, 74, 80, 86, 92, and 96 by Ben Brody

Printed in the United States of America

A catalog record of this book is available from the Library of Congress.

ISBN: 978-1-4833-7546-5

This book is printed on acid-free paper.

SUSTAINABLE FORESTRY INITIATIVE

Certified Chain of Custody

Promoting Sustainable Forestry

www.sfiprogram.org

SFI-01268

SFI label applies to text stock

15 16 17 18 19 10 9 8 7 6 5 4 3 2 1

CONTENTS

PART II. PUNCTUATION

Visit the companion website at
www.resources.corwin.com/bernabeigrammar
for downloadable versions of all
the student essays and other resources,
including state testing correlation charts.

ACKNOWLEDGMENTS

For your good sense, high energy, extraordinary competence, and great hearts: Lisa Luedeke, Maura Sullivan, and Judi Reimer.

For dazzling Corwin Literacy teamwork, bumping, setting, and spiking the parts: Julie Nemer, Emeli Warren, Melanie Birdsall, Patrice Sutton, Rose Storey, and Leonardo March.

For so generously comparing notes about grammar and writing: Catherine D'Aoust, Suzi Lockamy, Shelley Fisette, Courtney Bauer, Kayla Shook, Gina Graham, Traci Kuenzi, Cindy Tyroff, Cynthia Candler, Carol Booth Olson, Kayla and Stephen Briseño, Elizabeth Perez, Maggie Ojeda, Kimberly Lipe, Mark Keenum, and Corbett and Deena Harrison.

For so many long-ago, thoughtful conversations that led to this book: Pat Schmitz, Mary Howard, Caroyl Green, Dan Kirby, Peter Medway, Phillipa Stratton, Barry Lane, Chris Goode, Julie Cason and Sherry Long, Cindy Tyroff, and Jeff Anderson.

For your teaching legacies and fine friendship: Dottie Hall, Patricia Sue Gray, Kim Grauer, and Jennifer Koppe.

For making coffee, whizzing through computer quirks, and cooking therapeutic migas: Alicia Narvaez.

And for knowing everything important, my family: Johnny, Matilde, Julian, Bert, and Dixie.

INTRODUCTION: WHAT'S A KEEPER?

When my daughter Matilde was 4, she and I lived briefly on the family farm in Kentucky. One day in the basement, I sat writing in my journal and watching her play. She was clearly playing school, and her dolls were her students. When I asked her about it, she told me that she was going to be a teacher when she grew up.

"And when you are a teacher, what are you going to teach your students to do?"

"All the best things."

What a simple utterance. I sat, stunned, thinking back over the assignments I'd handed out to students, and how few of these I'd consider "the best things."

I decided that from that moment on, I'd dedicate myself to teaching only the best things. I'd make time for daily writing, giving the students time to record their lives. Everything we'd do would be worth keeping, worth remembering. Keeping things you want to remember in your life—that's what journals are for. And we'd just figure out how to use these daily entries for other academic purposes.

A few years later, one of my high school students wrote a journal entry about going back and reading from her own first grade journal. She captured the magic of looking back to see how that little person used to think. She also captured the need for us to make room in our precious class time for daily writing time. Naturally, I kept a copy of her journal entry. And I'd bet that Katie, like hundreds of her peers, still has her journal.

By: Katie Edgar
January 22, 2001

Today I found one of my old journals when I was getting ready for school. It was so funny what I wrote about. I didn't have correct spelling or punctuation either. It was my "daily log" from 1st grade or 2nd grade. It was cool though, because when I read it I knew what that little girl (me) was thinking and doing that day. I am so glad you are making us write journals now. It is like a time capsule of different experiences that we have been through. Also, a time capsule of memories. I just wish my next teacher will do this, because I don't have discipline to write in a journal each day.

Oh, also on the "Daily Log," that I would write in when I was younger, at the end of each one I would write:

P.S. Have a good day, see ya sooon! Have a good year!

It was so funny!

In the years that followed, I found ways to use these daily entries for other academic purposes, including grammar instruction, the topic of this book. By embedding grammar lessons into my classes' daily journal time, I am able to focus on the things that kids struggle with most—persistent problems in punctuation, usage, and sentence structure—and to do so in a context that is meaningful. I also created a "Parts of Speech" sheet that I share in this book that helps students learn—and *remember*—how to make correct grammatical choices.

Have students tackled these most persistent problems? Have they internalized correctness? Have these lessons *worked*?

Maybe not every lesson, not every time, but the evidence is solid and clear, and not only from test scores. Sometimes the evidence is more personal, more meaningful. My seventh grader, Tori, posted this Mother's Day message for her mother on Facebook last year. While I'm certain her mother was touched by the thoughts, I was moved nearly to tears by her strikingly correct mechanics. For Tori, the lessons about there/their/they're, your/you're have become part of her breathing. They're keepers.

A few months ago, again while looking in on Facebook, I was astounded to see a photo posted by Mike, an ex-student. He was saying good-bye to his Parts of Speech sheet, from his journal from my class, which he had kept for twenty-five years.

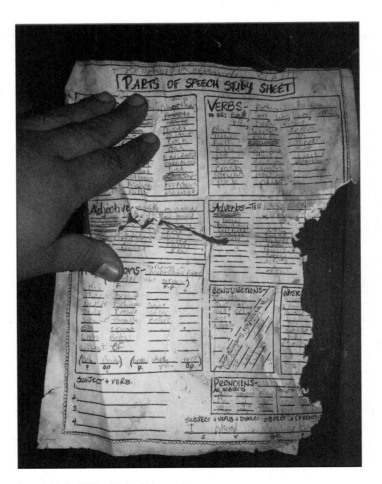

I had visited before with former students who had told me they had kept this sheet through their college years for quick reference, but this was a new record.

Since we have so little time with students, and since we will never be able to "cover" all of the curriculum, we have to make the choice to share with them the best of what we know, leaving out anything meaningless or unnecessary. We have time only for the best authors, the best poetry, the best ways of living, the best ways to learn the most valuable things.

We have to offer all the best things we know, but only students will reveal to us which ones are the *keepers.*

TEACHING GRAMMAR IN CONTEXT—SO WHAT'S THE PROBLEM?

What's the big mystery about teaching grammar within the writing process?

For years, teachers have known we should teach grammar, not in isolation, but within the context of student writing. The *Writing Next* research report even says that "traditional grammar instruction is unlikely to help improve the quality of students' writing" (Graham & Perin, 2007, p. 21). In fact, students actually lose ground in their growth when treated to doses of traditional grammar instruction, separated from writing or reading. And most teachers agree that we should weave grammar into authentic writing.

But nobody has known *how.*

The report says that focusing "on the function and practical application of grammar within the context of writing produces strong and positive effects on students' writing" (Graham & Perin, 2007, p. 21).

But they don't say how to *do* it.

Meanwhile, in other states and certainly here in Texas, statewide writing test scores are placing more and more emphasis on grammar fundamentals, and scores have plummeted. In fact, the "revising and editing" multiple-choice section of the tests can make or break a student's scores. Schools are desperate for a systematic and thorough process for teaching grammar without reverting to Warriner's grammar exercises.

This book offers a more kid-friendly approach to teaching grammar. I teach grammar in the context of their writing—in students' journals—in a way that actually transfers into students' talking, their thinking, and their writing. I'm sure my combination is not the only way to teach grammar in context, but it's one way. And it's worked.

I call these lessons *keepers* because they are lessons that last. My students keep them, refer to them, and even internalize them. They are lessons students find valuable. I keep doing them, because I haven't found another way to teach grammar that has this effect.

Keepers don't separate grammar from breathing or reading or writing. Students record the keepers in their journals, creating grammar they're going to keep. *Keep-able* pieces.

A teacher friend of mine recently said to me, "If you're about to give me one more thing to do, I am going to burst." I get that. Every teacher understands how she feels. These lessons don't ask you to add to your curriculum. You can teach them right within the context of whatever else you're doing—without losing track of what you've covered.

And let's face it: pedagogy doesn't help at all if kids aren't learning.

OVERVIEW OF THIS BOOK

There are three central practices at the core of this book that weave together, each involving thorny problems in student understanding and achievement:

1. **Daily journal writing,** which increases writing practice *and* allows students to implement and practice grammar lessons

2. **Interactive dialogues** that model for students how to make grammatical choices

3. **A "Keepers 101" tracking sheet and a "Parts of Speech" sheet,** so that we can systematically keep track of what we've taught and students can keep track of what they've learned

   Below, I will explain the importance of each.

1. Why Journal Writing?

Most students don't write daily. At the end of the year, many parents receive the year's writing in a thin folder containing a scant handful of pages. No wonder kids are having difficulty. They can't learn without practice. One of the foundational beliefs of the National Writing Project is that students must write frequently. The Common Core Standards ask that "students write routinely over extended time frames . . . and shorter time frames . . . for a range of tasks, purposes and audiences" (see http://www.corestandards .org/wp-content/uploads/ELA_Standards.pdf, p. 41).

But most teachers don't know how to "let them write" without overdirecting the writing, burdening themselves with impossible grading loads, and choking the autonomy of students. Daily journal writing solves part of this problem, and if students learn grammar while they're doing it, then teachers feel even more justified devoting class time for what they may often otherwise have considered wasted.

2. Why an Emphasis on Interactive Dialogue?

Central to this book is Vygotsky's (1978) notion that social interaction plays an integral role in the formation of thought, that our "out loud" speech becomes our "inner speech." This element of social interaction is the missing link in systemic grammar instruction, and in any grammar instruction books I've ever seen.

As Jerome Bruner put it,

> Let me propose that interior intellectual work is almost always a continuation of a dialogue. This is not a new point. Its most famous exponent is the Russian psycholinguist Vygotsky, who argues that the development of thought in the child is dependent upon his entering a dialogue and that, in time and with practice, the dialogue becomes internalized. (Bruner, 1962, p. vii–viii)
>
> —*Jerome Bruner,* On Knowing: Essays for the Left Hand

We must model interactive grammatical choices.

How does it work? When you, or any other literate person, are writing the word *their, there,* or *they're,* you have a tiny conversation with yourself as you choose which one to write. You have an inner dialogue with yourself. It just happens so fast that we can't hear it as it goes by. But if you could record your thought process and play it back in slow motion, you'd hear conversation at the moment of grammatical choice, something like, "Over there, t-h-e-re," or they are = they're. Based on these tiny conversations, you make your grammatical choice.

Our students who are developing readers and writers do not have these mental processes established yet. There is no mental dialogue like ours. So at the moment of grammatical choice, it's hit or miss—mostly miss.

However, if students have access to the language of these inner conversations, this inner speech, and practice them, they can actually become independent wielders of grammatical choices. I've seen this in my own classroom for over twenty-five years. But students have to be able to hear it with their ears first, before it can become internalized as a thought process. So you will find, in every lesson in this book, a "Practice the Conversation" section where students practice making a grammatical choice through speech.

> **PRACTICE THE CONVERSATION:**
> **A:** Who'd like to read the sentence?
> **B:** *They're leaving.*
> **A:** Perfect! And how do you spell *they're*?
> **B:** T-h-e-y-apostrophe-r-e.
> **A:** I think you have the wrong *they're*.
> **B:** I'm pretty sure it's the right one.
> **A:** Can you prove it?
> **B:** Yes I can. *They are leaving.*
> **A:** You're so right! It's the right one.

Some of the theory behind this process also includes Frank Smith's idea that students learn vicariously from watching other students and from Jerome Bruner's work, especially in the area of "formatting" language protoconversations (Bruner & Watson, 1983).

3. Why the Tracking Charts?

When I began, I didn't have a systematic way to teach grammar in the context of writing. I taught responsively, largely in response to students' weaknesses, while leading them into new grammatical territories to help them develop more sophisticated syntax. But at the end of the year, like many of us, I had a disquieting little secret: I didn't know what all we had covered and what all I had left out.

A detailed tracking chart, the "Keepers 101" sheet, solves this murky problem for the teacher. But it also benefits students. It serves as a visual tool for their notes, a place they can turn to to remember and further internalize the inner conversations we practice. It also allows them to see concretely how the elements of grammar fit together into a whole, even if the pieces are taught separately.

The chart is used to keep track of what all you've covered. My students cut the margins off their copies and tape them into the backs of their composition books. Then, whenever we have a mini-lesson, we jot down something into the tiny little space. Sometimes we jot down a "proof word," sometimes an example.

You can teach anything on the chart at any time, in any order you like. You and your students can see at a glance all you've done together and what you'd like to cover at a later time. Everything on the chart fits together and is part of how we use language. You can add or delete anything, so everything you want and need to teach is there on the chart.

KEEPERS 101

Common errors (top chart - blank template)

Too Proof	Two Proof	To Proof	It's Proof	Its Proof	Who Proof	Whom Proof	Who's Proof	Whose Proof	Our Proof	Are Proof	Then Proof	Than Proof	A lot Proof

Common errors (left column):
- They're Proof
- There Proof
- Their Proof
- You're Proof
- Your Proof
- We're Proof
- Were Proof
- Where Proof
- Already Proof
- All ready Proof
- All right Proof
- Used to Proof
- Me/I Proof
- S/V Agr Proof

Punctuation
Commas in a series	Apostrophes in contractions
Commas in a letter	Apostrophes in possessions (Singular)
Commas in appositives	Apostrophes in possessions (Plural)
Commas after beginning phrases/clauses	No apostrophes on plurals
Commas before ending phrases/clauses	No apostrophes in verbs ending in "s"
Commas with direct address	Quotations: question marks inside
Commas in a date	Quotations: ending in punctuation
Commas between city and state	Hyphenated adjectives
Colons	Punctuating dialogue: chicken dance

Parts of speech
- Nouns Proof
- Verbs proof
- Adjectives proof
- Adverbs proof
- Pronouns (sub / obj)
- Prepositions
- Interjections
- Conjunctions FANBOYS AAAWWWUBIS

Direct objects / Indirect objects / Predicate nominatives / Predicate adjectives

Verbals: Participial phrases / Infinitives / Gerunds

Sentence wringer
1. Statement?
2. Verb?
3. How many? Joined how? (no / yes)

Pitchforking
- actions
- nouns
- ba-da-bing
- exclamations
- descriptions
- sounds
- smells
- contrasts
- participial phrases
- absolutes

Spelling rules
- Silent E
- Words ending in Y
- Words ending in consonants
- I before E
- Ce/ci/ge/gi

Capitalization
- Proper nouns
- Proper adjectives
- Letter closing
- First words in sentences
- First words in quotations
- Religions
- Titles

Right column: Less Proof / Fewer Proof / Lie Proof / Lay Proof / Should've Proof / Accept Proof / Except Proof / Loose Proof / Lose Proof / Affect Proof / Effect Proof

---

(bottom chart - handwritten answers)

Top row answers: Too — so/also; Two — 2; To — so also; It's — it is; Its — his; Who — he; Whom — him; Who's — who is; Whose — his; Our — your; Are — were; Then — now; Than — ; A lot — whole; More

Common errors answers:
- They're → they are
- There → here
- Their → our
- You're → you are
- Your → our
- We're → we are
- Were → are
- Where → here
- Already → not yet
- All ready → not ready
- All right → all wrong
- Used to →
- Me/I → to me
- S/V Agr → we were / we was

Punctuation answers:
- Commas in a series: and — cats, dogs, flies
- Apostrophes in contractions: dont = do not
- Commas in a letter: Dear Jake, Sincerely,
- Apostrophes in possessions (Singular): dog's bowl
- Commas in appositives: Nina, my friend, / 3 dogs's bowls
- Apostrophes in possessions (Plural): 3 dogs's bowls
- Commas after beginning phrases/clauses: Every day,
- No apostrophes on plurals: 3 dogs
- Commas before ending phrases/clauses: —,
- No apostrophes in verbs ending in "s": goes
- Commas with direct address: Mom,
- Quotations: question marks inside: "What?"
- Commas in a date: Oct. 10, 2014
- Quotations: ending in punctuation: "Oh."
- Commas between city and state: San Antonio, Texas
- Hyphenated adjectives: red-hot
- Colons: Like this: 1, 2, 3.
- Punctuating dialogue: "—." —. / "—," —.

Parts of speech answers:
- Nouns: a —, the —, some —s
- Verbs: I —, you —, he —s
- Adjectives: a — book, a — person, a — idea
- Adverbs: ran how? ran when? ran where?
- Pronouns: sub — I, she, we, they; obj — me, her, us, them
- Prepositions: (to what)
- Interjections: no! oh...
- Conjunctions FANBOYS AAAWWWUBIS: For, And, Nor, But, Or, Yet, So / After, as, Although, While, until, When, Who, Because, if, since

Direct objects: what? if since
Indirect objects: who / what
Predicate nominatives: she is Nina
Predicate adjectives: she is nice.

Verbals: Participial phrases: adj — tired, V + ing; Infinitives: to be; Gerunds: N → swimming

Sentence wringer: Psst! 1. I —, you —, he —s; no / yes fanboy; this or that; .B

Pitchforking: actions; nouns; ba-da-bing; exclamations: No! No! No!; descriptions: big, red, fluffy; sounds: ♪♪♪; smells: sss; contrasts; participial phrases: ing... ing...; absolutes: N + ing, n + ing

Spelling rules: Silent E: hope = hoping; Words ending in Y: city = cities; Words ending in consonants: hop = hopping; I before E: thief, receive, weigh; Ce/ci/ge/gi: ace/age

Capitalization: Proper nouns: Maggie; Proper adjectives: Chinese food; Letter closing: Sincerely,; First words in sentences: .B; First words in quotations: ..."If...; Religions: Catholic; Titles: Mrs.

Right column answers: Less → can count; Fewer → can count; Lie → down; Lay → something; Should've → should have; Accept → take; Except → but; Loose → tight; Lose → find; Affect → n.; Effect → v.

hi!

Sometimes kids wonder when we're going to be "done" with language; it seems to them that there's always more to learn. I like for them to see how it all fits together, and it *is* basically finite.

The "Keepers 101" sheet and the "Parts of Speech" sheet can be found in the appendices and on this book's companion website, **www.resources.corwin.com/bernabeigrammar.**

KEEPING JOURNALS

On the first day of school this year, one of my colleagues, Traci Smith, told me about having found a journal entry she'd written years earlier on another first day of school. She had read it to her daughter, Kassidy, now a fourth grader.

I asked Kassidy to tell me what that was like:

> This happened a few months ago. My mom was going through some piles of papers and found her old journal. She said, "Hey, I remember this!" She brought it over to the couch and read me a page. I was looking over her shoulder. It was about my first day of kindergarten. It said she was so sad because "my baby was leaving the house." She looked a little bit sad when she was reading it. I was really surprised that she wrote that. It was surprising because she wrote that in class and shared it with her students in middle school. It seemed like so long ago. I couldn't believe it. I couldn't remember that day. That was cool. I wanted to hear more of her journal. It was awesome. It makes me want to write a journal for my kids.

At the beginning of the year, when my students are launching their journals, I show them my journal and explain that this is a place to keep your life. Write down anything that happens, anything you'd like to remember, and you'll keep it. If someone makes you react, write down what they said, and you'll keep it. If you see something you'd like to remember, write it down.

These are students' best topics.

They're allowed to make up stories, write rants, anything at all, within the guidelines, which we all copy onto page five. (The first pages are for their title page and photos of people or things they care about.)

We write for ten minutes every school day. I read their journals every two or three weeks and give them a grade for just writing—ten entries, ten points each; twenty entries, five points each. I don't make comments or corrections of any kind; I put check marks only on the bottom of each page I read. If they do the writing, they have hundreds. On the other hand, if they'd like to ask me a question, I'll answer it in their journals. It can be a wonderful place for two-way communication, initiated by them.

What about errors? Their journals are for themselves, a place to get their ideas down, to play, to increase fluency. When their writing is for a more formal audience, errors are not okay. But in journals, they don't count at all.

What if they don't have anything to write about? We start the year with topic lists in the back of their journals, in case they come up blank any day. It's a great place for memory lists, for quick lists of all kinds. We conduct hunts for great quotations, truisms, and

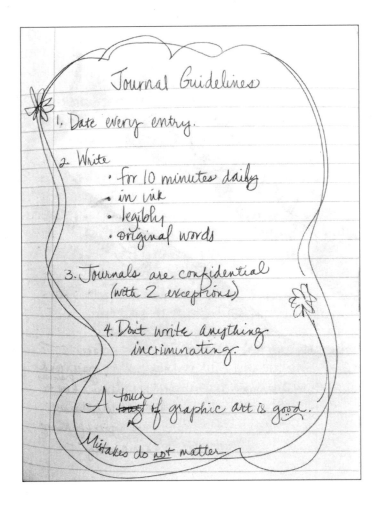

thoughts, and we add lists of these to the backs of their journals to be used as topics for writing. You can also ask them to jot down three things they could write about any day and compile these into a list for distribution. My students tape these compilations into the backs of their journals as another source of topics.

You may be wondering about **Guideline 3,** "Journals are confidential, with 2 exceptions." What are these exceptions? I explain to students that if I read that anyone is threatening to hurt them or if they're threatening to hurt someone (including themselves), I don't just check it and give them a grade; I will take some kind of action.

But if journals are confidential, how can you be sharing all these entries as part of this book? If you see a journal entry you think everyone would love to hear, ask the author for permission to publish it. You can also invite them to read aloud their entries when you have time, always allowing them the option of keeping them private. Students love hearing what other students write about. And they learn best from each other.

Guideline 4 needs a little explanation usually. I explain that negative comments about other people are not only hurtful if they're ever shared, but also they can actually be illegal. So I encourage them not to mention other people by name if they're expressing negative comments. When I've taught high school, I've also asked them not to commit to paper anything they did over the weekend, for instance, for which they could land in trouble.

The first time we write, I explain that I will time them, and they are to keep their pens moving. Ten minutes later, we look at what they wrote. If it's a half page, then that's the length of their typical entry. If it's a whole page, same thing. Throughout the year, their entries loosen up and become longer, generally. But the important thing is that they write whatever goes through their mind for ten minutes daily.

STAR POINTS

After this habit is established for a week or two, I pass out copies of the "Keepers 101" grammar chart. We trim the margins and tape it into the back. From that point on, I start each day with something from the grammar chart: a mini-lesson. I show them how to prove a grammatical choice and invite them to incorporate that day's lesson into the day's journal. If they use it (showing proofs) five or more times in that journal entry, I stick a star on the journal page when I grade it, and that entry counts double. Students call these "star points." They're not coerced, but they are encouraged to incorporate the day's grammar lesson into their journal writing. If we go on and continue to enact the proof dialogue out loud in class, we use a few volunteered journal examples from the students who opted to take the challenge. Students learn best from each other.

TWEAKING THE LESSONS

Of course, you will need to use a system that you like, and you will need to watch your students. You should adjust any of the directions in this book to suit your class. For instance, when the directions invite the students to use a proof five times in their journal, you might ask them to do three. Or do one. Use your judgment. After the journal writing, you may have the whole group listen to a few sentences with proofs students wrote and volunteer to share, or you might opt instead to have them grab a partner and share sentences—or share them with a small group.

Eventually, with students' permission, you might like to replace the journal entries in this book with those that your own students have written.

What About Reteaching, Formative Assessment, and Implementation Throughout the Year?

> Chris (on-air): If music is the pathway to the heart, as Voltaire suggested, then speech is the pathway to other people. Live in silence and you live alone.

> —From *Northern Exposure*,
> written by Henry Bromell

Reading, writing, and grammar are not separate subjects. They combine whenever we want to connect with other people. And kids constantly want to connect with others, as senders or receivers of messages, or both.

As students build a bank of grammar skills, they can begin to recognize these skills when they are used by others as well as point out how they have used the skills in their own speaking or writing. Implementation appears naturally in their reading and their writing as the year progresses. We can also encourage this.

For example, in their *reading* lives, they might

- Finish some independent reading time by copying down a sentence they notice in their book that shows something they learned on their grammar charts; over the sentence, they might include the proofs
- Use their cell phone cameras to take pictures of mistakes or correct usages in the world around them
- Imitate a sentence construction or interesting usage in their own writing

In their *writing* lives, they might

- Show proofs or labels (for anything we've covered) on anything they write, from journals to poems to formal essays
- Assign themselves practice any time on anything we've covered (like twenty-five prepositional phrases or fifteen there/their/they'res

Any of these activities can be used for formative assessment. And if you spot mistakes or signs that they're not getting something, it's good to reteach. Sometimes students make the best reteachers, so one potent type of reteaching is to ask students to review, or reteach, individual lessons.

The goal of all this is to create as many opportunities as possible for students to show their thinking, to show their thought processes at the moment of grammatical decisions. And if they are communicating with others in any form, they are making continuous grammatical decisions. The goal is decisions that are intentional and correct. The more they practice, the more likely they will internalize the correctness.

On the next page is a partial student essay that shows a student practicing several things she's learned.

ABOUT TESTING

What's testable? Of course, grammar conventions are part of most composition evaluation rubrics on any high-stakes test—mostly to the extent that the composition is readable. Most high-stakes tests also include revising and editing portions, but there are only a finite number of grammar rules that are commonly tested.

If you scrutinize the high-stakes testing in your state, or find your state in the State Testing Correlation Chart at the end of this book (and at **www.resources.corwin.com/ bernabeigrammar)**, you'll see the same grammar rules tested repeatedly. While most of these appear in a school's curriculum or standards around the second or third grade, often, the very same grammar rules plague students at the high school level. In this book, I've included lessons on all of these most persistent problems.

If you look at the sample questions from the high-stakes tests in your area, which I recommend, you may find a grammar rule not on this chart. Just add it. The goal for me in test prep is to hear students, after the test, say what Phillip said in his journal:

> Nothing was confusing in the multiple choice. It was all things we had on our grammar chart. So it was extremely easy.

Maggie Davis

Language Arts

March

The City Life; the Best Life

Nothing beats the city. Not the cows in the fields, not the lush green country side, and *definitely* not the bugs in every nook and cranny of my house. If you <u>were</u> looking *(are)* for me you would look one place and I would be <u>there</u>: the big city. It's *much* better <u>to be</u> in New York City, Las Vegas, or Miami <u>than</u> <u>to</u> be in the rural parts of Texas, Kansas, or Nebraska.

I am <u>four</u>, the city was the only thing I know. I <u>don't</u> know about the thousands of miles of nothing but fields, cattle, and wildflowers. It's the same schedule every day; wake up, school, Whataburger, Kim Possible, playtime, dinner, shower, and then bed. There is not enough time in the day for a little four year old to go drive for an hour just to look at grass and livestock. The city is home, the city is amazing, the city is perfect. Nothing is better than it.

I am seven and Sophie just moved to a small town that I hadn't heard of. Bergheim. I am at her little white house running around her property and what happens? I fall and sprain my ankle. I think that the city is safer and definitely better.

I am ten and I just had the most amazingly fun sleepover at Sophie's house. We played with her new puppies Juliette and Java, hopped around in the puddles on her

Many of the rules we learned as students actually aren't rules at all but conventions that change as the world changes. For example, I learned to spell out numbers up to one hundred, but nowadays, it's acceptable to use digits. I learned to underline major works and use quotation marks on short works; nowadays, changes in digital fonts and italics take care of a need for distinguishing titles. So those won't appear on a test. They're rules in transition.

With the digital age, letters have been largely replaced by e-mail, texts, tweets, and postings, so I suspect we won't see the formations of letter salutations and closings in tests as prominently as we did twenty years ago. I imagine that in another twenty years, words like *alot* and *alright* will be considered not quite as heinous as they are now. But some rules are absolute. It will never be correct to say, "The principal told Mrs. Koppe and I." *Whose* and *who's* will never be interchangeable. And even though we see comma splices running rampant as a stylistic tool in the novels we read, the same comma splices appear on tests at every grade level, from fourth to exit level.

It's relatively easy to pick up test points by teaching students how to nail the simple skills like common errors in object pronouns and apostrophe usage, but in my experience, the greatest gains are waiting to be harvested in the area of sentence formation. Students need to absolutely know how to identify (and remedy) a fragment or a run-on sentence, how to recognize a perfectly formed sentence, and how to combine sentences with several correct alternatives. In fact, sentence formation appears in multiple forms on every writing test.

In order to prepare our students for any test, we teachers need to watch, read, and learn what the psychometricians create for our students and make adjustments as our students need them.

WHAT THIS BOOK IS AND WHAT IT ISN'T

Grammar purists will probably hate this book. It's not intended to be another complete course in classical grammar but a practical tool for teachers who need their students to have a working knowledge of grammar and usage basics.

Why are so many journal entries in here by the same kids? For the most part, the journal entries came from my middle school students this year. Consequently, the same names will appear over and over—so will the titles of the books they have been reading.

What you're seeing is a snapshot of my classroom this year. The novels quoted at the top of each lesson were books students were reading during those days, and the journal entries were what they were thinking about during those days. We edited for clarity, correcting some mistakes that might have made readers want to turn the journal entries into proofreading activities, hunting for noticeable flaws. But the journal entries are not flawless; they are wonderful pieces that students sat down and wrote. They reflect changes in direction, genre switching, and all kinds of quirks that come from real middle school students writing for ten minutes daily. The entries are not for assessment; they're for language play.

LAST THOUGHTS

As teachers, we bring into our classroom every part of ourselves. The practices in this book began in me long before I read Vygotsky, before I discovered the brilliance of Jerome Bruner. They began in my childhood.

My mother was about as close to Maria von Trapp as you could get in Baytown, Texas, in the '50s. She talked to us, read to us, sang to us, and watched us play in the yard. She made word games and singing games with us, even turning unpleasant chores into something nearly gleeful. We four had wonderful childhoods, completely oblivious of the many treasures she was embedding into our breathing, years before I'd heard words like *engagement*, *interaction*, or *dialogics*—before I'd studied, internalized, and consciously employed the work of Lev Vygotsky or Jerome Bruner. We four emerged as adults whose natural language was generally correct English and whose general contact with others was natural conversation. Throughout my teaching life, I've drawn on these two—correctness and dialogue. I hope you'll find these lessons useful too, and that your students will discover plenty that they'll want to keep.

And ultimately, if they want to keep what they create, then it worked.

REFERENCES

Anderson, J. (2005). *Mechanically inclined: Building grammar, usage, and style into writer's workshop.* Portland, ME: Stenhouse.

Bruner, J. S. (1962). *On knowing: Essays for the left hand.* Cambridge, MA: Harvard University Press.

Bruner, J. S., & Watson, R. (1983). *Child's talk: Learning to use language.* New York, NY: W. W. Norton.

Graham, S., & Perin, D. (2007). *Writing next: Effective strategies to improve writing of adolescents in middle and high schools—A report to Carnegie Corporation of New York.* Washington, DC: Alliance for Excellent Education.

Noden, H. R. (1999). *Image grammar: Using grammatical structures to teach writing.* Portsmouth, NH: Heinemann.

Vygotsky, L. S. (1978). *Mind in society: The development of higher psychological processes.* Cambridge, MA: Harvard University Press.

SUGGESTED READINGS

Bruner, J. S. (1956). *A study of thinking.* New York, NY: Wiley.

Bruner, J. S. (1986). *Actual minds, possible worlds.* Cambridge, MA: Harvard University Press.

Vygotsky, L. S. (1962). *Thought and language.* Cambridge, MA: MIT Press.

Weaver, C. (1996). *Teaching grammar in context.* Portsmouth, NH: Boynton/Cook.

The "Parts of Speech" sheet, the "Keepers 101" sheet, all journal entries, "Practice the Conversation," "Write This on the Board," "State Testing Correlation Chart," and other resources are available on this book's companion website: **www.resources.corwin.com/bernabeigrammar**

PART I

COMMON ERRORS

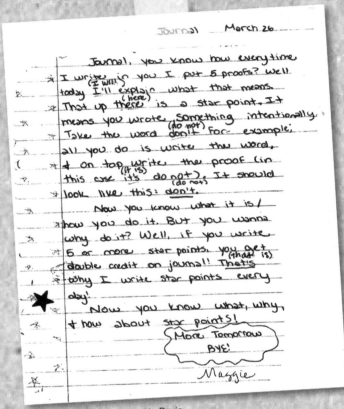

Journal   March 26

Journal, you know how every time
I write in you I put 5 proofs? Well
(I write)
today I'll explain what that means.
(here)
That up there is a star point. It
means you wrote something intentionally.
Take the word don't for example;
(do not)
all you do is write the word,
+ on top write the proof (in
(it is)
this case it's do not). It should
(do not)
look like this: don't.
    Now you know what it is/
how you do it. But you wanna
why do it? Well, if you write
5 or more star points, you get
(that is)
double credit on journal! That's
why I write star points every
day!
    Now you know what, why,
+ how about star points!
More Tomorrow
BYE!

Maggie

Correctness in writing is extremely important. When you read an essay and see, ". . . I could loose the game," that really stands out more than the good parts. You don't loose the game, you lose the game. Good mechanics can be the difference between good writing and great writing. Or in some cases, it's the difference between good writing and writing that belongs in the garbage can.

—Phillip Kaplan, eighth grade

Phillip is right about choosing the correct word. I like to begin students with this section to introduce the idea of "proof words." They aren't accustomed to arguing productively, and these work well to get them into the habit of questioning and proving. The proof practice builds their confidence and resilience when questioned.

After I introduce proof words, they are invited to use them in their journal writing for extra credit. At the end of the journal-writing time, I'll ask several students to read any sentence using that day's word. (The students have nicknamed the words "star points," as in "Ms. Bernabei, what's today's star point?") When students read a fresh sentence, I ask them to spell out the star point word. I then tell them they are wrong, and they act sad and shocked that they got it wrong. But next, they use the proof word to show me that they got it right! This way, even students who didn't take the invitation to use the proof words in their writing learn to use proofs by listening to other students. It helps those who are shy, those who need to hear it twice, or those who have other thoughts pressing. Everybody learns.

I usually start with there/their/they're to get the concept rolling. What grade level? Well, wherever students aren't using these words correctly: in my experience, every grade level between 5 and 12. After there/their/they're, we usually move to it's/its and you're/your and then skip around the chart as needed.

In the journal entry on the facing page, Maggie uses proofs and explains how they work at the same time.

1

THEY'RE

> 66 As for Tel Aviv, they're so accustomed to crisis and living under threatening 99
> scenarios—let's just say they're handling it well.
>
> —From *London Bridges* by James Patterson, found by Jake Torres

Teach it

1. Write this on the board

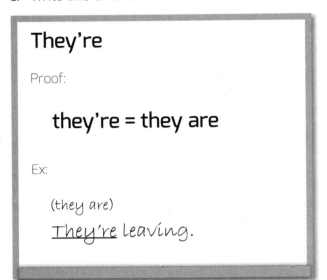

They're

Proof:

they're = they are

Ex:

(they are)
<u>They're</u> leaving.

PRACTICE THE CONVERSATION:

A: Who'd like to read the sentence?
B: *They're leaving.*
A: Perfect! And how do you spell *they're*?
B: T-h-e-y-apostrophe-r-e.
A: I think you have the wrong *they're*.
B: I'm pretty sure it's the right one.
A: Can you prove it?
B: Yes I can. *They are leaving.*
A: You're so right! It's the right one.

2. **Explain:**

   So many people have trouble with this word!

   *What does **they're** mean?*

   That's right. It means "they are."

   *So when you use **t-h-e-y-'-r-e**, you could substitute the words* they are *for it and listen. If it makes sense, then you have the right word.*

   *When you write **they're**, here is how you prove it:*

   • *Underline the word.*

   • *Write the proof over it—write* they are *in parentheses over the word **they're**.*

   The underline means I intentionally made a grammatical choice here. The proof above the word means that it's the correct choice.

3. **Ask:** *Now, who will try out this proof with me?* (Enact the conversation.)

4. **Say:** *Open to your grammar chart and find **they're**. Let's jot down the proof on the chart.*

Model it

5. Project the journal entry and read it.

6. Ask volunteers to read the sentences with **they're** aloud. Enact the conversation with several of them. Ask the others to explain why it's the right word.

Practice it

7. **Say:** *In your journal today, see if you can use the word **they're** at least five times, underlining each use. Write the proof over each one.*

August 28

I think that tomorrow, Thursday, the U.S. will attack Syria. There is a lot of bloodshed,

(they are)

and **they're** killing each other. And Assad used chemical weapons. **They're** killing their

(they are)

own people. Syria is a dangerous country right now. So many civilians have died over

there, people are dying without a scratch or a drop of blood, which is a sign of chemical

weapons. There is also no way of getting out except for escaping. Syria said if the U.S.

(they are)

attacks Syria, **they're** going to attack Israel, and so will Iran. They might be bluffing, but

(they are)   (they are)

nobody really knows what **they're** thinking. **They're** aware that it has happened before,

but I think Syria knows it will get destroyed by Israel, and I hope Iran knows, too.

—Ilan Sonsino
Grade 8

2

THERE

❝ There were a thousand things she wanted to say, but he was already looking away from ❞ her, pushing the button that would bring the elevator back up to the Institute floor.

—From *City of Glass: The Mortal Instruments*
by Cassandra Clare, found by Klarissa Martinez

Teach it

1. Write this on the board

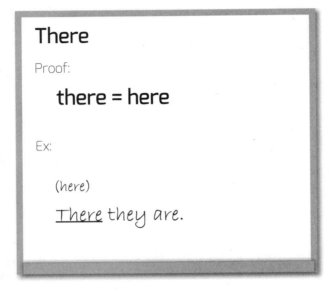

There

Proof:

there = here

Ex:

(here)

<u>There</u> they are.

PRACTICE THE CONVERSATION:

A: Read the sentence please?
B: *There they are.*
A: Perfect. Oh wait . . . how did you spell *there*?
B: T-h-e-r-e.
A: Oh no! That's not right!
B: I think it is.
A: Oh nooooo. I'm so sorry . . .
B: With all due respect, you're mistaken.
A: I don't think so!
B: *There they are. Here they are.*
A: You're right! It *is* t-h-e-r-e.
B: And I proved it.
A: You sure did. Excellent.

2. **Explain:**

So many people have trouble with this word!

*If you use **there**, you can test it by substituting the word* here *for it and listen. If it makes sense, then you have the right word.*

*So when you write **there**, here is how you prove it:*

Underline the word and write the proof over it.

Write here *in parentheses over the word **there**.*

The underline means I intentionally made a grammatical choice here. The proof above the word means that it's the correct choice.

3. **Ask:** *Now, who will try out this proof with me?* (Enact the conversation.)

4. **Say:** *Open to your grammar chart and find **there**. Let's jot down the proof on the chart.*

Model it

5. Project the journal entry and read it.

6. Ask volunteers to read the sentences with **there** aloud. Enact the conversation with each of them.

Practice it

7. **Say:** *In your own journal, try to use the word **there** at least five times, underlining each use. Write the proof over each one.*

February 14

Valentine's Day

So yesterday we took the writing benchmark and it was broken into two parts. *(here)* **There**

was a multiple choice section and two essays. On the multiple choice section there were

passages and they all had mistakes in them. While reading them, I wrote proofs if the

words were wrong and I highlighted misspelled words. *(here)* **There** were questions that asked

(here) if **there** needed to be semi-colons put in, and since I don't know where and how to use

them, that confused me.

On the two essays, I did a kernel before to organize my essay. While writing them, I

used dialogue, images, and AAAWUBBIS. However, I didn't use Ba-Da-Bings or pitchforks.

More Monday

BYE!

—Maggie Davis
Grade 7

3

THEIR

> 66 They had followed their orders and captured their prey. 99

—From *Maximum Ride—The Final Warning*
by James Patterson, found by Alicia Narvaez

Teach it

1. Write this on the board

Their

Proof:

their = our

Ex:

(our)

<u>Their</u> friends moved to California.

PRACTICE THE CONVERSATION:

A: Please read the sentence.
B: *Their friends moved to California.*
A: And how did you spell *their?*
B: T-h-e-i-r.
A: Ohhh, no. That's the wrong one.
B: I'm pretty sure it's the right one.
A: Can you substitute in the proof word?
B: *Our friends moved to California.*
A: *Their friends, our friends*, it works!
B: Okay then.
A: You nailed it! Perfect!
B: Thank you. Thank you very much.

2. **Explain:**

   Many people choose the wrong form of this word.

   *What does **their** mean?*

   That's right; it shows possession. Something belongs to someone.

   *Take a look at the substitute word. When you use **their**, you can substitute the word our for it and listen. If it makes sense, then you have the right word.*

   *When you write **their**, here is how you prove it:*

   Underline the word and write the proof over it.

   *Write our in parentheses over the word **their**.*

   The underline means I intentionally made a grammatical choice here. The proof above the word means that it's the correct choice.

3. **Ask:** *Who will volunteer to try out this proof with me?* (Enact the conversation.)

4. **Say:** *Open to your grammar chart and find **their**. Let's jot down the proof on the chart.*

Model it

5. Project the journal entry and read it.

6. Ask volunteers to read the sentences with **their** aloud. Enact the conversation with several students. Ask others to explain why it's the correct word, using the proof.

Practice it

7. **Say:** *In your journal today, see if you can use the word **their** at least five times, underlining each use. Write the proof over each one.*

September 2

Pet Peeves of Facebook

Something I can't stand in life is when I go on my Facebook and I check my news feed

and some girls will post a picture of themselves (also known as a selfie) and put as **their** *(our)*

caption, "I look so ugly . . ." I know that is just **their** way of asking for attention. (Or, *(our)*

fishing for attention.) They know that people will comment saying, "Oh, you're not ugly,

you're beautiful!" Which is what they want. Whenever I see **their** posts I always think, "If *(our)*

you think you look so ugly, then why would you post it for the public to see!"

Another thing on Facebook that annoys me is when people post statuses every

few seconds and they don't even have a reason for them. For example, they will post

something like, "Eating at Olive Garden!" Then they add a bunch of hashtags and a

picture of **their** food, "#food, #yummy #Olive #Garden #hungry #delicious." Seeing *(our)*

this, all I think is, "#No one cares!" They're just wasting **their** own precious time on *(our)*

these constant, worthless, statuses.

—Alyssa Rico
Grade 8

4

TOO

❝ He has outraged too many wise men and pleased too many fools to hide behind ❞
his too-appropriate pseudonym much longer.

—From *Ender's Game* by Orson Scott Card, found by Tori Shiver

Teach it

1. Write this on the board

Too

Proof:

too = so, also

Ex:

(so)
We were <u>too</u> frightened!

(also)
We were happy, <u>too.</u>

PRACTICE THE CONVERSATION:

A: Read the first sentence, please.

B: *We were too frightened!*

A: Great. How did you spell *too*?

B: T-o-o.

A: Oh no! That's not right.

B: Yes it is.

A: Prove it for me?

B: *We were so frightened.*

A: You're right! Can you read the second sentence now?

B: *We were happy, too.*

A: And how did you spell *too*?

B: T-o-o.

A: Sorry . . . that's not . . .

B: *We were happy also.*

A: You're right! It *is* t-o-o.

2. **Explain:**

   *People get this word wrong so often. When do we use **too**?*

   That's right. When there's "so much" of something.

   Or when it means "also."

   *So when you use **too**, substitute the word* so *or* also *for it and listen. If one of the substitute words makes sense, then **too** is the correct word.*

   *When you write **too**, here is how you prove it:*

   Underline the word and write the proof over it.

   Write so *or* also *in parentheses over the word **too**.*

   The underline means I intentionally made a grammatical choice here. The proof above the word means that it's the correct choice.

3. **Ask:** *Now, who will try out this proof with me?* (Enact the conversation.)

4. **Say:** *Open to your grammar chart and find **too**. Let's jot down the proof on the chart.*

Model it

5. Project the journal entry and read it.

6. Ask volunteers to read the sentences with **too** aloud. Enact the conversation with several students. Ask others to explain why it's the correct word, using the proof.

Practice it

7. **Say:** *In your journal today, see if you can use the word **too** at least five times, underlining each use. Write the proof over each one.*

February 7

Why I Don't Like Babies

I don't like babies because they are (so) **too** annoying! I also don't like babies because they

poop, (also) **too**. Well, we all poop, but in toilets! They poop on themselves. EWWWWWW!

And they always want attention and they have to have somebody change their diapers.

I always think they should get up and do it themselves. And we have to buy passyfires to

keep them quiet, but I'd rather buy Scotch tape and tape their mouths.

So now you know why I don't like babies. They're (so) **too** ugly to keep in your house!

They're (so) **too** stupid to be quiet! And it's (so) **too** hard to take care of a nasty (so) **too**-ugly baby!

—Carleigh Dentinger
Grade 6

---

5 TWO

❝ She was our age, biologically, and they had two fusion-clone teenaged daughters. ❞

—From *Forever Free* by Joe Haldeman,
found by Loretta Fautch

Teach it

1. Write this on the board

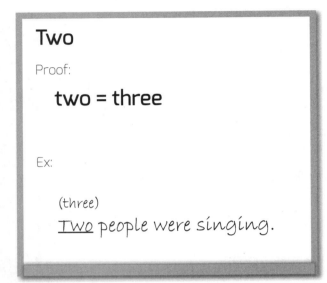

> **Two**
>
> Proof:
>
> ## two = three
>
> Ex:
>
> (three)
> <u>Two</u> people were singing.

PRACTICE THE CONVERSATION:

A: Will you please read the sentence?
B: *Two people were singing.*
A: Perfect! Wait . . . how did you spell *two*?
B: T-w-o.
A: Mmm, I don't think that's the right *too*.
B: Oh yes it is!
A: Can you prove it?
B: *Three people were singing.*
A: You're right! It's correct.

2. **Explain:**

   Every once in a while, people use the wrong word when they mean this one.

   *What does **two** mean? Yes, it's the number.*

   *So when you use **two**, you can substitute a different number, like* three, *for it and listen. If it makes sense, then you have the right word.*

   *When you write **two**, here is how you prove it.*

   • Underline the word and write the proof over it.

   • Write three *in parentheses over the word **two**.*

   The underline means I intentionally made a grammatical choice here. The proof above the word means that it's the correct choice.

3. **Ask:** *Now, who will try out this proof with me?* (Enact the conversation.)

4. **Say:** *Open to your grammar chart and find **two**. Let's jot down the proof on the chart.*

Model it

5. Project the journal entry and read it.

6. Ask volunteers to read the sentences with **two** aloud. Enact the conversation with several students.

Practice it

7. **Say:** *In your journal today, see if you can use the word* **two** *at least five times, underlining each use. Write the proof over each one.*

July 2

Scared Bananas

There was once a town of bananas called Tomatoville. In 1 Y.T. (year of tomatoes) bananas were slaves to the tomatoes and if a banana did something wrong, they would peel it. So, the bananas didn't want to be slaves, so they started an uprising and squashed all the tomatoes. Or so they thought. They ruled the town but still called it Tomatoville. The peeled bananas were like zombies to humans but [not] to bananas. So modern day bananas make movies about them, like my favorites Walking Peeled and World War P. So in 2015 Y.B. (year of bananas) a banana named Bob watched a movie with his friend Billy.

"Wow!" said Billy, "that movie was scary!"

"Whatever!" laughed Bob. "If Tomatoville was attacked by peeled bananas I would be the hero and squash them all."

But just as he said that an alarm went off. "Attention—all bananas grab your weapons and head to the Banana Facility if you're a male between 11 and 70!"

Bob and Billy ran straight to the Banana Facility and grabbed all the guns they could carry and ran straight to the commander.

"All soldiers and random banana citizens! Peeled bananas are everywhere!" he yelled as he ran off screaming. All the bananas spread out through the city and shot all the peeled bananas.

"That was easy," said Bob to Billy.

"Yeah!"

And they lived happily ever after. Until a human named Bobby peeled and ate them alive! MMMMWAAAHHH!!!
Bobby enjoyed the **two** *(three)* scared bananas. He went on to tell everyone how good those **two** *(three)* bananas were.
"One of the **two** *(three)* bananas was sweet and one of the **two** *(three)* bananas was soft," he said. "I wish I could've had more than just **two** *(three)* bananas," he said disappointedly. Then Bobby died of diabetes the minute after.

—E. J. Easterly
Grade 6

6

> **" ** "I've been trying not to ask you, but I'm giving up," I say. **"**
>
> —From *Allegiant* by Veronica Roth, found by Maggie Davis

Teach it

1. Write this on the board

> **To**
>
> Proof:
>
> to = ~~so, also, three~~
>
> Ex:
>
> (~~so, also, three~~)
> She drove the car <u>to</u> town.

PRACTICE THE CONVERSATION:

A: Will you please read the sentence?
B: *She drove the car to town.*
A: Perfect. Which *to* did you use?
B: T-o.
A: I think it should be *too.*
B: Nooo. *She drove the car so town.*
A: That doesn't work, does it?
B: *She drove the car also town.*
A: Nope, that sounds crazy.
B: *She drove the car three town.*
A: That's not the right proof either, is it? You're right! None of those proofs works.
B: So it's t-o.
A: You're absolutely right!

2. **Explain:**

This is such a simple word, but people make mistakes with it all the time.

*When do we use **to**? Basically, we use this word whenever we want it to sound like **to** and t-o-o or t-w-o don't work.*

*So whenever you use **to**, you try to substitute the words so, also, and three and listen. If none of these makes sense, then you have the right word.*

*When you write **to**, here is how you prove it:*

- *Underline the word.*

- *Write the three wrong proofs over it, with a line through them to show that they don't work. Write so, also, three in parentheses over the word **to**.*

The underline means I intentionally made a grammatical choice here. The proof above the word means that it's the correct choice.

3. **Ask:** *Now, who will try out this proof with me?* (Enact the conversation.)

4. **Say:** *Open to your grammar chart and find **to**. Let's jot down the proof on the chart.*

Model it

5. Project the journal entry and read it.

6. Ask volunteers to read the sentences with **to** aloud. Enact the conversation with several of them or ask them to explain using the proof.

Practice it

7. **Say:** *In your journal today, see if you can use the word __to__ at least five times, underlining each use. Write the proof over each one.*

September 16

Inventions That Should Be Real

There are many different things being made every day all around the world. Some

(so, also, three)

inventions I would love **to** be real are number 1: an animal communicater so we could

(so, also, three)

always know what they are saying and we can talk **to** them. Another cool invention

would be a car that runs on air/water. I have heard that it has been invented already,

but it would be nice if they would actually start selling them. I have also heard of a

(so, also, three)

pen that you touch on the color you want and it changes **to** that color so you can write

with any color you want. I'm not sure if it's invented yet but it should be. It would also

(so, also, three)   (so, also, three)

be cool **to** have waterproof phones without having **to** buy a case to make it waterproof.

And lastly a food maker of some sort, or a bathroom in your car, or separaters from

others. Those are just a few things I would definitely buy.

—Alyssa Rico
Grade 8

7

IT'S

>   ❝ I imagine it's the feeling Eve had as she bit into the apple. ❞
>
> —From *A Northern Light* by Jennifer Donnelly, found by Tori Shiver

Teach it

1. Write this on the board

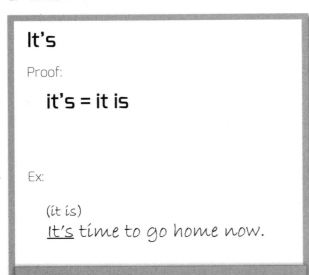

It's

Proof:

it's = it is

Ex:

(it is)
<u>It's</u> time to go home now.

PRACTICE THE CONVERSATION:
A: Will you read the sentence?
B: *It's time to go home now.*
A: Perfect. How did you spell *it's*?
B: I-t-apostrophe-s.
A: Hmm . . . nope. That's not correct.
B: Yes, it is.
A: No, it's not.
B: *It is time to go home now.*
A: Oh! You're right! Great job.

2. **Explain:**

   This is one of the big ones. So many people write it's, *and it's often wrong.*

   *What does **it's** mean?*

   That's right. It means "it is." And that is the only thing it means.

   *So every time you use **it's**, substitute the words* it is *for it and listen. If it makes sense, then you have the right word.*

   *When you write **it's**, here is how you prove it:*

   • *Underline the word.*

   • *Write the proof over it. Write* it is *in parentheses over the word **it's**.*

   The underline means I intentionally made a grammatical choice here. The proof above the word means that it's the correct choice.

3. **Ask:** *Who is ready to try out this proof with me?* (Enact the conversation.)

4. **Say:** *Open to your grammar chart and find **it's**. Let's jot down the proof on the chart.*

Model it

5. Project the journal entry and read it.

6. Ask volunteers to read the sentences with **it's** aloud. Enact the conversation with them.

Practice it

7. **Say:** *In your journal today, see if you can use the word __it's__ at least five times, underlining each use. Write the proof over each one.*

March 6

I just finished reading the book called *Smashed*. The book is interesting and disturbing a

bit but I enjoyed reading the book. I like the book in a way. It was more detailed about the

character's life so the reader can have a picture in his or her mind of how the character

(it is)
might be. __It's__ kind of sad that Katie's mom never comes that often to be with her kids.

(it is)
__It's__ sad how her friends tried to protect or warn her that the guy Alec she is with is bad.

(it is)   *(it is)*
__It's__ hard to know who to trust and __it's__ bad when you really think they are the people they

say they are.

                                       —Genesis Thomas
                                           Grade 7

8

ITS

Teach it

1. Write this on the board

Its

Proof:

its = his

Ex:

The computer was broken,
(his)
but <u>its</u> monitor still worked
fine.

PRACTICE THE CONVERSATION:

A: Go ahead and read the sentence.

B: *The computer was broken, but its monitor still worked fine.*

A: Yes. But wait . . . how did you spell *its*?

B: I-t-s.

A: You mean *apostrophe s*?

B: No. No apostrophe.

A: I think you should put an apostrophe.

B: Not this time!

A: Can you prove that for me?

B: *The computer was broken but his monitor still worked fine.*

A: His monitor, its monitor, that's right. Perfect!

2. **Explain:**

   This word is a mess. Lots of people put an apostrophe in it because it sounds possessive. But it never gets an apostrophe.

   Its *is a pronoun. It's like the word* his *or* her. *Is there an apostrophe in that? We like h-i-'-s friend. Nope, that would be crazy.*

   So a great substitute word is his. *When you use* **its**, *substitute the word* his *for it and listen. If it makes sense, then you have the right word.*

   When you write **its**, *here is how you prove it:*

   • *Underline the word and write the proof over it.*

   • *Write* his *in parentheses over the word* **its**.

   Remember, the underline means I intentionally made a grammatical choice here. The proof above the word means that it's the correct choice.

3. **Ask:** *Who will try out this proof with me?* (Enact the conversation.)

4. **Say:** *Open to your grammar chart and find* **its**. *Let's jot down the proof word on the chart.*

Model it

5. Project the journal entry and read it.

6. Ask volunteers to read the sentences with **its** aloud. Enact the conversation with several students.

Practice it

7. **Say:** *In your journal today, see if you can use the word **its** at least five times, underlining each use. Write the proof over each one.*

April 8

Well Hi!!! Have you ever had that dream where there are a bunch of crabs crawling on

you? Well, I'm at the beach right now and surprisingly the crab that is on me isn't biting

or pinching me at all!!! It's weird. Oh no!!! The crab's claws! I took (his) **its** claws!!! (his) **Its** claws are

what it uses to stand! I took (his) **its** feet, and ate them! (his) **Its** claws are tasty!!! (his) **Its** eyes, not so

tasty.

—Grayson Kyle
Grade 6

9

YOU'RE

❝ You're about as strong as a fart! ❞

—From *Ender's Game* by Orson Scott Card,
found by Miriam Stein

Teach it

1. Write this on the board

You're

Proof:

you're = you are

Ex:

(you are)
<u>You're</u> my favorite person!

PRACTICE THE CONVERSATION:

A: Read the sentence, please.
B: *You're my favorite person.*
A: Thank you! I like you too.
B: Uh. . .
A: Okay, but how did you spell *you're*?
B: Y-o-u-apostrophe-r-e.
A: No. I think you meant y-o-u-r.
B: That's not right. It's the other one.
A: Can you prove it?
B: *You are my favorite person.*
A: Yes! Right for two reasons!
B: I beg your pardon?
A: Just kidding. But you're right. You are right.

2. **Explain:**

    This word is misspelled more than just about any other word in English.

    *What does **you're** mean?*

    That's right. It means "you are."

    *When you use **you're**, substitute the words* you are *for it and listen. If it makes sense, then you have the right word.*

    *When you write **you're**, here is how you prove it:*

    • Underline the word and write the proof over it.

    • Write you are *in parentheses over the word **you're**.*

    The underline means I intentionally made a grammatical choice here. The proof above the word means that it's the correct choice.

3. **Ask:** *Now, who will try out this proof with me?* (Enact the conversation.)

4. **Say:** *Open to your grammar chart and find **you're**. Let's jot down the proof on the chart.*

Model it

5. Project the journal entry and read it.

6. Ask volunteers to read the sentences with **you're** aloud. Enact the conversation with several students; ask others to explain using the proof.

Practice it

7. **Say:** *In your journal today, see if you can use the word **you're** at least five times, underlining each use. Write the proof over each one.*

January 30

My Teacher's a Spy

My teacher's a spy, I know it! I also know (you are) **you're** wondering why but just read if you want to

find out. I even once told her "(you are) **You're** bad at being a spy," and she walked away. I even saw

her last night on the phone. She said the word *spy* so that proves she is one. If (you are) **you're** still

thinking she's not, (you are) **you're** dumb. Don't even finish reading this if (you are) **you're** **still** not believing

me. She even has a pencil that turns into a pen. Now that must have been given to her by

the C.I.A., which stands for Central Intelligence Agency. Or could it be from the A.I.C. (C.I.A.

backwards) Alaska Imports Cookies. Ya, that's it, she's trying to find out the secret formula

for our Texas cookies. I am going to stop my teacher and save the world.

"Honey, it's time for nap time!"

"5 minutes, Mom! (you are) **You're** so annoying sometimes, Mom."

OK, after nap time I will stop my teacher and save the world. Man, I'm a good detective.

—Asher Bar-Yadin
Grade 6

10 YOUR

> *Unless you're as stupid as a lamppost you've got to wonder what's coming off next, your arm? Your leg? Your neck?*
>
> —From *Bud, Not Buddy* by Christopher P. Curtis, found by Bryanna Ruggs

Teach it

1. Write this on the board

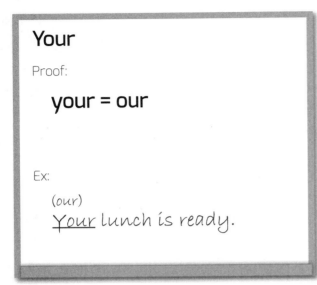

Your

Proof:

your = our

Ex:

(*our*)
<u>Your</u> lunch is ready.

PRACTICE THE CONVERSATION:

A: Read the sentence, please.
B: *Your lunch is ready.*
A: And how did you spell *your*?
B: Y-o-u-r.
A: You mean y-o-u-apostrophe-r-e?
B: No, I sure don't.
A: Can you prove your choice?
B: *Our lunch is ready.*
A: You're absolutely right!

2. **Explain:**

   This word is abused regularly by people of all ages.

   *What does **your** mean?*

   That's right. It tells whose.

   *So when you use **your**, you can substitute the word* our *for it and listen. If it makes sense, then you have the right word.*

   *When you write **your**, here is how you prove it:*

   • *Underline the word and write the proof over it.*

   • *Write* our *in parentheses over the word **your**.*

   The underline means I intentionally made a grammatical choice here. The proof above the word means that it's the correct choice.

3. **Ask:** *Now, who will try out this proof with me?* (Enact the conversation.)

4. **Say:** *Open to your grammar chart and find **your**. Let's jot down the proof on the chart.*

Model it

5. Project the journal entry and read it.

6. Ask volunteers to read the sentences with **your** aloud. Enact the conversation with several students. Ask others to explain the proof.

Practice it

7. **Say:** *In your journal today, see if you can use the word __your__ at least five times, underlining each use. Write the proof over each one.*

August 14

My First Day

My first day in class was nerve wracking cause you never know what's going to happen to

you. You can lose your balance, fall on the stairs, run into a pole. Embarrassing stuff, you

know? Like **your** (our) books can fall out of **your** (our) hand, or **your** (our) feet might feel sore and **your** (our) hand

might feel numb. Or what if a piece of pencil lead flew into **your** (our) eye!

   I kinda hate and like being new in school. I hate it cause you have no friends yet, and I

like it cause almost everyone wants to know who you are. AND I really didn't want to come

to JCC. I'm like: "I don't wanna go, what if . . ." What if was ALWAYS my excuse. Then I came

and I love this school. There's so much I can say about this school. . . .

   To be continued. . . .

—Klarissa Martinez
Grade 8

WHO

" Who are you fooling? Everyone knows those carrot sticks are just there to bring " the ranch from bowl to mouth.

—From *Eat This Not That! The Best (& Worst!) Foods in America!: The No-Diet Weight Loss Solution* by David Zinczenko, found by Ilan Sonsin

Teach it

1. Write this on the board

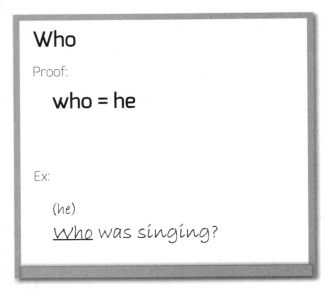

Who

Proof:

who = he

Ex:

(he)
<u>Who</u> was singing?

PRACTICE THE CONVERSATION:

A: Please read the sentence.
B: *Who was singing?*
A: Are you sure you should use *who* and not *whom*?
B: Positive.
A: Hmm . . . I'm not so sure.
B: I'm completely sure.
A: Can you prove that?
B: I sure can.
A: Today?
B: *He was singing?*
A: Perfect. You're completely right!

2. **Explain:**

It seems like nobody knows how to use who *and* whom.

Our ears don't hear when it's correct, so we can use a substitute word that our ears know well. Then it's easy to tell when to use who *and when to use* whom.

Whenever you use **<u>who</u>**, *you can substitute the word* she *or* he *for it and listen. If it makes sense, then you have the right word.*

When you write **<u>who</u>**, *here is how you prove it:*

- *Underline the word and write the proof over it.*
- *Write* he *in parentheses over the word* **<u>who</u>**.

The underline means I intentionally made a grammatical choice here. The proof above the word means that it's the correct choice.

3. **Ask:** *Now, who will try out this proof with me?* (Enact the conversation.)

4. **Say:** *Open to your grammar chart and find* **<u>who</u>**. *Let's jot down the proof on the chart.*

Model it

5. Project the journal entry and read it.

6. Ask volunteers to read the sentences with **<u>who</u>** aloud. Enact the conversation with several students.

Practice it

7. **Say:** *In your journal today, see if you can use the word **who** at least five times, underlining each use. Write the proof over each one.*

February 27

The Man Who Couldn't

So every story pretty much has a happy ending. For instance, all of the princess stories,

the Harry Potter series, the Percy Jackson series, I could go on for centuries. But I want to

change that. . . .

(he)
There once was a guy **who** was named Harold and he had the best life until he went to

the store and bought a rotten tomato with worms in it. When he bit into it he felt the most

(he)
horrific sensation anyone has ever sensated. He would be known for the man **who** had the

worst sensation ever. He spit out the rotten, black, wormy tomato and washed his mouth

out . . . with soap. Then he went to work and got some coffee. . . .

(he)
It was filled with rotten milk. Then he tried to do his famous back flip for a man **who** bet

he couldn't do it. . . .

He ended up having a back surgery after being rushed to the hospital. The other man

(he)
won $50.00. This was the story of the man **who** couldn't get picked to be in a happy story.

—Claire Weingart
Grade 6

12 WHOM

Teach it

1. Write this on the board

PRACTICE THE CONVERSATION:

A: Will you please read the sentence?
B: *She said this to whom?*
A: Uh oh . . . wait . . . I think *whom* isn't right.
B: It's right.
A: Can you prove it for me?
B: *She said this to him?*
A: Ah! You're right. It's right

2. **Explain:**

   Who *and* whom *are practically mystery words; so few people know when to use them correctly.*

   Our ears don't hear when it's correct, so we can use a substitute word that our ears do know well. Then it's easy to tell when to use who *and when to use* whom.

   Whenever you use **whom**, *substitute the word* him *for it and listen. If it makes sense, then you have the right word. Our ears know that we use* he *as a subject, and we use* him *as an object. We use* **who** *and* **whom** *the very same ways.*

   So let's keep it simple. When you write **whom**, *here is how you prove it:*

   • *Underline the word and write the proof over it.*

   • *Write* him *in parentheses over the word* **whom**.

   The underline means I intentionally made a grammatical choice here. The proof above the word means that it's the correct choice.

3. **Ask:** *Now, who will try out this proof with me?* (Enact the conversation.)

4. **Say:** *Open to your grammar chart and find* **whom**. *Let's jot down the proof on the chart.*

Model it

5. Project the journal entry and read it.

6. Ask volunteers to read the sentences with **whom** aloud. Enact the conversation with several students

Practice it

7. **Say:** *In your journal today, see if you can use the word **whom** at least five times, underlining each use. Write the proof over each one.*

April 9

Yesterday I was texting with Evan b/c I found a website with a bunch of hilarious shirts!

(him)
(With **whom** was I texting? With Evan.) It's called Noise Bot something. Anyway so when

(him)
I saw this website, I thought about him. (About **whom** was I thinking? About Evan.) There

were bunches of jokes that he would find funny. So I started texting them to him. (To

(him)   (him)
whom? To him. Evan.) So I sent him a link to the website for him to look at it. (For **whom**?

For Evan.) So he started texting the pictures to me too and I had a text joke war with him.

(him)
(With **whom**? With Evan.)

—Talia Delambre
Grade 6

13

WHO'S

" I know Mrs. Grimaldi, the lady who's always sitting by her window, and the old "
guy who walks up and down the street whistling like a bird.

—From *Wonder*, by R. J. Palacio, found by Phil Silberman

Teach it

1. Write this on the board

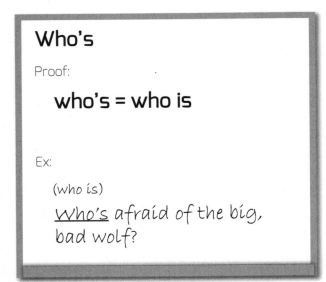

Who's

Proof:

who's = who is

Ex:

(who is)
<u>Who's</u> afraid of the big,
bad wolf?

PRACTICE THE CONVERSATION:

A: Read the sentence for me?
B: *Who's afraid of the big, bad wolf?*
A: Great. How did you spell *who's?*
B: W-h-o-apostrophe-s.
A: Oh wow . . . that's wrong.
B: I'm sure it's right.
A: Proof?
B: *Who's afraid . . . who is afraid?*
A: Perfect! You're so right.

2. **Explain:**

    People confuse who's *and* whose *all the time!*

    What does **who's** *mean?*

    That's right. It means "who is." It's a contraction.

    Any time you use **who's**, *you could substitute the words* who is *for it and listen. If it makes sense, then you have the right word.*

    When you write **who's**, *here is how you prove it:*

    *   *Underline the word and write the proof over it.*

    *   *Write* who is *in parentheses over the word* **who's**.

    The underline means I intentionally made a grammatical choice here. The proof above the word means that it's the correct choice.

3. **Ask:** *Who will try out this proof with me?* (Enact the conversation.)

4. **Say:** *Open to your grammar chart and find* <u>who's</u>. *Let's jot down the proof on the chart.*

Model it

5. Project the journal entry and read it.

6. Ask volunteers to read the sentences with **who's** aloud. Enact the conversation with them.

Practice it

7. **Say:** *In your journal today, see if you can use the word* **who's** *at least five times, underlining each use. Write the proof over each one.*

January 23

<u>Who's</u> the Greatest?

(who is)

Many people have different opinions about **who's** the best player in history. Some people

think that Michael Jordan is the best. I might think that Jordan is the best, but I don't think

that Larry Bird, or Hakeem Olajuwon is.

   I really do think that Tim Duncan is the best PF, and one of the best in history. But most

(who is)

people hate it when people say this. They can't accept the fact that a player **who's** not

really flashy can be the best. I'll always believe this.

<u>Who's</u> best?

Best Players	Team	Position
1. Michael Jordan	Bulls, Wizards	SF
2. Larry Bird	Celtics	PF
3. Tim Duncan	Spurs	PF/C
4. Hakeem Olajuwon	Rockets	PF/C
5. Julius Erving	Sixers	PF/C
6. Kobe Bryant	Lakers	SF/SG
7. Earvin "Magic" Johnson	Lakers	PG
8. Wilt Chamberlain	Lakers	PF
9. David Robinson	Spurs	C
10. Robert Horry	Lakers, Spurs, Rockets	SF/PF

—Ilan Sonsino
Grade 8

14

WHOSE

Teach it

1. Write this on the board

Whose

Proof:

whose = his

Ex:

(his)
Whose envelopes are these?

PRACTICE THE CONVERSATION:

B: *Whose envelopes are these?*

A: Hmm . . . how did you spell *whose*?

B: W-h-o-s-e.

A: I'm afraid that's completely wrong.

B: I'm afraid it's completely right.

A: Prove it?

B: *His envelopes are these?* That sounds weird.

A: Would you like to rearrange the words?

B: Okay, *these are his envelopes?*

A: These are his envelopes, these are whose envelopes? Yep, that's completely right.

B: All righty then.

A: . . .

2. **Explain:**

Here's a word that is often confused.

What does **whose** *mean?*

That's right. It's about ownership.

So when you use **whose**, *you can substitute the word* his *or* hers *for it and listen. You might also need to rearrange the question into a statement. Either way, if it makes sense, then you have the right word.*

When you write **whose**, *here is how you prove it:*

- *Underline the word and write the proof over it.*

- *Write* his *in parentheses over the word* **whose**.

- *The underline means I intentionally made a grammatical choice here. The proof above the word means that it's the correct choice.*

3. **Ask:** *Now, who will try out this proof with me?* (Enact the conversation.)

4. **Say:** *Open to your grammar chart and find* **whose**. *Let's jot down the proof on the chart.*

Model it

5. Project the journal entry and read it.

6. Ask volunteers to read the sentences with **whose** aloud. Enact the conversation with several students.

Practice it

7. **Say:** *In your journal today, see if you can use the word **whose** at least five times, underlining each use. Write the proof over each one.*

March 5

(his)
<u>**Whose**</u> book is that? That's his book. <u>**Whose**</u> (his) teacher is that? That's his teacher. My chum

(his)
chewed <u>**whose**</u> gum?

I don't know what to write about. Hmmm . . . I think I'll write a bunch of rhymes.

My frog stood on a log with a dog in the fog. That fat rat did not know how to spell cat even

(his)
though that rat was sitting on a mat that said "cat." <u>**Whose**</u> mat was it? It was the cat's.

Yo dog, I heard yo' and yo' dog like to yoyo. So I got yo' and yo' dog yoyos so yo' and yo' dog

(his)
can yoyo together. So <u>**whose**</u> yoyos are those?

—Nina De La Torre
Grade 7

---

15 WE'RE

Teach it

1. Write this on the board

> **We're**
>
> Proof:
>
> **we're = we are**
>
> Ex:
>
> (we are)
> <u>We're</u> in charge of the world.

PRACTICE THE CONVERSATION:

A: Will you please read the sentence?
B: *We're in charge of the world.*
A: Great. And how did you spell *we're?*
B: W-e-apostrophe-r-e.
A: Hmmm, that's not correct.
B: I believe it is.
A: Prove it for me?
B: *We are in charge of the world.*
A: You're right! It's correct! Good job.

2. **Explain:**

   We're, where, *and* were *are sometimes confused. Proof words will help us nail the right one.*

   What does **we're** *mean?*

   That's right. It means "we are."

   When you use **we're**, *substitute the words* we are *for it and listen. If it makes sense, then you have the right word.*

   When you write **we're**, *here is how you prove it:*

   • *Underline the word and write the proof over it.*

   • *Write* we are *in parentheses over the word* **we're**.

   The underline means I intentionally made a grammatical choice here. The proof above the word means that it's the correct choice.

3. **Ask:** *Now, who will try out this proof with me?* (Enact the conversation.)

4. **Say:** *Open to your grammar chart and find* **we're**. *Let's jot down the proof on the chart.*

Model it

5. Project the journal entry and read it.

6. Ask volunteers to read the sentences with **we're** aloud. Enact the conversation with several students.

Practice it

7. **Say:** *In your journal today, see if you can use the word **we're** at least five times, underlining each use. Write the proof over each one.*

August 19

WOW, the first journal entry, I hope it's good! Okay now I'm just staring off into space

cause I can't think of anything else to write about.

(we are)
Wait, I have an idea. **We're** gonna play a game. How about "I spy?" Do you want to

play? ☐ yes or ☐ no

(we are)
Well whatever you chose **we're** going to play anyway, but in order to play you must

(we are)   (we are)
sit in my seat. Then **we're** gonna start. **We're** starting in 3, 2, 1, go! ☐ yes or ☐ confirm.

Okay, I spy with my not-so-little eye something white and it has a lot of ink.

_____

Found it yet? It's the Journal =D.

(we are)
(**We're** not gonna play this game again!)

—Evan Katzman
Grade 6

16

WERE

66 Clary wondered what they were talking about. Politics? Opera? The high price 99
of tuna?

—From *City of Bones* by Cassandra Clare, found by Miriam Stein

Teach it

1. Write this on the board

> Were
>
> Proof:
>
> **were = are**
>
> Ex:
>
> (are)
> They <u>were</u> sitting right here.

PRACTICE THE CONVERSATION:

A: Read the sentence, please.
B: *They were sitting right here.*
A: How did you spell *were*?
B: W-e-r-e.
A: Hmmm . . . no, that's not right.
B: Yes, it is right.
A: I'm afraid not.
B: *They are sitting right here.*
A: I'm afraid you're right!
B: Don't be afraid.
A: Good job!

2. **Explain:**

   We're, where, and were *are sometimes confused. But you will never be unsure if you use proof words.*

   What does **were** *mean?*

   That's right. It's past tense of are.

   So are *is a perfect proof word. You substitute the word* are *for* **were** *and listen. If it makes sense, then you have the right word.*

   When you write **were**, *here is how you prove it:*

   • *Underline the word and write the proof over it.*

   • *Write* are *in parentheses over the word* **were**.

   The underline means I intentionally made a grammatical choice here. The proof above the word means that it's the correct choice.

3. **Ask:** *Now, who will try out this proof with me?* (Enact the conversation.)

4. **Say:** *Open to your grammar chart and find* **were**. *Let's jot down the proof on the chart.*

Model it

5. Project the journal entry and read it.

6. Ask volunteers to read the sentences with **were** aloud. Enact the conversation with them.

Practice it

7. **Say:** *In your journal today, see if you can use the word **were** at least five times, underlining each use. Write the proof over each one.*

Mexican Market

It was an extremely beautiful day, with the sun shining and a gentle breeze blowing. It

had just rained the day before and my family and I could smell the luscious earth, the

way you can after it rains. I was at the Mexican Market with my Uncle Joel, Aunt Julie,

(are)
and cousin Zula, who **were** visiting from Seattle.

(are)
As we walked around, we saw all the vendors and the stuff they **were** trying to sell. We

heard the mariachis and felt the beat inside our heart, thump-thump-thump. We smelled

(are)
the Mexican food. All of our senses **were** activated except for our sense of taste.

We sat down at the smooth gravel table at La Margarita. Uncle Joel ordered the family

platter. I could smell the meat on the grill as the chef prepared it.

After we ate, Aunt Julie, Zula, and I went to the park across the street. Some of the

(are)
sections **were** new, like the swing set. I could smell the almost fresh paint as Zula yelled,

"Push me! Push me!"

When everybody was satisfied, it was time to go back home. The Mexican Market was

fun. I would love to go again, and I'm sure Zula, Uncle Joel, And Aunt Julie would, too.

—Carmen Lizárraga
Grade 4

17

WHERE

❝ You know where I must start my search. **❞**

—From *Percy Jackson & the Olympians, Book Three:*
The Titan's Curse by Rick Riordan, found by Annabell Lang

Teach it

1. Write this on the board

> **Where**
>
> Proof:
>
> **where = here**
>
> Ex:
>
> (here)
> <u>Where</u> are the napkins?

PRACTICE THE CONVERSATION:
A: Will you read the sentence, please?
B: *Where are the napkins?*
A: Great! How did you spell *where*?
B: W-h-e-r-e.
A: Ohhh, I'm sorry to tell you, but that's not right.
B: It is right.
A: Prove it?
B: *Here are the napkins?*
A: Great. It is right. You can rearrange the sentence to listen to the proof if you need to.
B: Like what?
A: *I saw where you went.* Prove that one.
B: *I saw here you went . . . ?*
A: *You went here, you went where . . .*
B: Oh. Okay!

2. **Explain:**

We're, where, *and* were *are sometimes confused.*
But you will never be confused if you use the proof words.

When do we use **where**?

Of course—when we're asking about a place.

When you use **where**, *you can substitute the word* here *for it and listen. If it makes sense, then you have the right word.*

When you write **where**, *here is how you prove it:*

• *Underline the word and write the proof over it.*

• *Write* here *in parentheses over the word* **where**.

The underline means I intentionally made a grammatical choice here. The proof above the word means that it's the correct choice.

3. **Ask:** *Now, who will try out this proof with me?* (Enact the conversation.)

4. **Say:** *Open to your grammar chart and find* **where**. *Let's jot down the proof on the chart.*

Model it

5. Project the journal entry and read it.

6. Ask volunteers to read the sentences with **where** aloud. Enact the conversation with several students.

Practice it

7. **Say:** *In your journal today, see if you can use the word* **where** *at least five times, underlining each use. Write the proof over each one.*

March 7

(Part 3)

Later two more kids came, Blake and Lester. Blake asked, "Whose seat is this?"

"No one's."

"OK thanks."

Then Ender came and Abyus felt better. Then Abyus asked, "Who's not here?"

Then as a joke Ender said, "Who's not here? No really, who's the person over there

watching us? I don't know. Who is the one with the ugly face?"

"OK Ender, now you are just getting on my nerves. Wait, we just said who's like 5

times."

Then it hit Abyus, the guy who was watching them and Fox on the phone. It seemed

like he was planning somewhere. Probably in Hanger X but *(here)* **where** is Hanger X, *(here)* **where**

could it possibly be? He could still search for years and he still wouldn't know *(here)* **where** it

is. He would have to ask someone *(here)* **where** it is. Wait, why would they tell him *(here)* **where** top

secret Hanger X would be?

—Asher Bar-Yadin
Grade 6

18

OUR

❝ Do you think he was trying to get a rise out of me, or are all those ships really ❞ going to invade Commonwealth once Levana and I sign our Allegiance?

—From *Cress* by Marissa Meyer, found by Maggie Davis

Teach it

1. Write this on the board

> **Our**
>
> Proof:
>
> **our = your**
>
> Ex:
>
> (your)
> <u>Our</u> children are counting
> on us.

PRACTICE THE CONVERSATION:

A: Read the sentence, please.
B: *Our children are counting on us.*
A: Perfect. How did you spell *our*?
B: O-u-r.
A: No, you have the wrong word.
B: *Your children are counting on us.*
A: You're absolutely right!
B: Thank you.

2. **Explain:**

   *Sometimes people write the wrong word when they mean **our**.*

   *Which word is **our**? That's right. It's the pronoun, like* my *or* his.

   *So when you use **our**, you can substitute the word* your *for it and listen. If it makes sense, then you have the right word.*

   *When you write **our**, here is how you prove it:*

   • Underline the word and write the proof over it.

   • Write your *in parentheses over the word **our**.*

   The underline means I intentionally made a grammatical choice here. The proof above the word means that it's the correct choice.

3. **Ask:** *Who will volunteer to try out this proof with me?* (Enact the conversation.)

4. **Say:** *Open to your grammar chart and find **our**. Let's jot down the proof on the chart.*

Model it

5. Project the journal entry and read it.

6. Ask volunteers to read the sentences with **our** aloud. Enact the conversation with several students.

Practice it

7. **Say:** *In your journal today, see if you can use the word **our** at least five times, underlining each use. Write the proof over each one.*

April 24

The Water Cycle

The water cycle is cool. I wish I was a tiny rain drop so that I could live in a cloud. But

that's not important right now. What's important is that people are ruining it. I know we

(your)   (your)   (your)

have enough resources for **our** lives. But what about **our** kids, and **our** grandkids' lives?

                                                (your)

I can think of so many ways to stop pollution and wastefulness. Instead of using **our**

                                   (your)

gasoline cars, why don't we just use electric cars? And instead of using **our** power lines

and electricity, why don't we use solar power? I'm not one of those people who devotes

her life to saving the planet. But I do want to make a point.

—Miriam Stein
Grade 6

19

ARE

❝ We are gone. ❞
—From *Matched* by Ally Condie,
found by Kaylee Gurr

Teach it

1. Write this on the board

> **Are**
>
> Proof:
>
> ### are = were
>
> Ex:
>
> (were)
> <u>Are</u> you going to San
> Antonio?

PRACTICE THE CONVERSATION:

A: Will you read the sentence?
B: *Are you going to San Antonio?*
A: Great. How did you spell *are*?
B: A-r-e.
A: Oooh, no, that's not right.
B: Oh, yes it is.
A: No, I think it's wrong.
B: I can prove it. *Were you going to San Antonio?*
A: You're right! I'm so wrong!

2. **Explain:**

   It's a simple word, but people mix it up with other words frequently.

   When do you use **are**?

   Yes, as a verb in a sentence, as in "I am, you are . . ."

   When you use **are,** *you can substitute the word* were *for it and listen. If it makes sense, then you have the right word.*

   When you write **are,** *here is how you prove it:*

   • *Underline the word and write the proof over it.*

   • *Write* were *in parentheses over the word* **are**.

   The underline means I intentionally made a grammatical choice here. The proof above the word means that it's the correct choice.

3. **Ask:** *Now, who will try out this proof with me?* (Enact the conversation.)

4. **Say:** *Open to your grammar chart and find* **are**. *Let's jot down the proof on the chart.*

Model it

5. Project the journal entry and read it.

6. Ask volunteers to read the sentences with **are** aloud. Enact the conversation with several students.

Practice it

7. **Say:** *In your journal today, see if you can use the word **are** at least five times, underlining each use. Write the proof over each one.*

October 16

We're all infected; the numbers lower quickly every day. You might be thinking, "Well,

what do you mean we're all infected? It's not like we ^(were) **are** all dead?" Well, I mean that the

disease is so bad it's now in the air. It is extremely contagious and we all have it as long

as we ^(were) **are** breathing air.

    Meaning that, as soon as we die we will all come back as a zombie. So far we have

already lost many. In the 8th grade we have lost 3 out of 12 and many more in other

grades. The school is our safe house. Unfortunately we cannot stay at school because

then the dead would start noticing where all the living ^(were) **are** and would break in. So every

week day we can only stay 8 hours at the school. Then we have to go back into the

zombie-filled world. We can return home which most of us do but we have to always have

all the windows and doors blocked and lights off. We have to be quiet, too. We can't leave

without being prepared or making sure there ^(were) **are** very few zombies in the streets and if

not we have to snipe some with a silent sniper rifle to avoid attracting attention to the

house. No one can be left alone or behind. We work together. No one is stupid enough

to work alone in this crewel world. Those who do work alone because they believe he/

she is good enough to survive alone have already been bitten along time ago or it's just

a matter of time before they do get bit. Those who ^(were) **are** alone because their group was bit

should find a new group as soon as possible. And the biggest group possible. All groups

welcome new people. You can never have enough help in the apocalypse. It is sad that it

took a zombie apocalypse for everyone to get along and help work together. Before the

apocalypse lots of people didn't get along. People bareley worked together, and if they

did, they never welcomed just anyone. Everything is different in the apocalypse.

—Alyssa Rico
Grade 8

THEN

" Then he morphed [into a] Lunar royal guard. **"**

—From *Cress* by Marissa Meyer, found by Maggie Davis

Teach it

1. Write this on the board

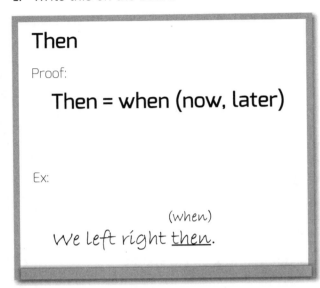

Then

Proof:

Then = when (now, later)

Ex:

(when)
We left right <u>then</u>.

PRACTICE THE CONVERSATION:
A: Will you please read the sentence?
B: *We left right then.*
A: Great. Wait . . . did you say *then*? Or *than*?
B: Then. T-h-e-n.
A: Oh no. I'm afraid that's wrong.
B: No, I'm afraid it's right.
A: Can you prove that?
B: Sure. *We left right then. We left right when.*
A: Perfect! You're right.
B: Thank you. Thank you very much.

2. **Explain:**

   Lots of people confuse the words then *and* than. *Today let's look at **then**.*

   *What does **then** mean?*

   That's right. It tells "when."

   *So when you use **then**, you can substitute the word* when *for it and listen. If it makes any sense, then you have the right word.*

   *When you write **then**, here is how you prove it:*

   • *Underline the word and write the proof over it.*

   • *Write* when *in parentheses over the word **then**.*

   The underline means I intentionally made a grammatical choice here. The proof above the word means that it's the correct choice.

3. **Ask:** *Now, who will try out this proof with me?* (Enact the conversation.)

4. **Say:** *Open to your grammar chart and find **then**. Let's jot down the proof on the chart.*

Model it

5. Project the journal entry and read it.

6. Ask volunteers to read the sentences with **then** aloud. Enact the conversation with several students.

Note: If one of your students discovers that *when* doesn't sound right on some usages of **then**, feel free to use alternative proof words, like *now* or *later.*

Practice it

7. **Say:** *In your journal today, see if you can use the word **then** at least five times, underlining each use. Write the proof over each one.*

March 27

I was in the 3rd grade when I got my first Facebook. Back **then** *(when)*, Facebook was really

popular and everyone thought me and my friend were so cool because we were the only

ones.

    Actually a few weeks ago I looked back to my old Facebook (it took forever) and **then** *(when)*

I found all of these super embarrassing pictures and statuses. I was crying from laughter

at my dumb posts and all of these "selfies" we took back **then** *(when)*, when we were 10 and 11!

Who even does this stuff at that age? **Then** *(when)* Facebook got old when Instagram came out

and it all repeats from there.

—Kaylee Gurr
Grade 8

THAN

66 They combed every inch of the room for more than an hour, but were forced **99** finally, to conclude that the locket was not there.

—From *Harry Potter and the Deathly Hallows* by J. K. Rowling, found by Madeleine Restaino

Teach it

1. Write this on the board

Than

Proof:

than = more than

Ex:

(more than)
She is taller <u>than</u> I am.

PRACTICE THE CONVERSATION:

A: Read the sentence, please.
B: *She is taller than I am.*
A: Did you mean *than*? Or *then*?
B: T-h-a-n, than.
A: Hmm. . . . I think that's the wrong word.
B: I don't think so.
A: Prove it for me?
B: *She is taller more than I am.*
A: Oh! It works. You're right.
B: It sounds funny that way though.
A: And that's why you use it only to listen.
B: So it's still right.
A: It sure is. Good job.

2. **Explain:**

   Many people confuse the words than *and* then.

   *What does **than** mean?*

   Yes! We use it when we're comparing things.

   *So if you use **than**, you can substitute the words* more than *for it and listen. If it makes any sense, then you have the right word.*

   *When you write **than**, here is how you prove it:*

   Underline the word and write the proof over it. Write more than *in parentheses over the word **than**.*

   • *The underline means I intentionally made a grammatical choice here.*

   • *The proof above the word means that it's the correct choice.*

3. **Ask:** *Now, who will try out this proof with me?* (Enact the conversation.)

4. **Say:** *Open to your grammar chart and find **than**. Let's jot down the proof on the chart.*

Model it

5. Project the journal entry and read it.

6. Ask volunteers to read the sentences with **than** aloud. Enact the conversation with several students.

Practice it

7. **Say:** *In your journal today, see if you can use the word* **than** *at least five times, underlining each use. Write the proof over each one.*

November 13

(more than)
The thing I'm most proud of more **than** anything in the world is my little brother Angel.

He has been growing up really fast. I see him and it reminds me of when I was his age.

(more than)
The best part of having a brother is that you do more sports **than** what you do with a

sister. That is my opinion.

I teach him Spanish and Turkish. I got Spanish and Portuguese from my roots, which

is easier than learning the language in a school. I got Turkish from what they taught me

in my old school.

It's fun having a little brother, but the disadvantages are him telling your mother about

(more than)
the bad things you do rather **than** the good things you do for him. Another disadvantage

(more than)
is that he is much smaller **than** you are, so you have to take care of him. But after you

teach him what to do and what not to do, it's really fun having a little brother.

The hobbies I teach him are drawing, soccer, and a lot more. But after all the fighting

we're still best friends and brothers for life!!

—Jacob Torres
Grade 7

22

A LOT

> ❝ I know being in a house with three girls sounds terrible, Jerry, but it's a lot better ❞ than being with a boy who's a couple of years older than you.
>
> —From *Bud, Not Buddy* by Christopher Curtis,
> found by Bryanna Ruggs

Teach it

1. Write this on the board

A lot

Proof:

a lot = a whole lot

Ex:

(a whole lot)
There was <u>a lot</u> of food at the party.

PRACTICE THE CONVERSATION:

A: Please read me the sentence.
B: *There was a lot of food at the party.*
A: Great! How did you spell *a lot?*
B: A . . . space . . . l-o-t.
A: Space? Isn't it one word? A-l-o-t?
B: No.
A: Yes, I believe it's one word.
B: No, it's actually two words.
A: Can you prove that?
B: *There was a whole lot of food at the party.*
A: Oh! You're so right! *A lot* is two words.

2. **Explain:**

   Many people write a lot *as one word, but that's considered substandard English. It's actually two different words, like a bunch or a group or a ton of something. You wouldn't write "I saw acrowd of people" or "We saw aherd of cows," and the same reasoning applies to **a lot**.*

   *So when you write **a lot,** here is how you prove it:*

   • *Write a whole lot in parentheses over **a lot**.*

   • *Underline **a lot**.*

   The underline means I made a grammatical choice here. The proof above the word means that it's the correct choice.

3. **Ask:** *Now, who will try out this proof with me?* (Enact the conversation.)

4. **Say:** *Open to your grammar chart, and let's find **a lot**. Let's jot down the proof on the chart.*

Model it

5. Project the journal entry and read it.

6. Ask volunteers to read the sentences with **a lot** aloud. Enact the conversation above to hear why **a lot** is written as two words.

Practice it

7. **Say:** *In your own journal, try to use **a lot** at least five times in what you're writing today, underlining each use. Write the proof over each one.*

February 24

Today for Texas History class, I'm going to teach the whole class **a lot** (a whole lot) about the

Reconstruction after the Civil War. It's going to be very cool to teach Ms. Koppe's class. I

wish we could teach **a lot** (a whole lot) more often about something. I am excited and nervous to teach

but I read chapter 19 and read **a lot** (a whole lot) of the book, so I think I will do just fine. It's **a lot** (a whole lot) of

fun to be a teacher for a day. I got **a lot** (a whole lot) of things for my locker yesterday. It was fun too.

—Genesis Thomas
Grade 7

23

ALREADY

> **❝** There was already bruises comin' on her arms. **❞**
>
> —From *To Kill a Mockingbird* by Harper Lee,
> found by Lindsay Weingart

Teach it

1. Write this on the board

Already

Proof:

already = soon

Ex:

         (soon)

The cat <u>already</u> had her kittens.

PRACTICE THE CONVERSATION:

A: Will you read the sentence, please?

B: *The cat already had her kittens.*

A: And how did you spell *already*?

B: A-l-r-e-a-d-y.

A: One word?

B: That's right, one word. *Already.*

A: Oh no! You're wrong!

B: I don't think so . . .

A: Can you prove it for me?

B: *The cat soon had her kittens.*

A: You're right! It's one word, *already.*

2. **Explain:**

   People often confuse <u>already</u> *with all ready.*

   *What does the single word **already** mean?*

   That's right. It means "by this time," or by a certain time.

   *Whenever you use **already**, you could substitute the word* soon *for it and listen. If it makes any sense, then you have the right word.*

   *When you write **already**, here is how you prove it:*

   • *Underline the word and write the proof over it.*

   • *Write* soon *in parentheses over the word **already**.*

   The underline means I intentionally made a grammatical choice here. The proof above the word means that it's the correct choice.

3. **Ask:** *Who will try out this proof with me?* (Enact the conversation.)

4. **Say:** *Open to your grammar chart and find **already**. Let's jot down the proof on the chart.*

Model it

5. Project the journal entry and read it.

6. Ask volunteers to read the sentences with **already** aloud. Enact the conversation with several students.

Practice it

7. **Say:** *In your journal today, see if you can use the word **already** at least five times, underlining each use. Write the proof over each one.*

September 16

Yesterday I was riding in the car going to my gymnastics meet. I don't know why, but

I was a little nervous. The first event we were going to was bars, and (soon) **already** I knew

something was wrong. We usually didn't go to bars first. We had (soon) **already** practiced,

practiced, and practiced at the gym, but today I guess I wasn't focused because when it

was time for my turn I fell on my hip. I got back up and finished my routine. I was so mad

that I had fallen and when I saw my score my heart sank. I had gotten an 8.55. I couldn't

believe that I had (soon) **already** started off bad.

—Annabell Lang
Grade 6

24

ALL READY

" Having received confirmation from Klein that the plane and the El Al crew also "
were [all] ready, Harel gave his operatives the go-ahead.

—From *Hunting Eichmann* by Neal Bascomb,
found by Ilan Sonsino

Teach it

1. Write this on the board

> All ready
>
> Proof:
>
> ## all ready = not ready
>
> Ex:
>
> (not ready)
> The class is <u>all ready</u> for vacation.

PRACTICE THE CONVERSATION:

A: Will you please read the sentence?

B: *The class is all ready for vacation.*

A: How many words are *all ready?* One or two?

B: Two.

A: Oh, I think you meant to use the other one.

B: I don't think so.

A: Can you prove it?

B: *The class is not ready for vacation.*

A: You're right! Perfect.

2. **Explain:**

   Lots of people confuse all ready with already.

   *What does **<u>all ready</u>** mean?*

   That's right. It means "all prepared." So a handy substitute is the opposite: not ready.

   *If you use **<u>all ready</u>**, you can substitute the opposite, the words* not ready, *and listen. If it makes sense, then you have the right words.*

   *When you write **<u>all ready</u>**, here is how you prove it:*

   • *Underline the word and write the proof over it.*

   • *Write* not ready *in parentheses over the words **<u>all ready</u>**.*

   The underline means I intentionally made a grammatical choice here. The proof above the word means that it's the correct choice.

3. **Ask:** *Now, who will try out this proof with me?* (Enact the conversation.)

4. **Say:** *Open to your grammar chart and find **<u>all ready</u>**. Let's jot down the proof on the chart.*

Model it

5. Project the journal entry and read it.

6. Ask volunteers to read the sentences with **<u>all ready</u>** aloud. Enact the conversation with several students.

Practice it

7. **Say:** *In your journal today, see if you can use **all ready** at least five times, underlining each use. Write the proof over each one.*

March 24–March 28

I tried to ask what was going on but it was like my vocal cords didn't want to cooperate

so all that came out was "mlaaahhh!"

"I think he's trying to speak," said a doctor. "He may be ready."

Since I couldn't ask what was going on, I had to see for myself. Without thinking I

pushed myself up to a sitting position and absorbed all the information I could. I was

in a lab/hospital room that had no windows, so I was guessing I was underground. I

looked down at my hands and was horrified by what I saw. My body is different. I'm still

Caucasian but I'm more tan and I don't have freckles on my hands. That explains why I

can't talk right now. I still have the same brain but not the same organs.

"What did you do to me?!" I finally managed to scream.

"You almost died, but we took your brain and inserted it into another body," a doctor

explained with a shocked face.

(not ready)

"Why would you do that?! I yelled. Wow. My voice is more stern and **all ready** to

command, but completely different. In fact, everything about me feels different.

"If you would like, we could change you back and you will be dead again," the

same doctor said.

"You still haven't answered my question!" I yelled. "Why did you change me?!" With

every word I scream, I feel more and more powerful. It's strange; I feel heat in my body

(not ready)
all ready for something.

"The world is in war. Longer and fiercer than we imagined. We need a super soldier,"

he stated. "We need you."

Me? Why me? What is so special about me? "Why me?" I asked.

"Because you are using 90% of your brain," said the doctor with a stern look.

90% of my brain? But, humans only use 10% of their brain.

"You have powers unimaginable. You must learn how to use those powers against our

enemies, or else we lose the war. You, and of course our nuclear weaponry, is our only

hope."

"What if I'm not ready to become your 'super soldier!'" I said in a serious voice.

The doctor's hand slipped into his pocket and pulled out a . . . gun!

"Then we will have to unalive you, if you know what I mean." The doctor cocked his

automatic pistol and pointed it at me.

(not ready)
"When do we start?!" I suddenly felt **all ready** to go.

—E. J. Easterly
Grade 6

Notes

25

ALL RIGHT

" Well, it's all right, anyway, Jim, long as you're going to be rich again some time
or other. "

—From *The Adventures of Huckleberry Finn*
by Mark Twain, found by Tori Shiver

Teach it

1. Write this on the board

> ### All right
>
> Proof:
>
> ## all right = all wrong
>
> Ex:
>
> (all wrong)
> Everything is <u>all right</u>.

2. **Explain:**

   *Do you know what mistake lots of people make with this? They write it as one word: alright.
   And that's not correct.*

   *What does **all right** mean?*

   Exactly! It means something like "okay."

   *Whenever you use **all right**, you can substitute the opposite—the words* all wrong *for it and listen. If it
   makes sense, then you have the right word.*

   *When you write **all right**, here is how you prove it. Underline the word and write the proof over it. Write*
   all wrong *in parentheses over the words **all right**.*

   *The underline means I intentionally made a grammatical choice here. The proof above the word means
   that it's the correct choice.*

3. **Ask:** *Now, who will try out this proof with me?* (Enact the conversation.)

4. **Say:** *Open to your grammar chart and find **all right**. Let's jot down the proof on the chart.*

Model it

5. Project the journal entry and read it.

6. Ask volunteers to read the sentences with **all right** aloud. Enact the conversation with several
   students.

Practice it

7. **Say:** *In your journal today, see if you can use the word **all right** at least five times, underlining each use. Write the proof over each one.*

ADS SECTION—INSANITY WEEKLY

(all wrong)
ALL RIGHT!

My amazingly Fail-a-licious Machine is here; doesn't

do anything right, drinks, smokes, takes drugs, swears,

hates English, and never bathes

It's only $1,999.99

Can I bet one of you idiots will buy one?

(all wrong)
ALL RIGHT!

CAR SALE   '70 CHEVROLET CHEVELLE

Running: no   Roof: no   Spare Tire: no   Paint: no

MPG: 00001125682   SS: barely Tires: 2

(all wrong)
It's **all right** to drive!

(all wrong)
ALL RIGHT!

You don't need a 3-speed Artichoke Juicer. But wait! Going to sell

you one.

Use this to order: Quantity: _____

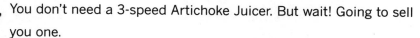

Address: _____

Credit Card #: _____

Price: $100.00

WOW! WHAT A GREAT DEAL!

$100.00 for something you'll never use.   WOOAH!

(all wrong)
ALL RIGHT!

*Subscribe 1 yr - $25.00

—Preston Oliver
Grade 6

26

LESS

66 If you're looking to indulge, skip the American cheese and reward yourself with a 99
few slices of bacon—it has less saturated fat and sodium.

—From *Eat This, Not That* by David Zinczenko, found by Phillip Kaplan

Teach it

1. Write this on the board

> **Less**
>
> Proof:
>
> ## Can you count them? No.
>
> Ex:
>
> (uncountable)
> We have <u>less</u> furniture
> than we used to.

PRACTICE THE CONVERSATION:

A: Will you please read the sentence?

B: *We have less furniture than we used to.*

A: Great. Just one second. I think you meant *fewer*, not *less*.

B: No, you wouldn't say fewer furniture. You could say fewer *pieces* of furniture, because you can count pieces. But *furniture* is not countable.

A: You're right! Good job.

2. **Explain:**

   Fewer *and* less *are sometimes confused. This logic will help you figure out which is correct.*

   *What does **less** mean?*

   *That's right, it means not as much of something. Something singular. You **can't** count whatever you're talking about (like sugar, time, patience).*

   *When you use **less**, ask yourself this: Can I count whatever I'm talking about? If you can't, then the word **less** is correct.*

   *When you write **less**, here is how you prove it:*

   • *Underline the word and write the proof over it.*

   • *Write* uncountable *in parentheses over the word **less**.*

   The underline means I intentionally made a grammatical choice here. The proof above the word means that it's the correct choice.

3. **Ask:** *Now, who will try out this proof with me?* (Enact the conversation.)

4. **Say:** *Open to your grammar chart and find **less**. Let's jot down the proof on the chart.*

Model it

5. Project the journal entry and read it.

6. Ask volunteers to read the sentences with **less** aloud. Enact the conversation with several students.

Practice it

7. **Say:** *In your journal today, see if you can use the word* **<u>less</u>** *at least five times, underlining each use. Write the proof over each one.*

May 22

You know what makes me mad? I'll tell ya. Whenever you're at a restaurant and you drink

soda with too much ice. Like c'mon lady/dude. You've had someone give you too much

(uncountable)   (uncountable)
ice and want **<u>less</u>** of it. Even if you want **<u>less</u>**, you can't do anything about it because it

would be rude to ask to have your drink sent back. If you were to return the drink there

(uncountable)
would probably be spit in your food. The smartest thing to do is ask for **<u>less</u>** ice so they

(uncountable)   (uncountable)
actually give **<u>less</u>**. One more tip, make sure you ask for **<u>less</u>** ice every time you get a refill.

—Maggie Davis
Grade 7

---

27 FEWER

> The police always preferred it that way: fewer witnesses to interview, less paperwork.

—From *From Beirut to Jerusalem* by Thomas Friedman,
found by Ilan Sonsino and Phillip Kaplan

Teach it

1. Write this on the board

Fewer

Proof:

Countable? Yes!

Ex:

(countable)

We have <u>fewer</u> chairs than we used to.

PRACTICE THE CONVERSATION:

A: Will you please read the sentence?

B: *We have fewer chairs than we used to.*

A: Good. But wait! Don't you mean *less chairs*?

B: No, I sure don't.

A: How do you know you should use *fewer*?

B: You can count chairs. So you use *fewer*.

A: You're right! It's correct! Good job.

2. **Explain:**

   Fewer *and* less *are sometimes confused. This logic will help you figure out which is correct.*

   *What does **a few** mean?*

   That's right. It means "several." You could count whatever you're talking about (like pencils, persons, papers).

   *When you use **fewer**, ask yourself if you could **count** whatever you're talking about. If you can, then the word fewer is correct.*

   *When you write **fewer**, here is how you prove it:*

   • *Underline the word and write the proof over it.*

   • *Write* countable *in parentheses over the word **fewer**.*

   The underline means I intentionally made a grammatical choice here. The proof above the word means that it's the correct choice.

3. **Ask:** *Now, who will try out this proof with me?* (Enact the conversation.)

4. **Say:** *Open to your grammar chart, and find **fewer**. Let's jot down the proof on the chart.*

Model it

5. Project the journal entry and read it.

6. Ask volunteers to read the sentences with **fewer** aloud. Enact the conversation with several students.

Practice it

7. **Say:** *In your journal today, see if you can use the word* **fewer** *at least five times, underlining each use. Write the proof over each one.*

March 10

Cooking Show

I am going to do a cooking show on *"fewer."* Here are the contestants: Zach Prescott,

Lauren Messer, Ben Brody. Give it up for the contestants. Oo yeah. The three contestants

have to pick a different amount of the three core ingredients which are rice, beans and

ground beef. They can add any other ingredients they want for their soup, though. Zack

(countable)   *(countable)*
picks **fewer** grains of rice than Lauren does. Ben picks **fewer** grains of rice than Lauren

(countable)
does but more than Zack picks. Zack picks **fewer** beans and meat than Lauren and Ben,

(countable)
but Ben picks **fewer** than Lauren. Now they have their three core ingredients. Now they

(countable)
start cooking. Lauren adds a little spice to her soup but Ben adds **fewer** grains of spice

to his soup but also adds some salt and pepper. Zach adds some spinach and salt to his

(countable)
soup, but Ben and Lauren do the same but **fewer** pieces than Zach does. They finished

cooking and now it's time for the judges to try it out and give first second and third place.

Ben's definately tastes the best so he gets first. Lauren gets second and I get third.

—*Zack Prescott*
Grade 6

28

LIE

“ I need to lie down. ”

—From *A Nest for Celeste* by Henry Cole,
found by Missy Puente

Teach it

1. Write this on the board

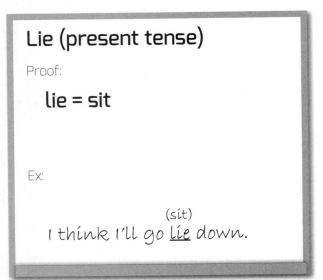

Lie (present tense)

Proof:

lie = sit

Ex:

(sit)
I think I'll go <u>lie</u> down.

PRACTICE THE CONVERSATION:

A: Read the sentence, please.

B: *I think I'll go lie down.*

A: Don't you mean *go lay down*?

B: Nope.

A: Prove that?

B: *I think I'll go sit down.*

A: Good!

2. **Explain:**

   There are not too many Americans who use this word correctly.

   When should we use lie, *and when should we use* lay?

   We lie down, but we hold something in our hands and lay it down.

   When you use **lie**, *you can substitute the word* sit *for it and listen. If it makes sense, then you have the right word.*

   When you write **lie**, *here is how you prove it:*

   • *Underline the word and write the proof over it.*

   • *Write* sit *in parentheses over the word* **lie**.

   The underline means I intentionally made a grammatical choice here. The proof above the word means that it's the correct choice.

3. **Ask:** *Now, who will try out this proof with me?* (Enact the conversation.)

4. **Say:** *Open to your grammar chart and find* **lie**. *Let's jot down the proof on the chart.*

   Note: It can get confusing when we use the past tense of this word. It goes like this:

   Today I will lie down; yesterday I lay down; I have lain down every day this month.

   Proofs: Today I will sit down; yesterday I sat down; I have sat down every day this month.

Model it

5. Project the journal entry and read it.

6. Ask volunteers to read the sentences with **lie** aloud. Enact the conversation with several students.

Practice it

7. **Say:** *In your journal today, see if you can use the word **lie** at least five times, underlining each use. Write the proof over each one.*

April 30

(sit)   (sit)
Usually I **lie** down at around 11, but yesterday I decided to **lie** down about 30 minutes

(sit)   (sit)
earlier. I tried to **lie** down in my bed earlier than when I usually **lie** down to go to bed, to

see if I would have less trouble getting up out of bed the next morning. Unfortunately, it

didn't work. In second period, I almost gave up. I was about to lay my head on my desk

in defeat when Dan and I found out that for the bridge lab in science class, we would

have to build an arch bridge. I kept forcing myself to be in a positive attitude, so that

(sit)
Dan wouldn't give up, with me following him. (We can't **lie** down on this job.) I could

lie, saying that building such a constructively flawed bridge would make us the best

constructors in the class. I am scared about our grade being based on how it is built, not

how it stands or withstands more weight.

—Jonah Katzman
Grade 8

29

LAY

> Because we were the first school to arrive, we got to run around the field all we wanted until the teachers told us it was time to lay out our sleeping bags on the ground and get good seats.

—From *Wonder* by R. J. Palacio, found by Annabell Lang

Teach it

1. Write this on the board

Lay

Proof:

   lay = put

Ex:

                    (put)
He should <u>lay</u> the candle
on the table.

PRACTICE THE CONVERSATION:

A: Please read the sentence.

B: *He should lay the candle on the table.*

A: Oh no, you mean *lie the candle on the table*, right?

B: No, I do not.

A: How can you prove that?

B: *He should put the candle on the table.*

A: Ah! You're right!

B: When you're putting something with your hands, you should use *lay*, not *lie*.

A: Perfect! Well done.

2. **Explain:**

This is a word that gives most Americans trouble.

When should we use lie, and when should we use lay? We lie down, but we hold something in our hands and lay it down.

*So whenever you use **lay**, you can substitute the word put for it and listen. If it makes sense, then you have the right word.*

*When you write **lay**, here is how you prove it:*

* *Underline the word and write the proof over it.*
* *Write put in parentheses over the word **lay**.*

The underline means I intentionally made a grammatical choice here. The proof above the word means that it's the correct choice.

3. **Ask:** *Now, who will try out this proof with me?* (Enact the conversation.)

4. **Say:** *Open to your grammar chart and find **lay**. Let's jot down the proof on the chart.*

   Note: It can get confusing when we use the past tense of this word.

   It goes like this: Today I will lay the pencil down; yesterday I laid the pencil down; I have laid the pencil down every day this month.

   Proofs: Today I will put the pencil down; yesterday I put the pencil down; I have put the pencil down every day this month.

Model it

5. Project the journal entry and read it.

6. Ask volunteers to read the sentences with **lay** aloud. Enact the conversation with several students.

Practice it

7. **Say:** *In your journal today, see if you can use the word* __lay__ *at least five times, underlining each use. Write the proof over each one.*

April 30

Today, I'll finish up a PowerPoint presentation. I started by **laying** (put) down the crucial

information first. Then, I **laid** (put) down the pictures and videos on the sides. Next I recorded

some audio of myself talking in the background to shake things up a bit and engage the

audience. In addition to audio, I may **lay** (put) down some music on a few slides. After I **lay** (put)

down everything I need, I will add the finishing touches: the theme, the background;

the color scheme, and the animations and transitions. After the finishing touches are

complete, I'll **lay** (put) my work out in front of me and marvel at the great presentation I made.

Once the reflection period is over, I'll save it and proceed to receive a 100% on it. If you

do this, the presentation can't be bad.

—Robert Jackson
Grade 8

Author's note: In the third sentence of this journal entry, the student could have incorrectly

used *lay* instead of *laid*, used "put" as the proof, and assumed it was the correct word.

This is a reminder that we have to do all of that tense-checking orally as we do proof

conversations. The important thing is that they associate the meaning "put" with the

word *lay* and don't confuse it with *lie*.

30

SHOULD'VE

> ❝ Should've taken less time with so many reminders of Tali all around me, but ❞ being in a room she might never see again scared me more than any guard I'd ever crossed.

—From *The Shifter* by Janice Hardy, found by Angelica Martinez

Teach it

1. Write this on the board

Should've

Proof:

should've = should have

Ex:

(should have)
You <u>should've</u> washed the dishes.

PRACTICE THE CONVERSATION:

A: Will you read the sentence?

B: *You should've washed the dishes.*

A: Perfect. How did you spell *should've*?

B: S-h-o-u-l-d-apostrophe-v-e.

A: Apostrophe? Nooo.

B: Oh yesssss.

A: Can you prove that?

B: *You should have washed the dishes.*

A: Well, you're so right! By the way, do you remember the only two reasons we use apostrophes?

B: Contractions and possessions.

A: And plurals?

B: Nope, not plurals. Just contractions and possessions.

A: You nailed it! Wonderful.

2. **Explain:**

   Lots of people make this mistake: should of.

   It sounds right when you say it out loud, but it's not ever right if you write it like that.

   *What does **should've** mean?*

   That's right. It means "should have." It's a contraction. The apostrophe marks the place where letters are taken out.

   *So whenever you use **should've,** you can substitute the words* should have *for it and listen. If it makes sense, then you're using the right spelling.*

   *When you write **should've**, here is how you prove it:*

   • *Underline the word and write the proof over it.*

   • *Write* should have *in parentheses over the word **should've**.*

   The underline means I intentionally made a grammatical choice here. The proof above the word means that it's the correct choice.

3. **Ask:** *Now, who will try out this proof with me?* (Enact the conversation.)

4. **Say:** *Open to your grammar chart and find **should've**. Let's jot down the proof on the chart.*

Model it

5. Project the journal entry and read it.

6. Ask volunteers to read the sentences with **should've** aloud. Enact the conversation with several students.

Practice it

7. **Say:** *In your journal today, see if you can use the word **should've** at least five times, underlining each use. Write the proof over each one.*

October 18

List of Ironic Sentences!

1. Did you hear about the fire house that burned down?

2. My dog got run over by an animal rescue van.

3. My doctor died of the flu.

4. That cow is lactose intolerant.

5. I'm a peanut farmer but I'm so allergic to nuts that they make me die.

6. The man who invented the Segway accidently rode one off a cliff.

COMMENTS:

- (should have)
  The firehouse **should've** had better equipment.

- (should have)
  My dog **should've** been inside. [**Note:** my dog did not really get run over.]

- (should have)
  The doctor **should've** lived.

- (should have)
  The cow **should've** died by now.

- (should have)
  The peanut farmer **should've** been smarter.

- (should have)
  The man **should've** not died.

—Miriam Stein
Grade 6

31

USED TO

" Between you and me, I'm still trying to get used to the whole flying-kid thing. "

—From *School's Out—Forever* by James Patterson,
found by Angelica Martinez

Teach it

1. Write this on the board

Used to

Proof:

used to = in the past

Ex:

(in the past)
We <u>used to</u> be friends.

PRACTICE THE CONVERSATION:

A: Read the sentence, please.
B: *We used to be friends.*
A: How did you spell *used to*?
B: U-s-e-d space t-o.
A: You put a "d" in there?
B: Yes, I did.
A: You didn't need that.
B: Yes, I did.
A: Can you prove that for me?
B: *In the past, we used to be friends.*
A: Aha. Perfect. You're right.

2. **Explain:**

   Lots of people leave off the "d" in used to. It's hard to hear that "d," so it's a natural mistake.

   *What does **used to** mean?*

   *Yes, it means that "something happened in the past"; it **used to** happen.*

   *When you use **used to**, you can add the phrase* in the past *and listen. If it makes sense, then you have used the past tense correctly.*

   *When you write **used to**, here is how you prove it:*

   • *Underline the words and write the proof over it.*

   • *Write* in the past *in parentheses over the words **used to**.*

   The underline means I intentionally made a grammatical choice here. The proof above the words means that it's the correct choice.

3. **Ask:** *Now, who will try out this proof with me?* (Enact the conversation.)

   Note: If the proof doesn't work because the sentence is one like "I'm not used to eating chili in spaghetti," just add an alternate proof, like *accustomed to*.

4. **Say:** *Open to your grammar chart and find **used to**. Let's jot down the proofs on the chart.*

Model it

5. Project the journal entry and read it.

6. Ask volunteers to read the sentences with **used to** aloud. Enact the conversation with several students.

Practice it

7. **Say:** *In your journal today, see if you can use the words <u>**used to**</u> at least five times, underlining each use. Write the proof over each one.*

January 30

The Last Clip

(<u>C</u>ool <u>L</u>ike <u>I</u>ndians <u>P</u>OW!)

He's the Clipasaurs' greatest ancestor. He's billions of years old. There <u>**used to**</u> *(in the past)* be Clips

everywhere, but now there aren't. Uh . . . they're dead. And there's only one left. His

name is—you don't even know—he's so cool and wise.

February 2

Now, he <u>**used to**</u> *(in the past)* be sad that he was the last Clip, but not anymore. He hid himself in a

deep cave and meditated for billions of years. While he meditated he learned. He <u>**used to**</u> *(in the past)*

learn very slowly but now very quickly. And he knows that he's the last ever Clip hiding

in his cave. He wakes up and there he is, hibernating, the last Clip. He <u>**used to**</u> *(in the past)* run wild,

but now the Clipasaurs are on his trail. Clips are the biggest species of Clipasaurs there

are. The last Clip was about four times the size of the evil Clipasaurs.

February 3

But there were thousands of evil Clipasaurs and only one of him. He knew it'd be

nearly impossible to defeat them, but he knew he had to try. And so he went to the evil

Clipasaurs' lair and simply knocked down the door. The Clipasaurs said, "Hey, come on

in! We're having a party!"

February 6

The Clip walks in and screams, "Your party's over!" (Cheesiest thing ever!)

Ya know what? I don't feel like writing a story today.

—William Kavy
Grade 6

32

ME/I

Teach it

1. Write this on the board

> ### Me/I
>
> Proof:
>
> ### Break them up.
>
> Ex:
>
> (I talked)
> ~~My father and~~ I talked
> (about me)
> about ~~my sister and~~ <u>me.</u>

PRACTICE THE CONVERSATION:

A: Read the sentence, please.

B: *My father and I talked about my sister and me.*

A: Are you sure it's not *my father and me?*

B: Yes. You wouldn't say *me talked.* You'd say *I talked.*

A: Perfectly done. Now let's look at the end of that sentence.

B: Okay.

A: It should be *my sister and I.*

B: That may sound more educated, but it's actually wrong.

A: Prove that, please.

B: *My father talked about my sister. My father talked about I.* See? That's wrong. *My father talked about me. Me* is the correct word here.

A: You're absolutely right. *Me* is right.

B: Ha ha.

A: . . .

2. **Explain:**

   When do we use I, *and when do we use* me? *Believe it or not, many people use the wrong pronoun. Even educated people often get this one wrong. There's an easy way to know for sure which one is correct.*

   When you're deciding whether to say **someone and I** *or* **someone and me,** *just drop the other person from the sentence and listen to the word* **I** *or* **me** *by itself. Your ear will know which is correct.*

   When you write **someone and me/I,** *here is how you prove it:*

   • *Underline the word and write the proof over it.*

   • *Take the other person out of the sentence and write your choice in parentheses over the word.*

   The underline means I intentionally made a grammatical choice here. The proof above the word means that it's the correct choice.

3. **Ask:** *Now, who will try out this proof with me?* (Enact the conversation.)

4. **Say:** *Open to your grammar chart and find* **me/I**. *Let's jot down the proof on the chart.*

Model it

5. Project the journal entry and read it.

6. Ask volunteers to read the sentences with **someone and me/I** aloud. Enact the conversation with several students.

Practice it

7. **Say:** *In your journal today, see if you can use __someone and me/I__ at least five times, underlining each use. Write the proof over each one.*

February 26

The Time I Went to Get My Dog!

It was a hot summer day when I got my dog. I remember distincktively it was August

(I ran)

4th, 2013 when we went to the stinky pound. **My brother Ariel and I** were running back

and forth in the halls. But we didn't find one we wanted. But then I saw a small room

(I walked)

with cages of dogs. **My brother and I** walked in and I saw the dog I wanted. My brother,

mom, and dad sat at a table and waited until I got the dog out of the cage. My mom and

dad had to talk about it for a while. They didn't look convinced but when **my brother, the**

(I made)

dog and I made puppy faces, we all laughed and then my parents looked at each other.

(told me)

My parents told **Ariel and me** we could get the dog. We were so happy! That was a great

(for me)

day for **my brother and me**.

—Tamara Weiss
Grade 6

33

SUBJECT/VERB AGREEMENT

We was all as glad as we could be, but Tom was the gladdest of all, because he had a bullet in the calf of his leg.

—From *The Adventures of Huckleberry Finn* by Mark Twain, found by Dan Meishar

Teach it

1. Write this on the board

Subject/verb agreement

We was going.

It don't matter.

One (of my brothers) **are** here.

The **boys** (with the band) **is** talented.

Measles are a dangerous disease.

There **is** some **problems** in these sentences.

They is all the same problem.

Proof:

(plural) (singular)
We was going

(plural) (plural)
We were going.

PRACTICE THE CONVERSATION:

A: Pick a sentence from the list and read it out loud.

B: Hmm . . . okay. *It don't matter.*

A: Great. Do you see a problem with subject/verb agreement?

B: I do. It should be *it doesn't matter.*

A: Can you prove that?

B: Sure. *It* is singular. *Do* is plural. They don't match.

A: *Do?* It doesn't say *do.* It says *don't.*

B: And that means *do not.*

A: Right.

B: So we wouldn't say *it do.* That's a subject/verb agreement problem.

A: Good.

B: So they should both be singular. *It doesn't.*

A: It doesn't what?

B: Matter.

A: Ha ha. Very good.

2. **Explain:**

   Listen to this first sentence. We was going. *Can you pinpoint the one word causing the problem in this sentence? That's right,* was. *Who can explain what's wrong with it? It should be* were, *that's right.*

   It seems obvious, but this is a widespread problem. It's called **subject/verb agreement**. *How can a subject and verb agree? What does that mean? Yes. If the subject is singular, the verb must be singular too. If the subject is plural, the verb must be also.*

   Whether we hear subject/verb mismatches informally from people we know or formally on the news, they are mistakes.

   If you notice yourself choosing a verb that agrees with the subject, show your thinking:

   • *Underline the subject and the verb.*

   • *Then write singular or plural over the subject and the verb. If they match, you don't have an agreement problem.*

   The underline means I intentionally made a grammatical choice here. The proof above the word means that it's the correct choice.

3. **Ask:** *Now, who will try out this proof with me?* (Enact the conversation.)

4. **Say:** *Open to your grammar chart and find* **subject/verb agreement (s/v agr.)**. *Let's jot down the proof on the chart.*

Note: If the problem is deeper than this and your students don't know the singular versus plural forms of common words, you might consider giving them a list for their reference.

Model it

5. Project the journal entry and read it.

6. Ask volunteers to read the sentences aloud. Enact the conversation with several students.

Practice it

7. **Say:** *In your journal today, see if you can notice **subject/verb agreement** at least five times, underlining each use. Write the proof over each one.*

May 2

        (plural)   (plural)
I love playing soccer, but there **are** some **things** that make the games less than perfect

   (plural)   (plural)   (plural)
experiences. **All** of the soccer games I play in **are** mostly in the afternoon. **All** of these ex-

    (plural)   (singular)
football coaches always **have** games early in the morning. **One thing** that really annoys me at

   (singular)   (plural)
the games **is** the behavior of some of the parents. It seems that **all** of the parents of this one

     (plural)   (singular)
team always **scream and cheer** unnecessarily and at inappropriate times. Every single **one** of

   (singular)   (plural)   (plural)
my teammates **says** how annoying they are. **All** of my teammates **are** determined to win so

(plural)
they aren't mocked by the parents. Hopefully we won't play them this weekend because they

are always in the same tournaments that we're in.

             —Jonah Katzman
               Grade 8

34

ACCEPT

66 Gollum ate nothing, but he accepted the water gladly. 99

—From *The Lord of the Rings: The Two Towers*
by J. R. R. Tolkien, found by Julian Ponce

Teach it

1. Write this on the board

PRACTICE THE CONVERSATION:

A: Will you please read that sentence?

B: *Will they accept this idea?*

A: Good! But wait . . . how did you spell *accept*?

B: A-c-c-e-p-t.

A: Oohhh, no, you've got the wrong one. Sorry.

B: I don't think so.

A: Can you prove it?

B: *Will they take this idea?*

A: You're right! It's correct!

B: Thank you. I thought so.

2. **Explain:**

Lots of people confuse this word with except.

*What does **accept** mean?*

Yes, it means "take."

So when you use accept, you can substitute the word take for it and listen. If it makes sense, then you have the right word.

*When you write **accept**, here is how you prove it:*

• *Underline the word and write the proof over it.*

• *Write take in parentheses over the word **accept**.*

The underline means I intentionally made a grammatical choice here. The proof above the word means that it's the correct choice.

3. **Ask:** *Who will try out this proof with me?* (Enact the conversation.)

4. **Say:** *Open to your grammar chart and find **accept**. Let's jot down the proof on the chart.*

Model it

5. Project the journal entry and read it.

6. Ask volunteers to read the sentences with **accept** aloud. Enact the conversation with several students.

Practice it

7. **Say:** *In your journal today, see if you can use the word **accept** at least five times, underlining each use. Write the proof over each one.*

November 25

Cognitive Dissonance on Benjamin Franklin

While doing research on Benjamin Franklin, I saw how diligent, honest and hardworking

(take)

of a man he was, and I definitely agreed and **accepted** his brilliance and greatness, until

I stumbled upon some intriguing details about him. I figured out that Benjamin Franklin

(take)

was a very dirty man. I could **accept** the fact that he may have liked to drink a lot, but I

(take)

couldn't **accept** quite a few things about him. He had multiple affairs and especially with

women who weren't even near his age. I saw that Benjamin Franklin liked to fool around

(take)

with married women and was a very big chick magnet, and that he **accepted** this as

something that wasn't wrong and was a fine thing to do. I didn't expect this at all and I

definitely saw how much of a cognitive dissonance moment that I had just experienced

(take)

about Benjamin Franklin that was very hard for me to **accept**.

—Dan Meishar
Grade 8

35

EXCEPT

> 66 None of the animals could form any ideas as to what this meant, except old 99 Benjamin, who nodded his muzzle with a knowing air, and seemed to understand, but would say nothing.
>
> —From *Animal Farm* by George Orwell, found by Lee Kaplan

Teach it

1. Write this on the board

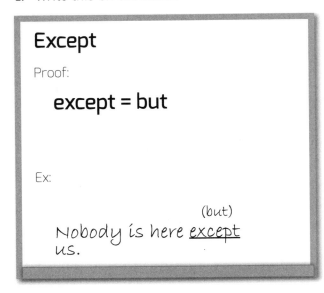

Except

Proof:

except = but

Ex:

(but)

Nobody is here <u>except</u> us.

2. **Explain:**

    Many adults confuse accept *and* except. *When you use* **except,** *you can try substituting* but *and listen to how it sounds. If it sounds right, you have the right word.*

    When you write **except,** *here is how you prove you have the right word:*

    • *Underline the word and write the proof over it.*

    • *Write* but *in parentheses over the word* **except.**

    The underline means I intentionally made a grammatical choice here. The proof above the word means that it's the correct choice.

3. **Ask:** *Now, who will try out this proof with me?* (Enact the conversation.)

4. **Say:** *Open to your grammar chart and find* **except***. Let's jot down the proof on the chart.*

Model it

5. Project the journal entry and read it.

6. Ask volunteers to read the sentences with **except** aloud. Enact the conversation with several students.

Practice it

7. **Say:** *In your own journal, try to work the word **except** at least five times, underlining each use. Write the proof over each one.*

September 20

Short Story

[NOT REAL!]

As I looked up at the dark sky, I thought three more days, only three more and then they

would all know what had happened on that day so many years ago . . .

(but)
. . . **except** my current wife didn't know what had happened back then.

(but)
. . . **except** now I am a changed man (I hope).

Now I am John Henson, not that man anymore.

I was born in South Virginia but moved around till I ended up here in Louisiana where

that incident took place in the swamps.

(but)
. . . **except** it all happened so fast . . .

[What do you think so far?   Go Phil!!]

—Phil Silberman
Grade 8

36

LOOSE

" Chloe was still smiling, her body loose, soft, and warm in my arms, when the cab "
dropped us off in front of my building on 125th street.

—From *Zoo* by James Patterson, found by Jake Torres

Teach it

1. Write this on the board

> ### Loose
>
> Proof:
>
> ## loose = tight
>
> Ex:
>
> (tight)
> His dentures were so <u>loose</u>
> he couldn't smile.

2. **Explain:**

    Many people mix up the words loose *and* lose.

    *What does **loose** mean? That's right. It means "not tightened."*

    *When you use **loose**, you can substitute the word* tight *for it and listen. If it makes sense, then you have the right word.*

    *When you write **loose**, here is how you prove it:*

    - *Underline the word and write the proof over it.*

    - *Write* tight *in parentheses over the word **loose**.*

    The underline means I intentionally made a grammatical choice here. The proof above the word means that it's the correct choice.

3. **Ask:** *Now, who will try out this proof with me?* (Enact the conversation.)

4. **Say:** *Open to your grammar chart and find **loose**. Let's jot down the proof on the chart.*

Model it

5. Project the journal entry and read it.

6. Ask volunteers to read the sentences with **loose** aloud. Enact the conversation with several students.

Practice it

7. **Say:** *In your journal today, see if you can use the word **loose** at least five times, underlining each use. Write the proof over each one.*

March 27

In my house there is an office instead of a dining room. My family always eats in the

kitchen so we figured a dining room would be lost space in the house. In the office room

my sister and I do most of our homework. On a school day the table would be filled

(tight)

with **loose** papers. On the wall are three bookshelves with all kinds of books. Some of

(tight)

the books are so old that they have **loose** pages. Other books that my parents bought

(tight)

decades ago have interesting marks and bookmarks. I once found a **loose**-leaf paper with

a grociery list in a book. On another wall is a large dry-erase board. One of the screws of

(tight)   (tight)

the board was so **loose** that it fell over. Well, I just wrote the word **loose** five times!

—Michael Squire
Grade 8

---

37   LOSE

> " The slothful and lazy not only lose the game—they lose at life. "
>
> —From *The Limit* by Kristen Landon, found by Alicia Narvaez

Teach it

1. Write this on the board

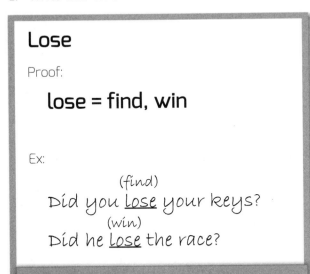

Lose

Proof:

lose = find, win

Ex:

(find)
Did you <u>lose</u> your keys?
(win)
Did he <u>lose</u> the race?

PRACTICE THE CONVERSATION:
A: Please read the sentence.
B: *Did you lose your keys?*
A: Great. How did you spell *lose*?
B: L-o-s-e.
A: Ooh. No. That's not right.
B: I believe it's right.
A: Can you prove it?
B: *Did you find your keys?*
A: Perfect! It's correct. You're right.

2. **Explain:**

   Many people mix up the words loose *and* lose.

   *What does **lose** mean?*

   Yes, it means something like "to misplace."

   It can also mean "to not win," like at a game or sport.

   *Whenever you use **lose**, you can test if it is correct by substituting the opposite word.*

   - *You can substitute* find *for* misplace.

   - *Or you can substitute* win *for* not win.

   Then listen. If one of those makes sense, you have the right word.

   *When you write **lose**, here is how you prove it:*

   - *Underline the word and write the proof over it.*

   - *Write* find *or* win *in parentheses over the word **lose**.*

   The underline means I intentionally made a grammatical choice here. The proof above the word means that it's the correct choice.

3. **Ask:** *Now, who will try out this proof with me?* (Enact the conversation.)

4. **Say:** *Open to your grammar chart and find **lose**. Let's jot down the proof on the chart.*

Model it

5. Project the journal entry and read it.

6. Ask volunteers to read the sentences with **lose** aloud. Enact the conversation with several students.

Practice it

7. **Say:** *In your journal today, see if you can use the word **lose** at least five times, underlining each use. Write the proof over each one.*

November 3

This week's fantasy football was pretty interesting. I was **losing** *(win)* to Phillip 60–153. Then

I had two receivers play. One got me 15 points, and the other got me 81 points. In my

mind, any player who gets over 15 fantasy points has had a good week. But anyway,

I am now trailing Phillip 150–103. I still have one player left to play. He is one of the

best in the NFL. He never **loses.** *(win)* He got me 52 points last week. While I was watching

the Texans game (when my guy got 81 points), I remembered that fantasy basketball

was going on, so I ran to my phone to see if I won. I never **lose.** *(win)* I won and I thought to

myself, one down, a lot more to go. No one likes to **lose,** *(win)* especially me.

Just one more Ba-da-bing:

   I walked into the gym after not going for a month. I shot my first basket, and I thought,

I still got it.

November 5

Today is Tuesday. I did **lose** *(win)* to Phillip by 16 points. I am now 6–3. I play Phillip again this

week and all of my starters are playing so it should be better.

   Start pushing myself harder. Great vocabulary quiz. I just got an 84 on my test, but I

am winning in fantasy basketball 11–2. The Spurs also won in double overtime yesterday

so that made my day ok too.

—Ethan Weingart
Grade 8

AFFECT

" You don't think your breathing is affected, my dear boy? You seem to breathe " quickly.

—From *Great Expectations* by Charles Dickens, found by Jonah Katzman

Teach it

1. Write this on the board

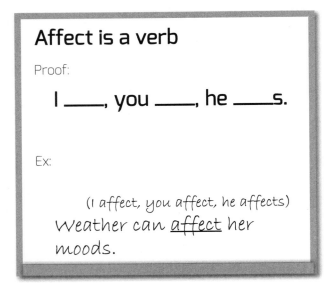

Affect is a verb

Proof:

I ____, you ____, he ____s.

Ex:

(I affect, you affect, he affects)
Weather can <u>affect</u> her moods.

PRACTICE THE CONVERSATION:

A: Read the sentence, please.
B: *Weather can affect her moods.*
A: Great. How do you spell *affect*?
B: A-f-f-e-c-t.
A: Oh no . . . that's not the right word.
B: I'm afraid it is.
A: Can you prove it?
B: *Weather can affect her moods.* I affect, you affect, he affects. Affect is a verb.
A: Perfect! It is a verb!

2. **Explain:**

Many people often mix up effect *and* affect.

*What does **affect** mean?*

That's right. It means something like "make a change." It's a verb, an action.

*So when you use **affect**, write the verb proof for it and listen. If it makes sense, then you have the right word.*

*When you write **affect**, here is how you prove it:*

• Underline the word and write the proof over it.

*• Write I __, you __, he __s in parentheses over the word **affect**.*

The underline means I intentionally made a grammatical choice here. The proof above the word means that it's the correct choice.

3. **Ask:** *Now, who will try out this proof with me?* (Enact the "Practicing conversation.")

4. **Say:** *Open to your grammar chart and find **affect**. Let's jot down the proof on the chart.*

Model it

5. Project the journal entry and read it.

6. Ask volunteers to read the sentences with **affect** aloud. Enact the practicing conversation with several students.

Practice it

7. **Say:** *In your journal today, see if you can use the word **affect** at least five times, underlining each use. Write the proof over each one.*

January 30

Yesterday we did an 11-minute essay in class. The topics we wrote about were very

different. I didn't expect it to be so diverse. I thought most people would've thought to

write about futuristic stories/movies. I'll write an 11-minute essay anytime, they're very

fun. For my movie I picked *Munich* directed by Steven Spielberg. It's my favorite movie,

(I affect, you affect, he affects)
and this really **affected** me. This made it really easy to use in an 11-minute essay, because

I think it looks at all aspects of life, such as: revenge, anger, guilt, sorrow, vengeance,

hatred, pursuing peace, affection, and an "eye for an eye." The main idea of this movie

(I affect, you affect, he affects)
is to show how the killing **affected** the leader of the group, but also how he got through

(I affect, you affect, he affects)
the guilt, and knew he was **affecting** the world in a good way. He had trouble with this

thought, because he didn't know if he was doing good or bad. In life, everybody wants to

(I affect, you affect, he affects)
affect the world, but how they will do it is the question.

—Ilan Sonsino
Grade 8

39   **EFFECT**

❝ Peeta rolls his eyes at Haymitch. "She has no idea. The effect she can have. ❞

—From *The Hunger Games* by Suzanne Collins,
found by Anael Ashkenazi

Teach it

1. Write this on the board

> **Effect is a noun**
>
> Proof:
>
> a/an _____, the _____,
> some _____.
>
> Ex:
>
>   (an effect, the effect, some effect)
> Weather has an <u>effect</u> on
> her moods.

PRACTICE THE CONVERSATION:

A: Will you please read the sentence?
B: *Weather has an effect on her moods.*
A: How do you spell effect?
B: E-f-f-e-c-t.
A: I'm sorry, but you have the wrong word.
B: No, I believe it's the right word.
A: How do you know?
B: Effect is a noun.
A: What's the noun proof?
B: An effect, the effect, some effect.
A: So prove that effect is a noun here?
B: *Weather has an effect, the effect, some effect. On her moods.*
A: . . . Perfect. That *is* the right word.

2. **Explain:**

   Many people mix up effect *and* affect.

   *What does **effect** mean?*

   That's right. It means something like "result." It's a noun, a thing.

   *So when you use **effect**, write the noun proof for it and listen. If it makes sense, then you have the right word.*

   *When you write **effect**, here is how you prove it:*

   • *Underline the word and write the proof over it.*

   • *Write a/an __, the __, some __ in parentheses over the word **effect**.*

   The underline means I intentionally made a grammatical choice here. The proof above the word means that it's the correct choice.

3. **Ask:** *Now, who will try out this proof with me?* (Enact the conversation.)

4. **Say:** *Open to your grammar chart and find **effect**. Let's jot down the proof on the chart.*

   Note: *Effect* can be a verb sometimes, as in *to effect change.* A good proof in this case is "to effect = to cause." Most of the time, though, the noun proof works.

Model it

5. Project the journal entry and read it.

6. Ask volunteers to read the sentences with **effect** aloud. Enact the conversation with several students.

Practice it

7. **Say:** *In your journal today, see if you can use the word **effect** at least five times, underlining each use. Write the proof over each one.*

May 1

Effects

(an effect, the effect, some effect)
Today I need a good grade in school! Bad grades have an **effect** on whether I go to high

(an effect, the effect, some effect)
school or not. High school will have an **effect** on my life majorly. I need to go to high

(an effect, the effect, some effect)
school because if I don't, it will obviously have even more of an **effect** on my life. This is

(an effect, the effect, some effect)
why studying has a big **effect** on school and your progress in school. If I get bad grades,

(an effect, the effect, some effect)
it will have a visible and lasting **effect** on my mom's attitude at the end of the day. If I

(an effect, the effect, some effect)
fail, I can have an **effect** on my mom because she will have to home school me or take

(an effect, the effect, some effect)
me to summer school every day of the summer. This can have an **effect** on both of us

(an effect, the effect, some effect)
but I think that this will have an **effect** on me more because it's having an **effect** on my

education.

(an effect, the effect, some effect)
Doing this journal entry is going to have a positive **effect** on my grade majorly. If this

(an effect, the effect, some effect)
journal entry sucks it will have a short-term **effect** on me and it will have a long-term

(an effect, the effect, some effect)
effect on whether I go to high school or not!

—Layne Dentinger
Grade 8

PART II

PUNCTUATION

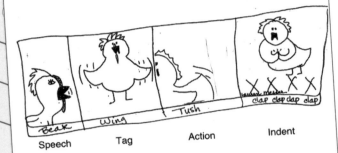

| Speech | Tag | Action | Indent |

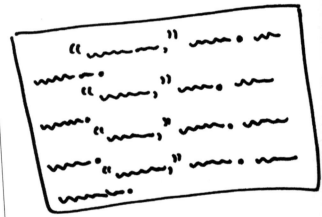

> Punctuation is the tone of people's voices. Without punctuation, no one would breathe at all. Ever.
>
> —Lindsay Weingart

I've heard a research rumor that grammar acquisition is 75 percent oral. This seems especially true for the dynamics of punctuation. If writing is drawing speech on paper, as pioneering psycholinguist Lev Vygotsky proposed (1978), then punctuation guides our voices when we re-create speech from the paper. In other words, as writers, we use punctuation so that readers can hear the speech of the writer, complete with breathing, pauses, and all kinds of vocal gestures.

Even though these cues aren't as necessary in students' familiar world of texting, they are still necessary in the business and legal worlds. Every one of our students will need to be able to navigate those worlds. They may not all become lawyers, but they will all come into contact with laws, wills, decrees, and contracts in their lives. They need to be competent, literate citizens and family members.

This section includes most of the rules of the basic literacy rules of punctuation. On the grammar chart, students will write proofs for some of the rules; they'll write examples for others.

The issue of sentence correctness is so important that it has its own chapter.

APOSTROPHES—CONTRACTIONS

❝ I think it's best that we show our new foster families that we're very . . . **❞**

—From *Bud, Not Buddy* by Christopher Curtis,
found by Bryanna Ruggs

Teach it

1. Write this on the board

Apostrophes in contractions

Proof:

don't = do not

Ex:

(did not)
She <u>didn't</u> leave yet.

PRACTICE THE CONVERSATION:

A: Will you read me that sentence?

B: Sure. *She didn't leave yet.*

A: How did you spell "didn't"?

B: D-i-d-n-apostrophe-t.

A: You used an apostrophe? What are the two reasons we use apostrophes?

B: Contractions and possessions.

A: And which is this?

B: A contraction.

A: Hmm . . . I don't think so.

B: It is!

A: Prove it?

B: *She did not leave yet.*

A: Perfect! It is a contraction.

2. **Explain:**

   There are only two reasons we use apostrophes: contractions and possessions.

   When we contract two words, we shrink them into one word.

   Wherever we leave out letters, we mark that with an apostrophe. It's almost like we took a scalpel and cut those letters out, and we close the wound with a tiny stitch, the apostrophe.

   When you use an apostrophe in a contraction, this is how you prove it:

   - *Underline the contraction. This means "I made a grammatical choice here."*
   - *The proof above the word shows that it's the correct choice.*

3. Pass out the practice conversation.

4. **Ask:** *Now, who will try out this proof with me?* (Enact the conversation.)

5. **Say:** *Open to your grammar chart, and let's find **apostrophes in contractions**. Let's jot down an example of a proof on the chart.*

Model it

6. Project the journal entry and read it.

7. Ask for a volunteer to read aloud each of the sentences with the contractions. Each time, reenact the practicing conversation above. This allows students to hear why the word gets an apostrophe, to hear proof that it is a **contraction**—and to internalize the language of the conversation.

Practice it

8. **Say**: *In your journal today, try to use at least five examples of **apostrophes in contractions**, underlining each use. Write the proof over each one.*

January 30

My Dog Toby

Bad things he does
• Bites
• Chews shoes, clothes, socks
• Poops and pees
• Sheds fur
• Nails are too sharp
• Throws up sometimes

(he is)   (he is)   (I am)

He's a very bad dog but I love him to death. **He's** very small and big, but **I'm** just happy

(he is)   (did not)

he's my dog. It would be so boring if I **didn't** have him as a dog. "Name is <u>Toby</u>." He gets

(he is)

my clothes dirty by his shedding fur. **He's** so playful and his nails are very sharp, so my

dad clipped his nails.

- Golden retriever
- ~~Born November 4th~~
- Mom died after birth
- Has 5 brothers and sisters

—Kennedy Cantu
Grade 6

---

41 APOSTROPHES—POSSESSIONS

> **"** All my father's birds were bigger, and they picked on him, and made him **"**
> miserable.
>
> —From *The Neddiad* by Daniel Pinkwater,
> found by Kennedy Cantu

Teach it

1. Write this on the board

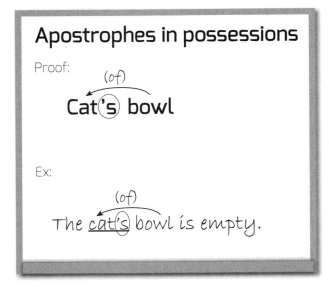

Apostrophes in possessions

Proof:

Cat('s) bowl *(of)*

Ex:

The <u>cat('s)</u> bowl is empty. *(of)*

PRACTICE THE CONVERSATION:

A: Read me the sentence please.

B: *The cat's bowl is empty.*

A: Great. How did you spell *cat's*?

B: C-a-t-apostrophe-s.

A: Hmm. I don't think you needed an apostrophe there.

B: I'm pretty sure an apostrophe goes there.

A: Why? What are the two reasons you would ever use an apostrophe?

B: Contractions and possessions.

A: Yes! But wait . . . which one is this?

B: It's a possession.

A: I don't think it is.

B: It absolutely is!

A: Can you prove it?

B: *The cat's bowl . . . the bowl of the cat . . .*

A: It's empty, isn't it? Great job.

2. **Explain:**

   There are only two reasons we use apostrophes: contractions and possessions.

   Possessions mean that something belongs to something. Use this process to test to see if a noun is possessive:

   - *Insert "of the" in between the two words.*

   - *Flip the positions of the two words; then read it to see if they sound like a possession.*

     Here are examples:

     the boy's bike = the bike of the boy

     my friend's feelings = the feelings of my friend

     the computer's hard drive = the hard drive of the computer

   So if you're going to use an apostrophe to show a possession, here's how you show your proof:

   - *Circle the apostrophe-s.*

   - *Draw an arrow from the possession (the thing) to the owner.*

   - *Write* of the *over the arrow, like the example on the board.*

   - *Now listen to it backward, like those examples.*

3. Pass out the practicing conversation.

4. **Ask:** *Now, who will try out this proof with me?* (Enact the conversation.)

5. **Say:** *Open to your grammar chart, and let's find **<u>apostrophes in possessions, singular</u>**. Let's jot down an example of a proof on the chart.*

Model it

6. Project the journal entry and read it.

7. One at a time, ask volunteers to read the sentences with the **singular possessive apostrophes** aloud. Ask them to use the proof to show how the apostrophe marks a possession.

Practice it

8. **Say:** *In your journal today, try to use at least five examples of* **apostrophes of possession**, *underlining each use. Write the proof over each one.*

August 29

My favorite soccer players are Messi, Nehmar, Pelé, Ronaldo, Ronaldihno and last Robihno.

They are my favorite soccer players. Messi—because he is the best in the world when it

comes to soccer, with 185 goals in 1 month. He was declared **2012(of)'s** best. Nehmar Jr.—He

is my favorite, because 1) he is Brazilian, 2) **Nehmar(of)'s** agility skills are great. Nehmar

was declared best shooter of all times. Pelé—He is my favorite because 1) Brazilian,

2) **Pele(of)'s** record won him awards, and he was the first person to be called the best in

1998. In 1997 Pelé retired. Ronaldo—Ronaldo is a good Portuguese soccer player.

Ronaldo(of)'s winnings are 95,000,000 euros for playing in Real, Madrid, and Portugal.

Ronaldo(of)'s free kicks are considered the best. Ronaldihno—Ronaldihno is my first favorite.

He made 23 goals in one game. **Ronaldihno(of)'s** skills and tricks are perfect. The last but not

least is Robihno, a good Brazilian soccer player. He is now playing for Milan, the Italian

League. What or who is your favorite soccer player?

—Jacob Torres
Grade 7

APOSTROPHES—PLURALS

> 66 High above a thick and prickly trunk, the branches of the trees drooped down like 99
> laundry hung out to dry, spreading their wide, flat leaves out in every direction,
> like a low, leafy ceiling over the Baudelaires' heads.
>
> —From *A Series of Unfortunate Events: The Ersatz Elevator*
> by Lemony Snicket, found by Lauren Messer

Teach it

1. Write this on the board

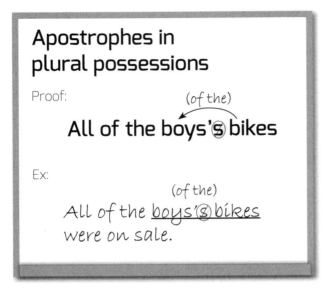

Apostrophes in
plural possessions

Proof:

         (of the)

All of the boys's bikes

Ex:

        (of the)

All of the boys's bikes
were on sale.

PRACTICE THE CONVERSATION:

A: Will you please read the sentence?

B: *All of the boys' bikes were on sale.*

A: Yes! How do you spell *boys'*?

B: B-o-y-s-apostrophe.

A: Apostrophe? Do you know the two reasons we use apostrophes?

B: I sure do. Contractions and possessions.

A: And which one is this?

B: It's a possession.

A: Can you prove it?

B: *The boys' bikes—the bikes of the boys . . .*

A: More than one boy?

B: Yep. Boys.

A: Great job.

2. **Explain:**

There are only two reasons we use apostrophes: contractions and possessions.

Possessions mean that something belongs to something. Use this process to prove that a noun is possessive:

- *Insert "of the" in between the two words.*
- *Flip the positions of the two words; then read it to see if they sound like a possession.*

But what happens when the word is plural? Where do you put the apostrophe? There's a simple way to look at this.

It's not just the apostrophe that shows the possession. It's the **apostrophe-s.** *So you think of a plural word (boys, cars, computers, horses, children) and add an* **apostrophe-s** *to those words, to show possession.*

If the word already has an "s," to show that it's plural, then you just **take off the second "s."** *You show it like this: The boys have cars . . . the boys's cars . . . the boys' cars. (It sounds stupid to pronounce the second "s," like "boyziz.")*

On the other hand, if we need to pronounce the "s," we keep it. The children have parents, the children's parents. We add the apostrophe-s and then don't take off the "s." It's simple, right?

3. **Ask:** *Now, who will try out this proof with me?* (Enact the conversation.)

4. **Say:** *Open to your grammar chart, and let's find* ***apostrophes in possessions***, ***plural***. *Let's jot down an example of a proof on the chart.*

Model it

5. Project the journal entry and read it.

6. Ask volunteers to read the sentences with the **plural possessions** aloud. Ask each of them to use the proof to hear how we add an apostrophe-s and then remove the unvoiced "s."

Practice it

7. **Say:** *In your journal today, try to use at least five **plural possessions,** underlining each use. Write the proof over each one.*

April 10

Tonight the Spurs play Dallas. The **Spurs's** *(of the)* record is the best in the league, and their players

are amazing. Their **players's** *(of the)* shots always fall and their **teammates's** *(of the)* passes are always crisp.

Spurs's *(of the)* fans are the best. The **fans's** *(of the)* cheers radiate through the arena. The game tonight will

be great. Dallas stinks. The Spurs are good and that's what makes the games always fun. Our

staff and coaches are the best. Even our arena rocks. The other **arenas's** *(of the)* capacities are not as

large as our San Antonio **Spurs's** *(of the)* AT&T Center. Spurs are the best, and that's all there is to it!

—Phillip Kaplan
Grade 8

43 NO APOSTROPHES—PLURALS

> " The whole mountaintop was in ruins—so many beautiful buildings and gardens " gone.

—From *The Last Olympian* by Rick Riordan, found by Claire Weingart

Teach it

1. Write this on the board

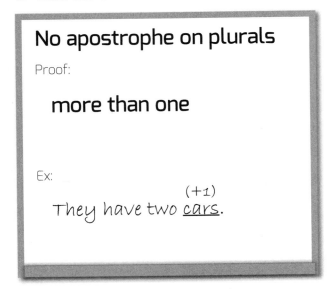

No apostrophe on plurals

Proof:

more than one

Ex:

                  (+1)

They have two <u>cars</u>.

PRACTICE THE CONVERSATION:

A: Please read the sentence.
B: *They have two cars.*
A: Great. How did you spell *cars*?
B: C-a-r-s.
A: Apostrophe-s.
B: No, no apostrophe.
A: Are you sure?
B: Yes.
A: Well, what are the two reasons we use apostrophes?
B: Contractions and possessions.
A: And which one is *cars*?
B: Neither. It's just a plural. Just more than one car. No apostrophe.
A: Perfect! Well done.

2. **Explain:**

   Misused, abused apostrophes are all over America. You can tell who is educated and who is not by looking at what they do with apostrophes. It's a basic literacy marker.

   So here's the rule. There are two reasons we use apostrophes: contractions and possessions. That's it.

   Do we use apostrophes on plurals? No.

   Do we use apostrophes on verbs ending in "s"? No.

   There are only two reasons we use apostrophes: contractions and possessions. (Have your students repeat three times "contractions and possessions.")

   When you write any word that's plural—which means more than one—and it ends with an "s," **don't put an apostrophe.** *Here is how to prove your choice:*

   - *Underline the word*
   - *Write the proof over it*
   - *Write "+1" in parentheses over the plural word*

   Remember, the underline means I intentionally made a grammatical choice here not to use an apostrophe. The proof above the word means that it's the correct choice.

3. **Ask:** *Who will try out this proof with me?* (Enact the conversation.)

4. **Say:** *Open to your grammar chart, and let's find the punctuation rule about* **no apostrophes on plurals***. Let's jot down the proof (+1) on the chart.*

   Note: There is an exception, of course. Plurals of acronyms, numbers, or other symbols need an apostrophe to show where the acronym stops and the plural "s" starts. (Does he know his ABC's? He got all A's. It was the 1980's; I don't show my students this until they have the rest of the rule down or until someone notices it and brings it up.)

Model it

5. Project the journal entry and read it.

6. Ask volunteers to read the sentences with the **plurals without apostrophes**. Ask them to use the proof to show why they intentionally shunned the cute little mid-air comma.

Practice it

7. **Say:** *In your journal today, try to use at least five **"apostrophe-less" plurals**, underlining each use. Write the proof above each one.*

February 19

From "He's the Stupidest Man in the World . . ."

(+1)
I don't always poke grizzly **bears,** but when I do . . . I always wear a meat necklace.

(+1)
I don't always ride **tricycles,** but when I do . . . I always make sure to put on my

knee and elbow pads.

(+1)   (+1)
I don't always jump off **cliffs,** but when I do . . . I make sure to leave my **parachutes**

at home.

(+1)
I don't always hit wasp **nests,** with a baseball bat but when I do . . . I cover myself

with honey beforehand.

—Lindsay Weingart
Grade 6

NO APOSTROPHES—VERBS ENDING IN S

> 66 Springtime, she thought, before the heat comes and crushes the leaves into pulp 99
> and withers the petals off the flowers.
>
> —From *City of Bones* by Cassandra Clare, found by Miriam Stein

Teach it

1. Write this on the board

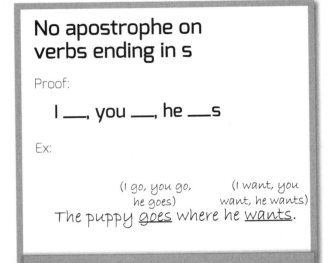

No apostrophe on
verbs ending in s

Proof:

I __, you __, he __s

Ex:

(I go, you go,
he goes)   (I want, you
want, he wants)

The puppy <u>goes</u> where he <u>wants</u>.

PRACTICE THE CONVERSATION:

A: Will you please read this sentence?
B: *The puppy goes where he wants.*
A: Do you see a word that ends with "s"?
B: *Goes.*
A: Great. It needs an apostrophe, doesn't it?
B: No. It doesn't.
A: What are the two reasons we use apostrophes?
B: Contractions and possessions.
A: Yes. Which one is this word?
B: Neither.
A: Then why is there an "s" on it?
B: It's just a word that ends with "s." It's a verb.
A: Can you prove that?
B: I go, you go, he goes. No apostrophes on verbs.
A: Great job.

2. **Explain:**

   It's important to know when to use apostrophes, and it's just as important to know when not to use them. Often, people use them where they don't belong.

   So here's the rule. There are two reasons we use apostrophes: contractions and possessions. That's it.

   Do we use apostrophes on plurals? No.

   Do we use apostrophes on verbs ending in "s"? No.

   There are only two reasons we use apostrophes: contractions and possessions. (Have your students repeat three times "contractions and possessions.")

   When you write a verb or any other word that ends in "s," don't put an apostrophe. Here is how to prove your choice:

   - *Underline the word and write the verb proof in parentheses over the word.*

   Remember, the underline means I intentionally made a grammatical choice here not to use an apostrophe. The proof above the word means that it's the correct choice.

3. **Ask:** *Who will try out this proof with me?* (Enact the conversation.)

4. **Say:** *Open to your grammar chart, and let's find the punctuation rule about* <u>**no apostrophes on verbs ending in "s."**</u> *Let's jot down an example (like goes) on the chart.*

   Note: If students don't already know the verb proof, you might want to teach it first.

Model it

5. Project the journal entry and read it.

6. Ask for volunteers to read each of the sentences with the <u>**verbs without apostrophes**</u> out loud. Ask them to use the proof and explain the no-apostrophes rule.

Practice it

7. **Say:** *In your journal today, try to use and at least five __verbs without apostrophes__, underlining each use. Write the proof over each one.*

February 7

(I am, you are, it is)

This entry **is** actually kind of personal and when I saw it in the topics list it made me

stop and think for a while. What do I think of my religion? I have always grown up

into a Christian family. Everyone in my family is hardcore Christian. But sometimes I

(I am, you are, it is)

think it's really annoying when everyone in my family **is** yelling at me to go to church

(I do, you do, it does)

and to get more into the Lord. **Does** it make me a bad person to say that I don't want

to? When you've experienced the things that I have, you kind of wonder if there really

(I am, you are, it is)(I do, you do, it does) (I help, you help, it helps)

is a God that **does** good and **helps** people. Of course I believe and will always be a

Christian but I can't help but wonder . . .

(I am, you are, it is)   (I get, you get, it gets)

Another thing **is** that I can't say anything jokingly to my mom because she **gets**

(I try, you try, it tries)

offended and **tries** to give me a holy message!!! No one can take a joke. Also, a lot of

Christians (at least at my church) are very judgmental and rude. If you have your eyes

open during prayer, or wear jeans to church, they give you bad looks!

I'm still young and right now, religion doesn't really matter to me. My family is

(I make, you make, it makes)

always pushing me to religion but I think it **makes** me want to get further away from it.

(Sorry for the rant. I didn't know how else to explain it.)

—Kaylee Gurr
Grade 8

45 COMMAS IN A SERIES

> 66 She chewed up a toothbrush pill, punched her pillows, and shoved an old 99 portable heater . . . under the covers.

—From *Uglies*, by Scott Westerfeld, found by Juliette Urrutia

Teach it

1. Write this on the board

Commas in a series

Ex:

(commas in series)
They had snow, rain,
sleet, and hail.

PRACTICE THE CONVERSATION:

A: Read the sentence, please.

B: *They had snow, rain, sleet, and hail.*

A: Great. Why are there commas after *snow, rain, sleet,* and *hail?*

B: Because these are items in a series.

A: That's right! Here's a question for you. Do you know which one of these commas is optional?

B: What do you mean?

A: You could leave out one of these commas if you want to. Which one?

B: The last one?

A: That's right. Do you know why?

B: Because of the word *and?*

A: . . . That's exactly right. The word *and* separates these items. So you could put the comma there if you want to, but that one is your choice. Good job!

2. **Explain:**

   One way we use commas is to show what goes together. Commas separate items in a list, also called items in a series.

   The underline under each comma means I intentionally made a grammatical choice here. The proof above the word means that it's the correct choice.

3. **Ask:** *Who will try out this proof with me?* (Enact the conversation.)

4. **Say:** *Open to your grammar chart and find* **commas in a series**. *Let's jot down an example on the chart. (Write a short example like 1, 2, 3, and 4.)*

Model it

5. Project the journal entry and read it.

6. Ask volunteers to read aloud each of the sentences with the items in a series. Ask them to use the proof to explain the rule.

Practice it

7. **Say:** *In your journal today, try to use at least five items with **commas in a series**, underlining each use. Write the proof over each one.*

March 28

When I grow up . . .

(commas in a series)
I could be a basketball player, a construction worker, a baby sitter, a soccer player,

(commas in a series)   (commas in a series)
a banker, a lawyer, a person who makes video games, a dancer, a singer, a teacher,

(commas in a series)   (commas in a series)   (commas in a series)   (commas in a series)
a lawn mower, a hunter, a lacrosse player, a fisher, a football player, an author, a

(commas in a series)   (commas in a series)   (commas in a series)
scientist, a doctor, a guitarist, a desiner, a sports comintator, a basketball coach, a

(commas in a series)   (commas in a series)
sports cards worker/owner, a principal, a gym teacher, and a counselor. You can do

anything you put your mind to!

—Jacob Fiero
Grade 7

46

COMMAS IN A LETTER

" "Dear Miss Gokey," it read. "

—From *A Northern Light* by Jennifer Donnelly,
found by Tori Shiver

Teach it

1. Write this on the board

> Commas in the
> opening of a
> friendly letter
>
> Ex:
>
> (friendly letter opening)
> Dear John,

PRACTICE THE CONVERSATION:
A: Will you please read the example?
B: *Dear John,*
A: Great. What comes after John?
B: A comma.
A: Yes! Why do we use a comma there?
B: Commas go after the opening of a friendly letter.
A: Perfect!

2. **Explain:**

    There are two different kinds of letters, informal friendly letters and more formal business letters. For the friendly letters, we start with a greeting, followed by a comma. This is called a salutation or an opening.

    So whenever you're writing to someone (on paper or digitally, even e-mail), if you begin with a greeting, it's correct to follow that greeting with a comma.

    *   *The underline under the comma means I intentionally made a grammatical choice here.*
    *   *The proof above the word shows that it's the correct choice.*

3. **Ask:** *Who will try out this proof with me?* (Enact the conversation.)

4. **Say:** *Open to your grammar chart and find **commas in a letter**. Let's jot down an example on the chart.*

    Note: On the grammar chart, you'll also find the comma at the ending of a letter, after the closing (like after *Sincerely,*). Though there's not a lesson specifically for this comma, you might want to teach that along with this lesson.

Model it

5. Project the journal entry and read it.

6. Ask for volunteers to read the beginnings of the letters aloud. Ask them to use the proof to hear why the openings contain commas.

Practice it

7. **Say:** *In your journal today, try to use at least one **letter opening**, underlining each use. Write the proof over each one.*

September 27

Today is Friday. I want to write a letter to our Hebrew substitute teacher. I think we

took advantage of her. At the moment I misbehaved I only thought about having fun. I

think, sometimes as students, we forget that teachers are here to help. They don't want

to punish us (at least I hope not) and all we want is to have fun at their expense. But I

thought about what it must've been like for her to try and teach us while we laughed the

whole time. Frustrating. So I want to tell her everything I just said now in a letter. I'll write

it at lunch. Here's what it will say:

(letter opening)
Dear Mrs. Grauer,

I would like to apologize for my behavior yesterday, I know that teachers are here to

help and I'm sorry for only thinking about the moment of fun, and not how frustrating it

must've been for you . . . eh . . . I'll be respectful again when I write it at lunch.

—Lee Kaplan
Grade 8

47

COMMAS IN APPOSITIVES

" But Benjamin pushed her aside and in the midst of a deadly silence he read: **"**
"Alfred Simmonds, Horse Slaughterer and Glue Boiler, Willingdon."

—From *Animal Farm* by George Orwell, found by Lee Kaplan

Teach it

1. Write this on the board

Commas in appositives

Ex:

(appositive)

Ms. Davis, our principal,
will be right with you.

PRACTICE THE CONVERSATION:

A: Please read the sentence.

B: *Ms. Davis, our principal, will be right with you.*

A: Perfect! But wait . . . do you use commas before and after *our principal*?

B: You sure do.

A: But why?

B: Those commas surround an appositive.

A: What's an appositive?

B: It's when you name and rename something. You use different words, but it's the same person or thing. If you read the sentence *without* the appositive, it will still make sense.

A: Great explanation.

B: . . .

A: . . .

2. **Explain:**

   An appositive is a way to rename something right after you say it. We put commas before and after appositives. How do you know it's an appositive?

   If you read the sentence without the appositive, you see that it still would make sense:

   "Ms. Davis will be right with you."

   The appositive just adds information.

   The underline means I intentionally made a grammatical choice here. The word appositive *above means that I know why I made that choice. I know the rule.*

3. **Ask:** *Who will try out this proof with me?* (Enact the conversation.)

4. **Say:** *Open to your grammar chart and find* **_commas in appositives_**. *Let's jot down an example on the chart.*

   Note: Some appositives (like my friend John or my sister Sally) don't need commas. Listen to the sentence, and if you pause, use commas.

Model it

5. Project the journal entry and read it.

6. Ask volunteers to read each of the sentences with the appositives aloud. Ask them to say the rule to explain why the commas are there.

Practice it

7. **Say:** *In your journal today, try to use at least five examples of __commas in appositives__, underlining each use. Write the proof over each.*

March 28

My Dream

Last night, I dremt about school. I know it's kinda weird, but the dream

was weird. So it all started by the parking lot by **the Alamo, the old** *(appositives)*

(appositives)
Texas shrine. It was about 2:30, and the shining sun was beating down

on my forehead. Then, out of nowhere, **Ms. Bernabei, the crazy ELA** *(appositives)*

teacher, walked out of an ice cream van and started chasing me. I don't

know why, but she was. Then, I suddenly was at school and **Ms. Black, a** *(appositives)*

cool teacher, had some taco eraser that was supposedly mine.

"Ms. Black," I started, "I know you are the one who stole my taco."

"No, this came out of nowhere."

Then she walked down the stairs by **the lockers, our storage units**. *(appositives)*

Ms. Bernabei, the ice cream van person, came by my locker which *(appositives)*

was 66, not 67, and yelled, "We don't have time to put stickers on our

lockers, young man!" Then **Maura, my sister,** woke me up. *(appositives)*

—Lauren Messer
Grade 6

> " Though she'd used up all her tranquilizer darts during the fight in Paris, she'd " been able to manufacture some weapons on her own—projectiles made out of welded nails.
>
> —From *Cress* by Marissa Meyer, found by Maggie Davis

Teach it

1. Write this on the board

Commas after beginning phrases or clauses

Ex:

(beginning phrase)
<u>After the play,</u> we went home.

(beginning clause)
<u>After we left the beach,</u> we went home.

---

2. **Explain:**

   Sometimes in a sentence, if you look for the main subject and verb, you find them not at the beginning, but after groups of words.

   If these groups of words would not stand alone as a sentence, then they are phrases or clauses. They should be separated from the main part of the sentence by a comma. If you listen to the sentence aloud, you hear a pause, and that is where the comma goes.

   Why does the group of words not have to stand alone as a sentence? Well, can you join two sentences with a comma? Never. But after any group of words that's less than a sentence, definitely, you use a comma.

   - When you use a comma for this reason, underline it and write **_beginning phrase_** above it.

   The underline means I intentionally made a grammatical choice here. The label above the word means that it's the correct choice.

3. **Ask:** *Who will try out the sentence with me?* (Enact the conversation.)

4. **Say:** *Open to your grammar chart and find **commas after beginning phrases**. Let's jot down an example on the chart.*

   Note: If students have trouble distinguishing a phrase from a sentence, teach them the sentence wringer (Lessons 66–71).

   If students have trouble distinguishing a clause from a sentence, teach them AAAWWWUBification (Lesson 75).

PRACTICE THE CONVERSATION:

A: Will you please read the first sentence?

B: *After the play, we went home.*

A: Why is there a comma after *play*?

B: We use commas after beginning phrases. *After the play* is a beginning phrase.

A: Isn't it a sentence by itself?

B: No.

A: How do you know?

B: There's no verb in it.

A: Great. So it's less than a sentence. What do we do?

B: We put a comma after it.

A: Good. Will you read the second sentence?

B: *After we left the beach, we went home.*

A: Why is there a comma after *beach*?

B: Everything before the comma isn't a whole sentence.

A: Are you sure?

B: Sure. It has a subject and verb, but the word *after* makes it less than a whole sentence.

A: Huh?

B: Listen to it by itself: *After we left the beach.* See? That's not a whole sentence.

A: Right. So what do we do?

B: We use a comma to separate a beginning phrase or clause. That one is a clause.

A: What's a clause?

B: It's anything with a subject and verb that doesn't stand alone as a sentence.

A: Great job.

Model it

5. Project the journal and read it.

6. Ask volunteers to read the sentences with the **commas after beginning phrases** aloud. Ask them to explain the rule.

Practice it

7. **Say:** *In your journal today, try to use at least five **commas after beginning phrases**, underlining each use. Write the proof over each one.*

August 28

(beginning phrase)
Ever since I could talk, I have always loved animals and babies. (beginning phrase) **When I was around 4 or**

5 years old, my dog had 11 puppies in one litter. I would often take naps with them. They

(beginning phrase)
were the sweetest things. **When I got older,** I had two beagles named Lucy and Lady who

(beginning phrase)
also had puppies. **When I was around 10 or 11,** I was often told that there's something

special about me when it comes to animals and babies. They say animals and babies

usually seem to like me better than others. I talked to my mom about it and she said,

"They can sense that you like them. They can tell you have a good heart."

(beginning phrase)
After that, every time I was around animals or babies I would pay attention to how they

acted around me compared to others. "They're right," I thought. I don't know how I never

noticed before. My family and friends say it's a gift, and they are absolutely right. Lots of

my friends have dogs, and even their dogs love me. I love dogs the most though because

(beginning phrase)
they're so sweet! I have 4 dogs of my own. We have a big back yard. **Out there in the**

yard, they love running and playing.

—Alyssa Rico
Grade 8

---

49 COMMAS BEFORE ENDING PHRASES/CLAUSES

> " The scudding clouds did look a bit fishy, rippled into scales by a high-altitude " wind.

—From *Uglies*, by Scott Westerfeld, found by Juliette Urrutia

Teach it

1. Write this on the board

> ### Commas before ending phrases or clauses
>
> Ex:
>
> (ending phrase)
>
> We went home at 6:00, just before sunrise.
>
> (ending clause)
>
> We left the beach after that, since our friends were already gone.

PRACTICE THE CONVERSATION:

A: Read the first sentence please.

B: *We went home at 6:00, just before sunrise.*

A: Why is there a comma after *6:00*?

B: Because the rest of the sentence is just a phrase.

A: And the rule?

B: You use a comma before an ending phrase.

A: Read the second sentence, please?

B: *We left the beach after that, since our friends were already gone.*

A: Why did you join two sentences with a comma? You know you can't do that.

B: Because . . . it's not two sentences. Look at the second part. It's not a whole sentence.

A: It's not?

B: Listen to it: *Since our friends were already gone.* That's not a whole sentence by itself.

A: Good job! So you use a comma.

2. **Explain:**

Sometimes in a sentence, if you look for the main subject and verb, you find them at the beginning. And after the main sentence, there is another group of words.

If these groups of words could not stand alone as a sentence, then they are phrases or clauses. They should be separated from the main part of the sentence by a comma. If you listen to the sentence aloud and you hear a pause, that is where the comma goes.

Why does the group of words have to not stand alone as a sentence? Well, can you join two sentences with a comma? Never. But for any group of words that's less than a sentence, definitely, you use a comma.

When you use a comma for this reason, how do you prove it?

*   Underline it and write **_ending phrase_** above it.

The underline means I intentionally made a grammatical choice here. The label above the word means that it's the correct choice.

3. **Ask:** *Who will try out the sentence with me?* (Enact the conversation.)

4. **Say:** *Open to your grammar chart and find **_commas before ending phrases_**. Let's jot down an example on the chart.*

    Note: If students have trouble distinguishing a phrase from a sentence, teach them the sentence wringer (Lessons 66–71).

    If students have trouble distinguishing a clause from a sentence, teach them AAAWWWUBification (Lesson 75).

Model it

5. Project the journal entry and read it.

6. Ask for volunteers to read the sentences with the **commas before ending phrases** aloud. Ask each of them to explain the rule.

Practice it

7. **Say:** *In your journal today, try to use at least five __commas before ending phrases__, underlining each use. Write the proof over each one.*

August 29

Have you ever wondered what your mission is in life? Last night, I didn't fall asleep

(ending phrase)
till around 11pm**, because I was thinking about that one simple, but yet so complex**

(ending phrase)
question. Not in a depressing way or anything. Just out of curiosity. If I'm to become

(ending phrase)
a pharmacist, I don't want to just sit behind the counter**, asking people for their name**

and what they've come to pick up. I'd like to help people. Make a difference. Find a cure.

Find a replacement for evil shots. Shots are and always have been one of my worst fears.

—Tori Shiver
Grade 8

---

50   COMMAS WITH DIRECT ADDRESS

" Isaac, perhaps you'd like to go first today. "

—From *The Fault in Our Stars* by John Green,
found by Phillip Kaplan

Teach it

1. Write this on the board

> ### Commas with direct address
>
> Ex:
>
> (direct address)
> <u>Lee,</u> are those sounds coming from you?
>
> Are those sounds coming
> (direct address)
> from you, <u>Lee</u>?

PRACTICE THE CONVERSATION:

A: Please read the first sentence.

B: *Lee, are those sounds coming from you?*

A: Why is there a comma after *Lee?*

B: Lee is someone's name, and you're talking to him, getting his attention.

A: That's right. What is that called?

B: A direct address.

A: Exactly. So why is there a comma?

B: We use commas after a direct address.

A: Great. Wait . . . always after? Look at the second sentence.

B: Oh well, the comma separates the sentence from the direct address, wherever it occurs.

A: That's the logic! Exactly.

2. **Explain:**

   Commas are used in many situations, and here is another one.

   *When we speak to someone and address them, it's called a **<u>direct address</u>**.*

   *We use commas to separate a **<u>direct address</u>** from the rest of the sentence.*

   *Look at the example sentence. The underline means I intentionally made a grammatical choice here. The proof above the word shows that I know why I made the choice; I know the rule about **<u>commas with a direct address</u>**.*

3. **Ask:** *Who will try out this comma rule with me?* (Enact the conversation.)

4. **Say:** *Open to your grammar chart and find **<u>commas with direct address</u>**. Let's jot down an example on the chart.*

Model it

5. Project the journal entry and read it.

6. Ask volunteers to read the sentences with **<u>commas with direct address</u>** aloud. Ask them to explain the comma rule.

Practice it

7. **Say:** *In your journal today, try to use at least five __commas with direct address__, underlining each use. Write the proof over each one.*

August 29

Squeaky (reading message):

HA HA HA HA! HA HA HA HA! HA HA GIBBER JABBER COUGH COUGH! I have

some AMAZINGLY TERRIBLE news for you. HA HA COUGH COUCH!

Jeff:	I wonder what that means*(direct address)*__, Squeaky.__
Squeaky:	I don't know*(direct address)*__, Jeff__.
Jeff:	Maybe we should ask . . . ! GRED! . . .
Squeaky:	DUN DUN DU-
Jeff:	STOP IT*(direct address)*__, Squeaky.__
Babalana:	What are you up to*(direct address)*__, Jeff?__
Jeff:	We found this note*(direct address)*__, Babalana.__
Babalana:	What does it say*(direct address)*__, Squeaky?__

Squeaky: M Hem (clears throat) HA H A HA HA, HA HA HA HA, HA HA

GIBBER JABBER COUGH COUGH! I have some AMAZING

TERRIBLE news for you, HA HA COUGH COUGH!

Babalana:	I think we should take it to . . . ! GRED! . . . *(direct address)*

Jeff:	*(direct address)* That's what I said**, Babalana.**
Babalana:	*(direct address)* Exactly**, Jeff.**
Squeaky:	Hey . . . ! GRED! . . .
Gred:	*(direct address)* *(direct address)* (Hiss) **Jeff, Squeaky,** and (hiss) most of all**, Babalana**!
Jeff:	Wow he must really hate yo-
Babalana:	*(direct address)* (Hiss) cough cough**, Jeff,** you know we've been mortal enemies since the day he told me he was jumping into the Grand Canyon.
Jeff:	*(direct address)* I know**, Babalana,** PRISON CHANGED ME! Ha ha ha ha ha!
Babalana:	*(direct address)* Umm**, Jeff,** WHERE'S GRED!?
Gred:	*(direct address)* (HISS!)**, Squeaky,** they'll never stop to notice that I'm going on the 12:30 p.m., air service, plane to Kawiwi, air plane #19, the airport at interstate 1930 and highway 2! HA HA HA, you'll never find me!!! I recorded this message.
Squeaky:	I WILL FIND YOU . . . ! GRED! . . . after they stop doing, that.

—Sara Toms
Grade 6

Notes

51 COMMAS IN A DATE

" South Ostelic, N.Y. "
June 19, 1906
My Dear—

—From *A Northern Light* by
Jennifer Donnelly, found by Tori Shiver

Teach it

1. Write this on the board

Commas in a date

Ex:

They were married on

(comma in a date)
<u>March 5, 2004</u>.

PRACTICE THE CONVERSATION:

A: Will you please read the sentence?

B: *They were married on March 5, 2004.*

A: Do you see a comma in this sentence?

B: I definitely do. It's in the date.

A: Why would someone put a comma there?

B: Well, it just separates the day and the year. It would be confusing without it.

A: So what's the comma rule here?

B: We use a comma to separate a day and a year.

A: Good!

2. **Explain:**

   Commas are used in many situations, and here is another one. When we write out the date, we use commas to separate the day from the year.

   Look at the example. The underline means I intentionally made a grammatical choice here.

   The proof above the word shows that I know why I made the choice; I know the rule about **commas in dates**.

3. **Ask:** *Who will try out this comma rule with me?* (Enact the conversation.)

4. **Say:** *Open to your grammar chart and find* **commas in dates**. *Let's jot down an example on the chart.*

Model it

5. Project the journal entry and read it.

6. Ask volunteers to read the sentences with **commas in dates** aloud. Ask each of them to explain the comma rule.

Practice it

7. **Say:** *In your journal today, try to use at least five **commas in dates**, underlining each use. Write the proof over each one.*

(comma in a date)

March 17, 2014

Deadly Duckies!

Blake Cobbler was 14 years old. He had a pet duck named Ripjaw. Ripjaw was a dwarf ducky. Ripjaw had big sharp teeth. That's why Blake got him. "What the flip!" Blake always said when Ripjaw bit him. OK, this story is STUPID! I'm going to write another one.

Characters! | Ship!

The Great Adventures of CATBUG!

St. Patrick's Day!

"Reporting for duty, sir!" Catbug said, as Jake told him to get into the control-room of the ship.

"Everybody on the planet below us is going crazy! I'm going to send you down there to see what's wrong," said Jake.

"But . . ."

"Bye, Catbug!" said Jake, and he sent Catbug down.

Everybody was wearing green four-leaf-clovers and shiny green glasses. "Wow, looks like they are celebrating St. Patrick's Day!" said Catbug.

"E-a-t clover!" said some crazy hobo in the alley with a cardboard box as a house.

"Wow, I don't like this place!" said Catbug. Catbug pulled the rope he was attached to so he can go back up to the ship.

"They are celebrating St. Patrick's Day!" said Catbug.

"Ooooooohhhh," said Jake.

—Shaine Carpenter
Grade 6

52 COMMAS BETWEEN CITY AND STATE

> "Four locations had been marked. New Beijing. Paris. Rieux, France."
>
> —From *Cress* by Marissa Meyer, found by Kaylee Gurr

Teach it

1. Write this on the board

Commas between city and state

Ex:

They were married in

(city, state)

Somerset, Kentucky.

PRACTICE THE CONVERSATION:

A: Will you please read the sentence?

B: *They were married in Somerset, Kentucky.*

A: Do you see a comma in this sentence?

B: I definitely do. It's after *Somerset.*

A: Why would someone put a comma there?

B: Well, it just separates the city from the state. It would be confusing without it.

A: So what's the comma rule here?

B: We use a comma to separate cities and states.

A: Good!

2. **Explain:**

   Commas are used in many different situations, and here is another one. We use commas to separate a city and state.

   *Look at the example sentence. The underline means I intentionally made a grammatical choice here. The proof above the word shows that I know why I made the choice; I know the rule about **commas between cities and states**.*

3. **Ask:** *Who will try out this comma rule with me?* (Enact the conversation.)

4. **Say:** *Open to your grammar chart and find **commas between cities and states**. Let's jot down an example on the chart.*

Model it

5. Project the journal entry and read it.

6. Ask volunteers to read the sentences with **commas between cities and states** aloud. Ask each to state the comma rule.

Practice it

7. **Say:** *In your journal today, try to use at least five **commas between cities and states**, underlining each use. Write the proof over each one.*

December 19

Weirdest City/Town Names in TEXAS

(commas between city and state)

1. **Spearman, TX**	13. **Round Rock, TX**
2. **Canadian, TX**	14. **Temple, TX**
3. **Canyon, TX**	15. **Franklin, TX**
4. **Tulia, TX**	16. **Crockett, TX**
5. **Dimmitt, TX**	17. **Marshall, TX**
6. **Past, TX**	18. **Pasit, TX**
7. **Seagraves, TX**	19. **New Boston, TX**
8. **Farwell, TX**	20. **Shepard, TX**
9. **Crane, TX**	21. **Huntsville, TX**
10. **Alice, TX**	22. **Palestine, TX**
11. **Kingsville, TX**	23. **Colorado City, TX**
12. **Mathis, TX**	24. **Nacogdoches, TX**

---

25. **Marathon, TX**

26. **Kermit, TX**

27. **Childress, TX**

28. **Sundown, TX**

29. **Dilly, TX**

30. **West, TX**

31. **Mexia, TX**

32. **Waco, TX**

33. **Whitehouse, TX**

34. **Liberty, TX**

35. **Humble, TX**

36. **Athens, TX**

37. **Plains, TX**

38. **Sugarland, TX**

39. **Texas City, TX**

40. **Junction, TX**

41. **Marfa, TX**

42. **Van Horn, TX**

43. **Muleshoe, TX**

44. **Mt. Pleasant, TX**

45. **Cooper, TX**

46. **Columbus, TX**

47. **Edna, TX**

48. **Victoria, TX**

49. **Goliad, TX**

50. **Universal City, TX**

51. **Italy, TX**

52. **Munday, TX**

53. **Graham, TX**

54. **Beeville, TX**

55. **Elkhart, TX**

56. **Paint Rock, TX**

57. **Asherton, TX**

58. **San Saba, TX**

59. **Throckmorton, TX**

60. **Waxahachie, TX**

These are all real places. I got them from a map in Mrs. Koppe's classroom.

—Lindsay Weingart
Grade 6

53 QUOTATIONS—QUESTION MARKS INSIDE

> " "Is she . . . ?" I hesitated. "Is she . . . ok?" "
>
> —From *The Killing Woods* by Lucy Christopher,
> found by Kennedy Cantu

Teach it

1. Write this on the board

Question marks
inside quotations

Ex:

(? inside ")

"What's the problem?" she asked.
She asked, "What's the
problem?"

PRACTICE THE CONVERSATION:

A: Read the sentence, please.

B: *"What's the problem?" she asked.*

A: Why is that question mark inside the quotation marks?

B: Well . . . everything inside the quotation marks is what someone said out loud.

A: Uh-huh . . .

B: And everything she said is just like in the word bubble.

A: Uh huh . . .

B: And when you see it in the word bubble, her words are a question that ends with a question mark.

A: Uh huh . . .

B: So the quote ends with a question mark and the quotation marks go after it.

A: Good!

2. **Explain:**

*Many people get confused about whether or not punctuation goes **inside** of quotation marks, especially when there are question marks involved.*

These three thoughts may help simplify the issue:

- *Quotation marks do the same job as word bubbles do in comics: They let the reader know what words are being spoken out loud by a person or character.*

- *If you draw a word bubble around these words (like in the example on the board), the words in the bubble will end with some kind of punctuation. In the example, it's a question mark.*

- *We don't usually use two punctuation marks in the same place, so if there's already a question mark, we don't need an additional comma or period.*

Look at the sentences in the example. In each, the underline means I intentionally made a grammatical choice here. How do I know I'm right?

- *The proof above the word shows that I know why I made the choice; I know the rule about **question marks going inside quotations.***

3. **Ask:** *Who will try out the thinking with me?* (Enact the conversation.)

4. **Say:** *Open to your grammar chart and find **question marks inside quotations**. Let's jot down an example on the chart.*

Model it

5. Project the journal entry and read it.

6. Ask volunteers to read the sentences with the **question marks in quotations** aloud. Ask them to explain the rule.

Practice it

7. **Say:** *In your journal today, try to use at least five **question marks in quotations**, underlining each use. Write the proof over each one.*

January 23

Totally Theresa Tells a Story

One time, like, a million years ago, some chick wanted to put on this stupid red coat

hood, and was all like, "Oh yeah, I gotta go to my grandma's house, like, totally." She got

on her bike and, like, rode into the forest. She was really tired, so she, like, tried to get to

her grandma's house faster.

(? inside ")

Then, some dude wolf came up and was like, "Hey, can I, like, have your cookies**?"**

"Uh, no, totally," she said.

So she, like, rode off to her old granny's house. When she got there, she was, like,

knocking on the door. The door, like totally creaked open and she was all like, "Hey

(? inside ")

Granny, you want some cookies**?"**

The granny wasn't really the granny. It was a wolf. She died.

The, like, END

—Lauren Messer
Grade 6

54

QUOTATIONS—ENDING IN PUNCTUATION

> 66 "That's sad," said Montag, quietly, "because all we put into it is hunting and 99 finding and killing."

—From *Fahrenheit 451* by Ray Bradbury, found by Dan Meishar

Teach it

1. Write this on the board

Quotations ending in punctuation

Ex:

You know I can see you.

(word bubble)

She said, "You know I can see you."

(word bubble with comma)

"You know I can see you," she said.

(interrupted word bubble)

"You know," she said, "I can see you."

PRACTICE THE CONVERSATION:

A: Read the first sentence, please.

B: *She said, "You know I can see you."*

A: How does it end?

B: After the word *you* is a period, then quotation marks.

A: Can you explain why the period is inside the quotation marks?

B: It's the end of the quote. If it were drawn as a word bubble, the period would be inside **the** word bubble.

A: Great. Will you read the second sentence?

B: *"You know I can see you," she said.*

A: Yes. Why isn't there a period after *you* in that sentence?

B: The end of the quote isn't the end of the sentence. So the sentence gets the period, and the end of the quote changes into a comma. The quotation marks go after the comma.

A: Excellent. And the third sentence?

B: Same logic.

A: Exactly.

2. **Explain:**

Many people get confused about what punctuation goes inside and outside of quotation marks.

Take a look at the three examples on the board.

- ***Example one:*** Quotation marks do the same job as word bubbles in comics: they tell the reader that someone is speaking out loud. If you draw a word bubble and put the spoken words in it, the words inside the bubble will end with some kind of punctuation. We end the quote with that punctuation, then show the end of the spoken words by using quotation marks.

- ***Example two:*** If the quote (the words spoken out loud) isn't the end of the whole sentence, don't end that quote with a period. Change it to a comma. Place the quotation marks after the comma.

- ***Example three:*** If you split a quote, use a comma (not a period) to end the first part of the quote and a comma before the continuation of the quote. It's all one sentence.

*In the examples on the board, the underline means I intentionally made a grammatical choice here. The proof above the word shows that I know why I made the choice; I know the rule about **quotations ending in punctuation**.*

3. **Ask:** *Who will try out this proof with me?* (Enact the conversation.)

4. **Say:** *Open to your grammar chart and find **quotations ending in punctuation**. Let's jot down an example on the chart.*

Model it

5. Project the journal entry and read it.

6. Ask volunteers to read aloud the sentences with quotations. Ask each volunteer to explain the rule about **_quotations ending in punctuation_**.

Practice it

7. **Say:** *In your journal today, try to use at least five **quotations ending in punctuation**, underlining each use. Write the proof over each one.*

January 21

Well, today Anael's back.

Yay, for some reason I missed Anael so much. I think it's just b/c I missed her

attitude.

Anyway, yesterday I was up in my room and came down the stairs and told my

(word bubble)
grandma, **"I feel so OLD."**

(word bubble)
She replied as a question, **"Why? You are only eleven."**

(word bubble)
I replied, **"Exactly."**

So yeah, I feel OLD.

—Bryanna Ruggs
Grade 6

55

HYPHENATED ADJECTIVES

❝ And this disease was called The Loneliness, because when you saw your home town dwindle to the size of your fist and then lemon-size and then pin-size and then vanish in the fire-wake . . . ❞

—From *The Martian Chronicles* by Ray Bradbury, found by Lee Kaplan

Teach it

1. Write this on the board

> ## Hyphenated adjectives
>
> Ex:
>
> The boy drank some
>
> (hyphenated adj.)
> <u>ice-cold</u> water.

> **PRACTICE THE CONVERSATION:**
> **A:** Will you please read the sentence?
> **B:** *The boy drank some ice-cold water.*
> **A:** Is *ice-cold* hyphenated?
> **B:** It sure is.
> **A:** Can you explain why?
> **B:** I can. The words are acting like one single adjective, describing the water. It wasn't just ice, and it wasn't just cold, it was ice-cold.
> **A:** That's a good explanation.
> **B:** Thank you.

2. **Explain:**

   Sometimes we put two words together to describe something. When we do that, we hyphenate them to show that they are now acting like one adjective.

   The underline means I intentionally made a grammatical choice here. The proof above the word means that I know why I made that choice; I know the rule.

3. **Ask:** *Who will try out this proof with me?* (Enact the conversation.)

4. **Say:** *Open to your grammar chart and find* **<u>hyphenated adjectives</u>**. *Let's jot down an example on the chart.*

Model it

5. Project the journal entry and read it.

6. Ask volunteers to read the sentences with the **<u>hyphenated adjectives</u>** aloud. Ask each of them to explain the rule regarding why there is a hyphen between the two words.

Practice it

7. **Say:** *In your journal today, try to use at least five **hyphenated adjectives**, underlining each use. Write the proof over each one.*

January 22

Yesterday I watched NBA basketball and college basketball too Texas played Kansas

State. It was a great game, and Texas won on a *(hyphenated adj.)* **three-point, buzzer-beating,** fade

away jumper from the corner with no time left. It's always a good game when there is

(hyphenated adj.) a **buzzer-beater** moment to win it. *(hyphenated adj.)* **Buzzer-beater** moments are what make basketball

fun. They're the equivalent of a last second Hail Mary in football, a Golden Goal in

soccer, an Overtime Sudden Death Slapshot in hockey, or a *(hyphenated adj.)* **walk-off** home run in

baseball. In basketball, when they sink a buzzer-beater, you immediately see the crowd

stand up, their arms extended above their heads, shouting and cheering. Then you

see the shooter get mobbed by his teammates. That's got to be the coolest thing

ever. Just like that, the game is over. One centimeter decides the game. And then it's

over. Tonight, once again, there are some great games on. And now, after seeing Lee's

journal, I too will attempt to draw a portrait of Ethan.

—Phillip Kaplan
Grade 8

56

COLONS

❝ I've gotten used to figuring things out on my own: how to put toys together, how ❞ to organize my life so I don't miss friends' birthday parties, how to stay on top of my schoolwork so I never fall behind in class.

—From *Wonder* by R. J. Palacio, found by Annabell Lang

Teach it

1. Write this on the board

Colons

Ex:

(colon)

He passed three <u>classes:</u>
math, English, and P.E.

(colon)

He had only one <u>wish:</u> to
graduate on time.

PRACTICE THE CONVERSATION:

A: Please read the sentence.

B: *He passed three classes: math, English, and P.E.*

A: Okay. Where is the colon?

B: Before *math, English, and P.E.*

A: Why would you use a colon there?

B: It shows that there is a list right after it.

A: Good! Now will you read the second example?

B: *He had only one wish: to graduate on time.*

A: Great. Why is there a colon in that sentence?

B: It's not a list. The colon here shows that the next thing is kind of like an announcement.

A: Exactly.

2. **Explain:**

   We use colons to show there is an announcement or a list coming.

   *When you use a colon, underline it and write **colon** above it.*

   The underline means I intentionally made a grammatical choice here. The label above the word means that it's the correct choice.

3. **Ask:** *Who will try out a sentence with a colon with me?* (Enact the conversation.)

4. **Say:** *Open to your grammar chart and find **colons**. Let's jot down an example on the chart.*

   Note: Of course, colons have other uses, like in the salutation of a business letter and in writing the time. But this mid-sentence use is the most prevalent and most tested.

Model it

5. Project the journal entry and read it.

6. Ask volunteers to read the sentences with **colons** aloud. Ask each of them to explain why a colon is used.

Practice it

7. **Say:** *In your journal today, try to use at least five **colons**, underlining each use. Write the proof over each one.*

September 30

For several years I've had this same

question, and this is my question*(colon)***:** I

understand that when you sit in a car

you move with the car because you

are connected to it. But what about

something that is not connected to the

car, but it is inside the car?

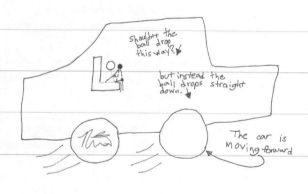

(colon)
For example**:** if you have a ball and

drop it on to your lap, will it fall on your

lap or will it go back as much as the

car went forward when the ball was

not touching anything? I have tried this

experiment before but the object does not fall back, it goes straight down into my lap.

Let me try to tell you in a picture.

—Nina De La Torre
Grade 7

57 PUNCTUATING DIALOGUE—CHICKEN DANCE

❝ "It's not so easy, stupid," Clarisse growled. ❞

—From *The Battle of the Labyrinth*, by Rick Riordan,
found by Annabell Lang

Teach it

1. Write this on the board

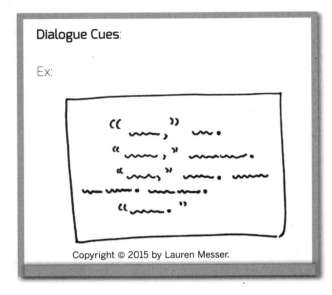

Dialogue Cues:

Ex:

Copyright © 2015 by Lauren Messer.

2. **Explain:**

   Almost everyone understands dialogue when we're reading it.

   But many people write dialogue only like this:

   "Blah blah," he said.

   "Blah blah," she said.

   They don't use the same kinds of patterns that their favorite authors use. So let's look at those patterns and see what we notice about what we already know.

3. **Ask:** *Who would like to enact this conversation with me on the patterns we notice?* (Enact conversation number 1.)

4. *Review the Chicken Dance.* (Demonstrations are available on YouTube.)

5. Ask for volunteers to demonstrate the Chicken Dance (only the chorus part).

6. **Say:** *Let's look at the chicken dance code.* (Show students the Chicken Dance Code). *Would someone like to enact this conversation with me?*

7. **Ask:** *Will someone read conversation number 3 with me?*

PRACTICE THE CONVERSATION:

A: Look at the squiggle dialogue. We don't know what the words are, but we know some things about them. What do we know about that first squiggle?

B: It's speech. They're words someone is saying.

A: Yes. And right after that? What do we know about that next squiggle?

B: That part tells who said it.

A: Right. We call that a tag. Now look at the second line. What do we know about that first squiggle?

B: It's more speech.

A: Is it the same person saying it?

B: No. It's someone else.

A: How can you tell it's someone else?

B: It's a new paragraph.

A: Good. And right after it, on the same line?

B: Another tag. It tells who said that part.

A: Yes. And the third paragraph?

B: It's speech and another tag and then something else.

A: What's that something else? The sentence at the end. What do we know about that?

B: We know it's something else, like action. Like "he slammed the door."

A: Good. And the last paragraph?

B: It's the other speaker's speech.

A: Excellent. You recognize several clues created by spaces and punctuation, which tell us what those words are doing: speech, tags, action, and indents.

B: Hey. That's almost like the chicken dance.

A: How could that be? Let's find out!

Chicken Dance Code

| Speech | Tag | Action | Indent |

Copyright © 2015 by Lauren Messer.

Practice it

8. **Say:** *Let's practice now by replacing the squiggles in the "Dialogue Cues" example with your own words.*

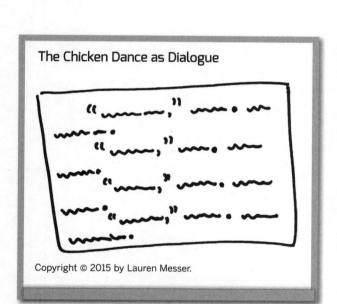

The Chicken Dance as Dialogue

Copyright © 2015 by Lauren Messer.

PRACTICE THE CONVERSATION 2: CRACKING THE CHICKEN DANCE CODE:

A: So how does this code work?

B: The beak part is speech.

A: Uh huh . . .

B: The wing part is like a tag. The wings are pointing, like "who said it?"

A: Okay . . .

B: The tushy part is action.

A: Uh huh . . .

B: And clap, clap, clap, clap is like indenting. Like hitting the space bar four times.

A: That's pretty brilliant.

B: Which means that if you used the code of the chicken dance and that you wrote dialogue for it, exactly as you dance it, the dialogue would look like this. Look at the Chicken Dance as Dialogue. (Show students the Chicken Dance as Dialogue.)

A: Let's dance that dialogue. Can you do the chicken dance and point to the dialogue at the same time?

B: Just watch me.

PRACTICE THE CONVERSATION 3: USING THE CHICKEN DANCE CODE FOR A VARIETY OF DIALOGUES

A: Not all dialogue is in that same pattern, though, is it?

B: Not in the books I read.

A: Then let's take a piece of dialogue from a book and rewrite it as a squiggle.

B: Okay . . .

A: Then you can change the squiggles to your own words.

B: Great!

A: Let's try that with the squiggles in the "Dialogue Cues" example on the board.

Example:

"What's everyone laughing about?" the teacher asked.

"I didn't do it," Lee said.

"Ooh, I get it," she said. She walked over to the closet, pulled out a can of room deodorizer, and sprayed.

"Thanks."

Note: For an additional explanation of this lesson, visit www.trailofbreadcrumbs.net.

PART III

CAPITALIZATION

April 9

Herobrine the Awakening: Part 7

So we go down into the cave and hear some voices. They say, "**Dude** it's the Apoe." *(1st word in quote)*

"**No** shut up! Someone will find us, Survivor 05. You survive. It's in your name." *(1st word in quote)*

"**Wait** Survivor05!" I whispered to Lazynathaniel. "**Wasn't** he in the prophecy?" *(1st word in quote)* *(1st word in quote)*

"**Yes**, he was," says Lazynathaniel. *(1st word in quote)*

"**Well**, let's go get them," I say. *(1st word in quote)*

Then I hear screaming, "**HELP**! HELP! HELP! meeee!!" *(1st word in quote)*

So me and Lazynathaniel rush down to find Herobrine about to kill Survivor 05. We pull out our diamond swords and put on our diamond armor and say, "**Leave** him alone, *(1st word in quote)*

Herobrine."

"**No** I will kill you all!!" Herobrine says. *(1st word in quote)*

"**No**! We will fight you and if we fail, there are others," Lazynathaniel says. *(1st word in quote)*

"**All** we have to do is enable spawning again," I say. *(1st word in quote)*

"**You** think that it's that easy, do you?!" Herobrine says. *(1st word in quote)*

"**Yes**, yes we do," me and the others say. *(1st word in quote)*

—Christian Westbrook
Grade 7

If you're just writing to write, like a journal entry, correctness is not so important. But if you're writing an essay for the King of the World, then yeah, it's important.

—Ben Brody, sixth grader

Nowadays, capitalization rules seem adrift. If you use all caps in any electronic writing, you're shouting. I don't remember anger having been a part of any of the capitalization conventions I grew up with. I do remember Winnie-the-Pooh capitalizing where he turned words into titles of different sorts (being a Bear of Very Little Brain). So perhaps writers have always wielded uppercase letters in play and for expression, as Ben did, above. Here is a mostly finite set of capitalization rules that students are expected to know and use in the literate world. These serve as the thick black lines on the coloring book page of literacy, and within those lines, there's room for play.

This section deals with the *hard-and-fast rules* of capitalization. And as with all hard-and-fast rules, there are exceptions.

We don't use proof words for this section. Instead, when students are showing their thinking about capitalization choices in their writing, they jot down the rule, or a very abbreviated form of it, over the word. On the chart, we jot down examples.

58 PROPER NOUNS

> " By the time we finally got to Westover Hall, it was getting dark, and she'd told " Annabeth and Thalia every embarrassing baby story there was to tell about me.
>
> —From *Titan's Curse* by Rick Riordan, found by Ben Brody

Teach it

1. Write this on the board

Capitalize proper nouns

Ex:

    (proper   (proper
noun—name) noun—place)
<u>Phil</u> flew to <u>Dallas</u> on

    (proper noun—name)
<u>Southwest Airlines</u>.

PRACTICE THE CONVERSATION:

A: Read the sentence, please.

B: *Phil flew to Dallas on Southwest Airlines.*

A: Great. Is Dallas capitalized?

B: It is.

A: Why?

B: We always capitalize proper nouns. Dallas is a specific place, which makes it a proper noun.

A: Are there any other proper nouns in this sentence?

B: Why yes, I do believe there are.

A: Like what?

B: Southwest Airlines is the name of a company, and Phil is a specific person. They are both proper nouns.

A: So they would get. . . .

B: Capitalized.

A: Perfect.

2. **Explain:**

   *We capitalize **proper nouns,** including persons' names, specific places, company names, and brands; titles of books, movies, songs, or other works; and names of religions, months, days of the weeks, and holidays.* (Have students record these in their journal.)

   *Look at the example sentence. The underline means I intentionally made a grammatical choice here. The proof above the word shows that I know why I made the choice; I know the rule about **proper nouns.***

3. **Ask:** *Who will try out this capitalization rule with me?* (Enact the conversation.)

4. **Say:** *Open to your grammar chart and find **capitalize proper nouns**. Let's jot down an example on the chart.*

   Note: On the grammar chart, you'll also find spots to add examples of proper nouns that are titles and religions.

Model it

5. Project the journal entry and read it.

6. Ask volunteers to read the sentences with the **proper nouns** aloud. Ask each of them to explain the rule, that we capitalize proper nouns.

Practice it

7. **Say:** *In your journal today, try to use at least five **proper nouns**, underlining each use. Write the proof over each one.*

March 26

(proper noun)
Titan Fall

(proper noun) (proper noun)
Finally I got to play the coolest game with over 75 awards. **Titan Fall** is like any

first person shooter except you get to run on walls. The coolest part is you get

(proper noun)
to use a **Titan**. In other words, you get to use a giant robot or you can have the

(proper noun)
robot follow you around. There are 3 **Titans**: the high defense tank class, the

(proper noun)
speedy assault class, and the main one who is on the cover of the game **Atlas**.

You can choose to be an assassin, which uses cloaking, or a pilot which often

looks like a clone trooper.

—Alex Melchor
Grade 7

59 PROPER ADJECTIVES

> " When I look at the Abnegation lifestyle as an outsider, I think it's beautiful. "
>
> —From *Divergent* by Veronica Roth, found by Claire Weingart

Teach it

1. Write this on the board

Capitalize proper adjectives

Ex:

(proper adjective—specific place)
Our <u>Italian</u> cousin rented a

(proper adjective—brand)
<u>Mustang</u> convertible.

PRACTICE THE CONVERSATION:

A: Read the sentence please.
B: *Our Italian cousin rented a Mustang convertible.*
A: Good! Why is *Italian* capitalized?
B: It's like a proper noun, but it's a proper adjective.
A: So . . . ?
B: So we capitalize proper adjectives.
A: What about the word *Mustang*? Is that a proper noun or a proper adjective?
B: It's . . . hmm . . . it tells what kind of convertible, so it's an adjective!
A: A proper adjective?
B: Yes, it's a brand. So it is capitalized.
B: Good work!

2. **Explain:**

   *We capitalize **proper adjectives**, including adjectives using persons' names, specific places, company names, and brands; titles of books, movies, songs, or other works; and names of religions, nationalities, months, days of the week, and holidays.*

   *Look at the example sentence. The underline means I intentionally made a grammatical choice here. The proof above the word shows that I know why I made the choice; I know the rule about **proper adjectives**.*

3. **Ask:** *Who will try out this proof with me?* (Enact the conversation.)

4. **Say:** *Open to your grammar chart and find **proper adjectives**. Let's jot down an example on the chart.*

Model it

5. Project the journal entry and read it.

6. Ask volunteers to read the sentences with the **proper adjectives** aloud. Ask each of them to use the proof to show that they know the rule.

Practice it

7. **Say:** *In your journal today, try to use at least five **proper adjectives**, underlining each use. Write the proof over each one.*

March 8

Today is Friday but it doesn't really feel like it. For dinner tonight our mom is

(proper adjective)   (proper adjective)
making **Thai** curry. She makes it and it tastes good. Our family loves **Asian** food.

(proper adjective) (proper adjective) (proper adjective)   (proper adjective)
We eat **Vietnamese, Chinese, Korean, Thai, Indian,** and **Japanese** foods. I think

most people would say they're all similar but I think there's a distinct taste and

flavor to all of them as they all use a unique blend of spices.

—Lee Kaplan
Grade 8

60

LETTER CLOSINGS

Teach it

1. Write this on the board

Capitalize the first word in a letter closing

Ex:

(closing)
<u>Your</u> friend,
Jennifer

PRACTICE THE CONVERSATION:

A: Will you please read the example?

B: *Your friend, Jennifer.*

A: Good. Now . . . why is *your* capitalized?

B: It's the first word in a letter closing.

A: Uh huh . . . so?

B: So the first word in this part of a letter should always be capitalized.

A: Right. What about the word *friend*?

B: No, just the first word.

A: Good. What is this part of a letter called?

B: The closing.

A: Perfect.

B: Thanks.

2. **Explain:**

   If you write a letter, you finish it with a closing.

   Capitalize the first word of the closing, in the line above your signature.

   *Look at the example. The underline means I intentionally made a grammatical choice here. The proof above the word shows that I know why I made the choice; I know the rule about **capitalizing the first word in a letter closing**.*

3. **Ask:** *Who will try out this proof with me?* (Enact the conversation.)

4. **Say:** *Open to your grammar chart, and find **letter closing**. Let's jot down an example on the chart.*

Model it

5. Project the journal entry and read it.

6. Ask volunteers to read the **letter closings** aloud. Ask each of them to explain the rule.

Practice it

7. **Say:** *In your journal today, try to use at least one **letter closing**, underlining each use. Write the proof over each one.*

April 3

Dear Timothy, age 33,

I know right now that you're riding in the flying car that you invented. I expect

you to be going to your laboratory to invent the time machine. Oh, and also after

that you will be flying to Texas because remember you're the governor. Wait a

minute—are your kids flying with the thrusters you made? Wow, your (or my)

kids are spoiled!

(closing)
Yourself,

Timothy, age 12

Dear Ms. Bernabei,

Would you like a free flying car and time machine? Any color, on me. And would

you like a robot body to replace your body . . . when . . . well, never mind.

(closing)
Your student,

Timothy

—Timothy Bates
Grade 7

61   FIRST WORDS IN SENTENCES

" When she said run, she meant it. **"**

—From *The Red Pyramid* by Rick Riordan,
found by Tamara Weiss

Teach it

1. Write this on the board

> # Capitalize the first word in a sentence
>
> Ex:
>
> (1st word in sentence)
> <u>He</u> considered enrolling
> in Clark High School.

PRACTICE THE CONVERSATION:

A: Read the sentence, please.

B: *He considered enrolling in Clark High School.*

A: Great. But wait . . . why is *he* capitalized? It's not a proper noun.

B: No, it's not. It's capitalized for another reason.

A: What other reason?

B: It's the first word in a sentence.

A: Respectfully, so what?

B: So this. Every sentence begins with a capital letter. That's the rule.

A: Smoothly done!

2. **Explain:**

   Every sentence begins with a capital letter. This is one of the first capitalization rules that schoolchildren learn as they begin to write sentences.

   The underline means I intentionally made a grammatical choice here. The proof above the word shows that it's the correct choice.

3. **Ask:** *Who will try out this proof with me?* (Enact the conversation.)

4. **Say:** *Open to your grammar chart and find **capitalize first words in a sentence**. Let's jot down an example on the chart.*

Model it

5. Project the journal entry and read it.

6. Ask volunteers to read a sentence aloud. Ask them to explain the rule: **first words of sentences** are capitalized.

Practice it

7. **Say:** *In your journal today, capitalize the __first word of every sentence__ and underline five of these. Write the proof over each one.*

February 6

My Dream

(1st word in sentence) (1st word in sentence) (1st word in sentence)
I'm HAPPY!!! HAPPY! HAPPY! HAPPY! **I** found out something AWESOME!! **Remember**

(1st word in sentence) (1st word in sentence)
that journal entry when I was SO HAPPY that I was a level six?! **Well** guess what! **GUESS**

(1st word in sentence) (1st word in sentence)
WHAT!! **I** just found out that I'm going to skip level six and train for level SEVEN!!! **I'm**

(1st word in sentence)
going to train with Megan and Morgan. (**These** people I just named, yeah they're level

(1st word in sentence)(1st word in sentence) (1st word in sentence)
SEVEN!!!) ☺ **It's** so perfect!! **I** get the leo, I get the scrunchy, and I get the bag!! **I** really

(1st word in sentence)
wish Miriam was here, so I could tell her the great news. ☹ **I** was learning how to do a

(1st word in sentence)
dismount yesterday on the beam. (**That's** where you run and do a front tuck at the end

of the beam!!)

—Annabell Lang
Grade 6

62

FIRST WORDS IN QUOTATIONS

" Then in a *muy, muy* soft voice, he said, "My name is Skippito Friskito. I . . . fear "
. . . not a . . . single bandito."

—From *Skippyjon Jones* by Judy Schachner, found by Julian Ponce

Teach it

1. Write this on the board

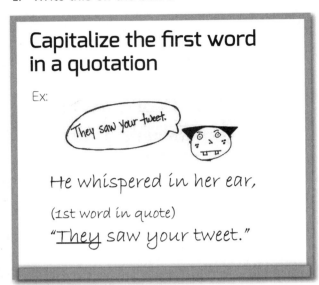

Capitalize the first word
in a quotation

Ex:

They saw your tweet.

He whispered in her ear,

(1st word in quote)

"<u>They</u> saw your tweet."

PRACTICE THE CONVERSATION:
A: Will you please read the sentence?
B: *He whispered in her ear, "They saw your tweet."*
A: Great. But why is the word *they* capitalized?
B: It's the beginning of the quote.
A: Yes, but it's not the beginning of the whole sentence.
B: True, but that doesn't matter. All quotes start with capital letters.
A: Aha. Nice work.

2. **Explain:**

   *We capitalize **the first words in quotations**, even if the quotation isn't the beginning of the sentence.*

   *Look at the example sentence. The underline means I intentionally made a grammatical choice here. The proof above the word shows that I know why I made the choice; I know the rule about **capitalizing first words in quotations**.*

3. **Ask:** *Who will try out this proof with me?* (Enact the conversation.)

4. **Say:** *Open to your grammar chart and find **capitalize first words in quotations**. Let's jot down an example on the chart.*

Model it

5. Project the journal entry and read it.

6. Ask volunteers to read the sentences with the quotations aloud. Ask each of them to state the rule: **first words in quotations are capitalized.**

Practice it

7. **Say:** *In your journal today, try to use <u>**quotations with capitalized first words**</u> at least five times, underlining each use. Write the proof over each one.*

April 9

Herobrine the Awakening: Part 7

(1st word in quote)

So we go down into the cave and hear some voices. They say, "**<u>Dude</u>** it's the Apoe."

(1st word in quote)

"**<u>No</u>** shut up! Someone will find us, Survivor 05. You survive. It's in your name."

(1st word in quote)   (1st word in quote)

"**<u>Wait</u>** Survivor 05!" I whispered to Lazynathaniel. "**<u>Wasn't</u>** he in the prophecy?"

(1st word in quote)

"**<u>Yes,</u>** he was," says Lazynathaniel.

(1st word in quote)

"**<u>Well</u>**, let's go get them," I say.

(1st word in quote)

Then I hear screaming, "**<u>HELP</u>**! HELP! HELP! meeee!!"

So me and Lazynathaniel rush down to find Herobrine about to kill Survivor 05. We

(1st word in quote)

pull out our diamond swords and put on our diamond armor and say, "**<u>Leave</u>** him alone,

Herobrine."

(1st word in quote)

"**<u>No</u>** I will kill you all!!" Herobrine says.

(1st word in quote)

"**<u>No</u>**! We will fight you and if we fail, there are others," Lazynathaniel says.

(1st word in quote)

"**<u>All</u>** we have to do is enable spawning again," I say.

(1st word in quote)

"**<u>You</u>** think that it's that easy, do you?! " Herobrine says.

(1st word in quote)

"**<u>Yes</u>**, yes we do," me and the others say.

—Christian Westbrook
Grade 7

PART IV

SPELLING

March 2

Ice C☐be People

One morning, in the land of Flames, there was a flame named Jack. Jack loved to burn things. One evening, his parents told him to come inside and eat. When he opened the door, a portal sucked him in. Where was he going? To the I**ce** (-ce) Cube World! I**ce** (-ce) cube people were everywhere! Then, he saw something horrid! A refri**ge**rator! (-ge) He instantly started running away from all the I**ce** (-ce) people. He bumped into an I**ce** (-ce) man. When he bumped him, the I**ce** (-ce) man melted.

"Murderer!" someone called out.

"Wait! I didn't!"

But the I**ce** (-ce) poli**ce** (-ce) grabbed him up. They wore anti-melt suits. They threw him into an anti-melt **ce**ll (-ce) with laser bars. One touch and an alarm goes off.

"Man, this sucks. I'm stuck in an anti-melt **ce**ll (-ce) with laser bars," Jack said. He looked outside and found out that the prison he was in was not only the most nonescapable prison, but the prison was secluded in the middle of the forest.

"Here's your food," a poli**ce**man (-ce) said as he slid i**ce** (-ce) cold fish under the bars. Jack wasn't sure if he should eat it or not. He thought it wasn't good.

"Well, no hurt in trying new foods," he said. He put the food in his mouth and started to die a slow, painful death. His veins were popping out so much they almost exploded, his pupils went fa**ci**ng (-ci) behind his head, and he was turning inside out. To make a long story short, he died and lived happily ever after.

The end

—Shaine Carpenter
Grade 6

Correctness is almost always important. Correctness completes the writing. But sometimes in writing, incorrectness is important. If you are quoting a person from a book such as *Flowers for Algernon*, and you are quoting Charlie, who is mentally ill, it is not only okay, but useful to make the spelling and grammar mistakes just as he talks.

—Ilan Sonsino, eighth grader

For many people, spelling seems impossible. Instead of memorizing hundreds of words, it's sensible and easier to learn a few basic spelling rules that work most of the time. Down the hall from me some years ago, a magnificent teacher named Pat Schmitz shared with me her go-to list of spelling rules, which have proven useful to me ever since.

One by one, I share these rules with students. They learn the dialogue that helps them check the rule, and they learn to talk themselves through the rule as they consider the spelling of a word. They show their thinking as they underline the words in their journal and write the spelling rule above them, or some very abbreviated form of the rule. Eventually, the dialogue becomes internalized, and they don't need to "show their work" with proofs.

Of course every spelling rule has many exceptions, but I find it best to teach the basics first or, as Harry Noden taught me, to oversimplify the directions at first. There are plenty of googlable resources for spine-tingling lists of exceptions, conditions, and nuances, and I welcome exploration of these by any of the grammatically intrepid or curious.

On the grammar chart, I've left room for additional spelling rules, in case you'd like to add some more of your favorites.

63

SILENT *E*

> Then Mr. Porter waited, hoping someone would fess up to writing it. But that, as you know, never happened.

—From *Thirteen Reasons Why* by Jay Asher, found by Tori Shiver

Teach it

1. Write this on the board

Silent E rule

Drop the final **E** from a word when adding –al, –ed, –ing, –able, –ate (suffixes beginning with vowels)

Ex:

      remove–removal
      date–dating
      love–lovable

Don't drop the final **E** from a word when adding any other suffix (suffixes beginning with consonants)

Ex:

      love–lovely
      care–careful

Ex:

    (silent e)   (silent e)
The <u>adorable</u> pup was <u>loved</u> by
   (silent e)   (silent e)
his <u>lovely</u> new <u>playmates</u>.

PRACTICE THE CONVERSATION:

A: Read the sentence at the bottom, please.

B: *The adorable pup was loved by his lovely new playmates.*

A: Great. Which of these words have a silent-E word as a root word?

B: Four of them. *Adorable, loved, lovely, playmates.*

A: Yes. And can you turn those into their silent-E roots?

B: Sure. *Adore, love, love, playmate.*

A: Why does the "E" stay on some of those words and get dropped on others?

B: The silent E has to stay on the word unless it's replaced by another vowel. So if the suffix starts with a vowel, the "E" can go. If there's no vowel, the "E" has to stay.

A: Good explanation!

B: Thank you.

2. **Explain:**

   Spelling is difficult for many people. Instead of memorizing hundreds of words, it's easier to learn a few basic spelling rules that work most of the time.

   This spelling rule involves **silent E**. *What happens to the* **E** *when we add a suffix? There's a simple rule that governs this.*

   Look at the example sentence. The underline means I intentionally made a grammatical choice here. The proof above the word shows that I know why I made the choice; I know the rule about **silent E**.

3. **Ask:** *Who will try out this spelling rule with me?* (Enact the conversation.)

4. **Say:** *Open to your grammar chart and find the spelling rule for the* **silent E**. *Let's jot down an example on the chart.*

Model it

5. Project the journal entry and read it.

6. Ask volunteers to read the sentences with the **silent E** aloud. Ask them to state the rule: we drop the **E** for suffixes beginning with vowels, and we keep the **E** for suffixes beginning with consonants.

Practice it

7. **Say:** *In your journal today, try to use at least five words ending with* **<u>silent E</u>**, *underlining each use. Change the ending of these words to try out the rule. Write the proof over each one.*

February 28

How to Survive a Horror Movie, Part 1

Tip one—don't be the stupid person. In all horror movies, there is at least one stupid

(silent e)
person who has no chance of **<u>surviving</u>**. That person is the person who, A—thinks it's a

good idea to split up. (If you're in a group, the killer will have a harder time killing you

if you are all together.) B—wants to go after the killer on their own because the killer

(silent e)
killed someone they **<u>liked</u>** or because they want someone to like them. C—thinks it's safe

(silent e)
<u>leaving</u> when it's clear it isn't.

Tip two—don't be the person who wants to take charge. The killer will kill that person.

March 3

How to Survive a Horror Movie, Part 2

(silent e)
Tip three—don't be the hero. Don't be the person who runs around **<u>saving</u>** everybody.

Don't save someone just to be killed right after.

(silent e)
Tip four—don't play by the **<u>rules</u>**. The killer will not be playing by the rules so why

should you? The killer will have special abilities to know where you are and since they

have wall hacks, they will be able to see you at all times.

—Nicholas Prewett
Grade 7

64 WORDS ENDING IN Y

> 66 By the time I was two, all my memories had words, and all my words had 99
> meanings. But only in my head. I have never spoken a single word. I am almost
> eleven years old.
>
> —From *Out of My Mind* by Sharon M. Draper, found by Layne Dentinger

Teach it

1. Write this on the board

Words ending in y

If you're adding a suffix to a word ending in **y**, look
at the letter before the **y**. If it's a vowel, just add "s."
If it's a consonant, change the **y** to an "i" and add the
suffix.

Ex:

    baby–babies
    country–countries
    monkey–monkeys
    holiday–holidays

Ex:

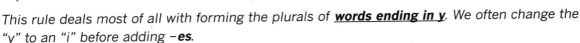

    (y to i)   (y to i)

The <u>ladies</u> went to <u>rallies</u> in six
(y to i)
<u>cities</u>.

PRACTICE THE CONVERSATION:

A: Will you please read the sentence?

B: *The ladies went to rallies in six cities.*

A: Great. Do you see any words that did end in "y"?

B: I do. *Ladies, rallies, cities.*

A: Exactly! But there is no "y" in them now?

B: No. In all three cases, the "y" has been changed to an "i."
Then –es is added.

A: Great. Would we do the same thing if one of the words was
highway?

B: No, we would not.

A: What would we do then?

B: We'd just add an "**s**." *Highways.*

A: How do you know when to change the "y" to an "i"?

B: You look at the letter before the "y." If it's a vowel, the "y" stays.
But if the "y" is the only vowel, it changes to an "i."

A: Excellent!

2. **Explain:**

*This rule deals most of all with forming the plurals of **words ending in y**. We often change the
"y" to an "i" before adding –**es**.*

*But does this always apply? No. If there is a **vowel** before the "y" (like keys or days), then we just add
the "s." But any other time, we change that "y" to an "i" before adding suffixes.*

*Look at the example sentence. The underline means I intentionally made a grammatical choice here. The
proof above the word shows that I know why I made the choice; I know the rule about **words ending in
"y.**"*

3. **Ask:** *Who will try out this spelling rule with me?* (Enact the conversation.)

4. **Say:** *Open to your grammar chart and find the spelling rule for **words ending in "y."** Let's jot
down an example on the chart.*

Model it

5. Project the journal entry and read it.

6. Ask volunteers to read aloud each of the sentences with underlined words. Ask them each to
state the rule: we change the "y" to an "i" before we add a suffix.

Practice it

7. **Say:** *In your journal today, try to use at least five plurals of **words that end in "y,"** underlining each use. Write the proof over each one.*

April 29

M = mom

D = dad

S = me

R = bro

A = sis

! = !

M: We should move to a different city.

D: I agree, we should go to Austin.

M: No, we should go to Corpus

Christi.

A: STOP FIGHTING!

D: Sweetie, we are NOT fighting.

R: UGH! Stupid cats.

M: What did they do, honey booboo?

R: They messed up my Lego set!

M: Ok, you can fix it, right?

R: Sure.

D: Well how would we sell this house?

R: Hey mom, hey mom, mom, mom.

M: (Ugh) what, honey?

R: My Lego guy has a yellow hand and a

blue hand!

M: (sarcastically) Cool, let Mommy and

Daddy talk.

R: Ok, fine.

D: Well first we would need to find jobs in

Austin—

M: Corpus, Ron!

D: Ok, first we would need to find jobs in

CORPUS so we could pay for another house.

M: Yeah we would.

S: (enters room suspiciously) What up yo?

M: Nothing.

D: We want to move to Aus—

M: CORPUS, Ron, Corpus.

D: fine. Corpus Christie, honey.

A: STOP IT GUYS!

M: We are NOT fighting!

S: DAD!!!

D: What!

S: How do you spell **cities**? *(y to i)*

D: Why!

S: It's my homework!

D: Figure it out.

M: It is c-i-t-

D: Susan! She can do it on her own!

M: Fine.

A: Stop FIGHTING!

M: WE ARE NOT FIGHTING!

D: Susan! Talk nicer to the kids!

M: You yell at them—

D: When they do the wrong thing!

M: Fine.

S: How do you spell **cities**?! *(y to i)*

D: Figure it out, Sara!

S: I tried!

M: Come here, Sara!

S: What?

D: Let me see your homework.

S: Ok.

R: I need toilet paper!

M: Amy, GET YOUR BROTHER TOILET

PAPER!

D: Ok, it starts with a C.

S: C-i-t-y-s, right?

D: No.

M: Guess again, honey.

D: Ok, so it's c-i-what?

S: I said c-i-t-y-s!

D: No, it has 2 i's and no y's.

D: Yes.

S: Ok, then c-i-t-y-s, citys.

M and D: NO!

S: ~~Dang it!~~

D: Don't say that, it hurts me to hear

you talk like your mother.

A: I didn't say the D word.

S: You call Amy a goody goody and she

can't cuss! And she's the **craziest** (y to i) baby.

(And I never learned to spell **cities** (y to i) until a while ago.)

A: No I'm not.

M: Stop it, you two. And Sara would be the

crazy baby.

D: Susan! They're not **babies** (y to i), they're just

kids.

M: Sara, do your homework.

S: But I don't know how to spell **cities** (y to i).

D: C-i-t-i-e-s. There, now finish your

homework.

S: Fine.

HW: ~~You live in San Antonio, TX. What is~~

San Antonio?

S: (writes) San Antonio is a city. A crazy

and happy city! One of the **craziest** (y to i),

happiest (y to i) **cities** (y to i) anywhere.

—Sara Toms
Grade 6

65

WORDS ENDING IN CONSONANTS

> " Once he saw her shaking a walnut tree, once he saw her sitting on the lawn "
> knitting a blue sweater, three or four times he found a bouquet of late flowers on
> his porch, or a handful of chestnuts in a little sack, or some autumn leaves neatly
> pinned to a sheet of white paper and thumb tacked to his door.

—From *Fahrenheit 451* by Ray Bradbury, found by Dan Meishar

Teach it

1. Write this on the board

Spelling rule—Doubling the consonants

When a word ends in one consonant, right after one vowel, double the consonant before adding a suffix.

Ex:

hop–hopping
map–mapping
hit–hitting

Ex:

(double consonant)   (double consonant)

Chef <u>snipped</u> and then <u>chopped</u>
(double consonant)

while <u>sitting</u> down.

PRACTICE THE CONVERSATION:

A: Read the sentence, please.

B: *Chef snipped and then chopped while sitting down.*

A: Great. What are the three underlined words?

B: *Snipped, chopped, sitting.*

A: Good. Now what's the spelling rule that applies to these words?

B: The consonants get doubled when you add a suffix like –ed or –ies.

A: Yes. So what were these words before? What are the root words?

B: *Snip, chop, sit.* They each end in one consonant after one vowel, which means the rule applies.

A: What would happen if you didn't double the consonant?

B: Well, a snipper would be a sniper.

A: Not good.

B: Nope.

A: Great work.

2. **Explain:**

   Spelling is difficult for many people. Instead of memorizing hundreds of words, it's easier to learn a few basic spelling rules that work most of the time.

   This spelling rule involves doubling up a consonant at the end of a word when we add a suffix.

   When does that happen? There's a simple rule that governs this. When a word ends in one consonant right after one vowel, we double the consonant before we add a suffix.

   It sounds complicated, but look at the example words. In hopped, *for example, if we didn't double the consonant, the past tense of* hop *would be* hoped.

   *Look at the example sentence. The underline means I intentionally made a grammatical choice here. The proof above the word shows that I know why I made the choice; I know the rule about **doubled consonants**.*

3. **Ask:** *Who will try out this spelling rule with me?* (Enact the conversation.)

4. **Say:** *Open to your grammar chart and find the spelling rule for the **doubled consonants**. Let's jot down an example on the chart.*

Model it

5. Project the journal entry and read it.

6. Ask volunteers to read the sentences with the **doubled consonants** aloud. Ask them to state the rule: we double the final consonant if there's one vowel in front of it, before we add a suffix.

Practice it

7. **Say:** *In your journal today, try to use at least five of these __doubled consonants__, underlining each use. Write the proof over each one.*

March 28

So we kept looking for the real thief. Since I am a real heli pilot and a really good spy,

I got in my heli. I flew basically in town and after a second I **spotted** *(double consonant)* something. It was

a young teen that was about 16 and he was packing up in his car something. I couldn't

quite tell what, though.

I hovered a little lower so I could see better. I noticed that there was a lot of money. I

thought why would a teen be the thief? Well I did more research and found a picture of

the thief. He was about in his 20's and had tattoos and looked like a thug.

So I found his address and told my friend to ride over there and check if he was there.

Why I did not go is because he knew that he had to leave the area, so he wouldn't be

caught. He most likely went to South Carolina.

So I flew my heli there and called my **buddy** *(double consonant)* to come here for backup because I

needed it. This guy was dangerous . . . he had guns and knives and dogs and bad guy

friends. So they were here.

The next day we found the house that he was staying at so we drove down in our high

tech car. I got my bullet-proof jacket on and my pistol. I kicked down the door. He was

shooting at us and loaded the bullets and hit me. It hurt but I was protected.

I ran and jumped on the thief, wrestled him to the ground. He was very strong. He had

a knife out. He was about to stab me but in astonishment I twisted his arm and **grabbed** *(double consonant)*

the knife. I **stabbed** *(double consonant)* him in the wrist so he would not get hurt that bad and **handcuffed** *(double consonant)*

him and was on my way.

My **buddy** *(double consonant)* searched the house and found the money, so we went to Texas and were

paid half of that money for solving the case. You would never guess this half of that

money was 10 trillion dollars.

—Zach Prescott
Grade 6

66

I BEFORE E

    ❝ Thomas was relieved that the pain in his skull had diminished. **❞**

—From *The Scorch Trials* by James Dashner, found by Evan Katzman

Teach it

1. Write this on the board

> I before E (except after C—or pronounced like an A, as in *neighbor* and *weigh*)
>
> Ex:
>
>   thief, chief, belief, relief, piece
>   After C: receive, perceive, conceive
>   Like A: neighbor, weigh
>
> Ex:
>
>   *(i before e)*   *(i before e)*
> The police <u>chief</u> began to <u>piece</u>
>
> together the clues left by the
> *(i before e)*
> <u>thieves</u>.

PRACTICE THE CONVERSATION:

A: Will you please read the example sentence?
B: *The police chief began to piece together the clues left by the thieves.*
A: How do you spell *chief*?
B: C-h-i-e-f.
A: How do you know it's spelled that way?
B: "I" before "E," except after "C."
A: Great.

2. **Explain:**

   This spelling rule comes in handy with lots of words we use often. It helps to say it aloud several times and memorize it:

   *"**I before E, except after C,** or pronounced like an A, as in* neighbor *and* weigh."

   *Look at the example sentence. The underline means I intentionally made a grammatical choice here. The proof above the word shows that I know why I made the choice; I know the rule about "**I**" before "**E**."*

3. **Ask:** *Who will try out this spelling rule with me?* (Enact the conversation.)

4. **Say:** *Open to your grammar chart, and find the spelling rule for "**I**" before "**E**." Let's jot down an example on the chart.*

Model it

5. Project the journal entry and read it.

6. Ask volunteers to read aloud the sentences with the underlined words. Ask them to state the rule:
   I before E, except after C.

Practice it

7. **Say:** *In your journal today, try to use at least five of **I before E** words, underlining each use. Write the proof over each one.*

February 25

Let's begin. Once upon a time, there was a giant, really mean grizzly bear. There was

also a boy named Boy. Boy had a lot of sheep. One day, Boy cried, "Grizzly bear!" but he

was lying. One day, the grizzly bear actually came. Boy cried, "Grizzly bear!" but nobody

(i before e)   *(i before e)*
believed him. So, Boy's sheeps' guts were all ripped out, with **pieces** left everywhere,

and Boy got mauled and was eaten alive.

(i before e)
"Tell you what," Boy's mom said, "he was a dumb, lying, **thieving** kid anyway." The

(i before e)
cops of that CSI show analyzed the body of Boy, and made a **brief** conclusion.

(i before e)
"Mrs. Boy," the **chief** said, "this is a homicide case, so we need to find the weapon."

"Hey, first of all, the weapon was the bear's teeth, and second, he just got mauled. It's

not like you can arrest a bear," Mrs. Boy said.

CSI cops were analyzing, searching, and spying over all the forest. When they found

the bear they said, "Hey, that's him. Cuff 'im."

The guy in the front slowly pulled out the handcuffs. He trotted up to the Grizzly Bear.

Soon enough, he was mauled, too. The cops were shocked, then shot the bear dead.

Mrs. Boy was surprised that the killer was finally brought to justice.

"Thank you, CSI!"

The End   Or is it?

So then, a (i before e) **brief** speech to the bear concluded that this was not the right bear. The

police (i before e) **chief** noticed that there was no evidence that made him the killer. The bear was

walking home after being let out of jail when a puzzle (i before e) **piece** had a picture of the real

killer. So they locked up Billy Bear.

—Lauren Messer
Grade 6

Notes

67 CE/CI/GE/GI

Teach it

1. Write this on the board

> Ce/ci/ge/gi = soft sounds
>
> Ex:
>
> face, fa<u>ci</u>al
> colle<u>ge</u>, colle<u>gi</u>al
>
> (Contrast this with <u>cap, cone, got, gutter</u>.)
>
> Ex:
>
> (–ce)   (–ge)
> She <u>glanced</u> at <u>General</u>
>   (–ci)
> Arnold, who <u>winced</u> during the
> (–ci)   (–ce)
> <u>fencing</u> <u>practice</u>.

PRACTICE THE CONVERSATION:

A: Will you please read the sentence?
B: *She glanced at General Arnold, who winced during the fencing practice.*
A: Great. Why are some words underlined?
B: They have soft "C" or soft "G" sounds.
A: Can you explain that?
B: A soft "C" sounds like an "S." A soft "G" sounds like a "J."
A: Yes. What's the spelling rule for those?
B: If a "C" or a "G" is soft, it's followed by an "E" or an "I," or sometimes a "Y."
A: That's right.

2. **Explain:**

   City cat. Giant gift. Both the "C" and "G" have two different sounds, soft and hard.

   The soft "C" sounds like an "S."

   The soft "G" sounds like a "J."

   There's a simple spelling rule to use for these different sounds.

   If the sound is soft, "C" or "G" is followed by an "I" or an "E" (or "Y"),

   If the "C" or "G" sound is hard, then it is followed by an "A," "U," or "O."

   Look at the example sentence. The underline means I intentionally made a grammatical choice here. The proof above the word shows that I know why I made the choice; I know the rule about soft sounds with **ce/ci/ge/gi**.

3. **Ask:** *Who will try out this spelling rule with me?* (Enact the conversation.)

4. **Say:** *Open to your grammar chart and find the spelling rule for words with* **ce/ci/ge/gi**. *Let's jot down an example on the chart.*

Model it

5. Project the journal entry and read it.

6. Ask volunteers to read the sentences with these words aloud. Ask them to tell the rule that causes a soft "c" or "g" sound.

Practice it

7. **Say:** *In your journal today, try to use at least five words with **ce/ci/ge/gi** underlining each use. Write the proof over each one.*

March 2

Ice C☐be People

One morning, in the land of Flames, there was a flame named Jack. Jack loved to burn

things. One evening, his parents told him to come inside and eat. When he opened the

door, a portal sucked him in. Where was he going? To the I**ce** Cube World! I**ce** cube
                                                          (-ce)   (-ce)

people were everywhere! Then, he saw something horrid! A refri**ge**rator! He instantly
                                                                  (-ge)

started running away from all the I**ce** people. He bumped into an I**ce** man. When he
                                        (-ce)   (-ce)

bumped him, the I**ce** man melted.
                    (-ce)

"Murderer!" someone called out.

"Wait! I didn't!"

But the I**ce** poli**ce** grabbed him up. They
          (-ce)   (-ce)

wore anti-melt suits. They threw him into an

anti-melt **ce**ll with laser bars. One touch and
           (-ce)

an alarm goes off.

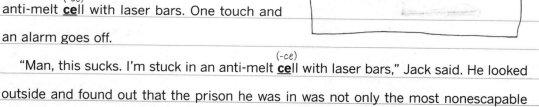

"Man, this sucks. I'm stuck in an anti-melt **ce**ll with laser bars," Jack said. He looked
                                             (-ce)

outside and found out that the prison he was in was not only the most nonescapable

prison, but the prison was secluded in the middle of the forest.

"Here's your food," a poli**ce**man said as he slid i**ce** cold fish under the bars. Jack
                          (-ce)   (-ce)

wasn't sure if he should eat it or not. He thought it wasn't good.

"Well, no hurt in trying new foods," he said. He put the food in his mouth and started

to die a slow, painful death. His veins were popping out so much they almost exploded,

his pupils went fa**ci**ng behind his head, and he was turning inside out. To make a long
                   (-ci)

story short, he died and lived happily ever after.

The end

—*Shaine Carpenter*
Grade 6

PART
V

FRAGMENTS

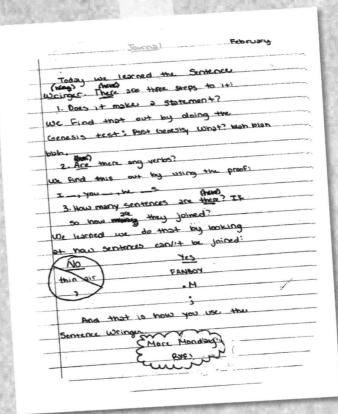

The greatest problem in fourth grade writing is sentence boundaries.
—Victoria Young, Texas Education Agency (January 31, 2013, at the Texas Council of Teachers of English Language Arts)

A period is life or death; if you forget to put a period, somebody might not stop to take a breath, and you need a breath to live. You could die.
—William Kavy, sixth grade

If students don't have sentence boundaries down cold, then the traditional ways of teaching sentence formation just aren't working. Some direct instruction is needed. What I have found that does work are the "paragraph overhaul" and the "sentence wringer." Though I usually teach the steps all at once (see Maggie's journal entry below), I've broken them down into smaller steps in these lessons.

Sentence wringers and paragraph overhauls aren't meant to be seat work. They're meant to be vehicles for *conversations*. As conversations, paragraph overhauls are dynamite. As seat work, paragraph overhauls accomplish nothing. It's that simple.

After students learn the dialogue of a sentence wringer, they are able to use it on any sentence anywhere. One of the most fruitful benefits is when they use it to disprove (or prove) the multiple choices on revision questions on tests.

"Hey!" I hear as we go over practice tests. "Look at A. Two sentences joined with thin air! And B is an AAAWWWUB-ified sentence. It's a fragment now!"

"D has a semicolon without sentences on either side."

"C is the only sentence!"

If you're not sure how the sentence wringer looks in a classroom, check the **www.resources.corwin.com/bernabeigrammar** book companion website, where you will find demonstration videos.

68

TWO-WORD SENTENCES

“ I flinched. ”

—From *The Host* by Stephenie Meyer,
found by Madeleine Restaino

Teach it

1. Write this on the board

> Two-word sentences
> Noun + verb
>
> Proof:
>
>
> (noun) + (verb)
> Boys laugh.

PRACTICE THE CONVERSATION:

A: Will you please read the two-word sentence?

B: *Boys laugh.*

A: Great. Is the second word a verb?

B: Yeppers.

A: Can you prove it?

B: I laugh, you laugh, he laughs.

A: Perfect. Is the first word a noun?

B: It sure is.

A: Can you prove that?

B: A boys, the boys, some boys.

A: It works perfectly in at least one of those, so it's definitely a noun. Right?

B: Right.

A: Well that's a perfect little two-word sentence. Thank you!

B: You're welcome.

2. **Explain:**

Two words can be a complete sentence. In fact, some of the most powerful sentences in the world are only two words. (I do.)

*The two parts of a **two-word sentence** are a noun (or pronoun, like in the sentence from The Host) and a verb.*

*All you need to do to prove that you have a basic **two-word sentence** is use the noun and verb proofs.*

To prove a noun, you put the word into every blank in this phrase: a __, the __, some __s.

To prove a verb, you put the word into every blank in this phrase: I __, you __, he __s.

3. **Ask:** *Now, who will try out this two-word sentence with me? (Enact the conversation.)*

Model it

4. Project the journal entry and read it.

5. Ask for volunteers to read each of the **two-word sentences** aloud. Ask them to use the proof to show how those two-word sentences are constructed.

Practice it

6. **Say:** *In your journal today, try to use at least five **two-word sentences**, underlining each use. Write the proof over each one.*

April 8

Nothing

Today I will write about . . . NOTHING.

You may be thinking, "But Nic, you just can't write about nothing."

And to this I say, "I do what I want. *(noun + verb)* __I can__. *(noun + verb)* __People should__."

Now there are some different ways of writing about nothing. The one way you

are thinking of is not the one I'm doing. *(noun + verb)* __It just isn't__.

This is the time where you may say, "If you're going to write about nothing,

then just do it!"

(noun + verb) __I will__. So here it is. Just __do it__. *(noun + verb)*

Did you enjoy that bit about nothing? *(noun + verb)* __I did__. Now you may think "There's

nothing there."

And to that I say, "Exactly."

—Nicholas Prewett
Grade 7

69

SENTENCE WRINGER—PSST! STATEMENT

" Go to the roof so I can capture the flag and gloat. "

—From *The Air Man*, by Francis A. Collins, found by Christian Westbrook

Teach it

1. Write this on the board

> ### Does it make a statement?
> ### "The Psst! Test"
>
> In the mall.   They left.
> There was a dog.   When he hollers.
> Any time it   In case of
> rains.   emergency.

PRACTICE THE CONVERSATION:

A: David, practice this with me. Look away.

A: Psst! David!

B: (looks) What?

A: In the mall.

A: (to the class) Did I tell him something? (listen and shake head) No. That wasn't a statement.

A: Let's do another one.

A: Psst! David!

B: (looks) What?

A: There was a dog.

A: Did I tell him something?

A: (Nod) Yes, I did. That was a statement. Let's do another one.

A: Psst! David!

B: (looks) What?

A: Any time it rains. Did I tell him something? No. That's the Psst! Test! And from now on, for the rest of the year, we can use this to try out sentences to see whether they make a statement.

2. **Explain:**

   Many people aren't absolutely positive about what makes a complete, correctly written sentence. Here's one step you can take to make sure that you have a real sentence between the capital and the period.

   *You give the words the **Psst! Test**.*

   Imagine someone walking up to you and saying the sentence right out of the blue. You'd listen to it and see whether they made a statement that you understand.

3. **Say:** *For the **Psst! Test**, I need one volunteer, someone who is quiet but would like to participate.* (Enlist one student, and let everyone listen as you teach them this process.)

   Okay, David. I'm going to ask you to look somewhere else. Then out of the clear blue, I'm going to say "Psst! David!" Then you look me right in the eyes and say, "What?" And no matter what else happens, don't say anything else. Ready to try it? (Enact the conversation.)

   Note: This doesn't completely determine whether the sentence is a correct sentence, but it's one way for students to learn to hear a fragment.

Model it

4. Project the journal entry and read it.

5. Ask for a volunteer to read each of the underlined sentences and try out the **Psst! Test** to see if the sentence makes a statement.

Practice it

6. **Say:** *Today while you're writing in your journal, think about the* **<u>Psst! Test</u>** *as you're writing. After journal time, you'll have a chance to pick out a sentence so that we can try the* **<u>Psst! Test</u>** *on it.*

October 6

<u>When I was little, I couldn't find my sister at the store.</u> She told me to go on the other

side and get my mom a candy, so I went and when I came back I could not find her.

Then I saw her. **<u>I ran to her and went to hug her.</u>** When I looked up at her to tell her that

I couldn't find her, it was another girl. **<u>I ran the other way</u>**. But my sister called me and

she was right behind the girl I hugged. **<u>When we got in the car</u>**. She started laughing

and so did I.

—Juliette Urrutia
Grade 7

70

SENTENCE WRINGER—IS THERE A VERB?

> " Tally realized that it was the same color as the cat–vomit pink of the sunset, with "
> a long snout and two pink little ears.
>
> —From *Uglies*, by Scott Westerfeld,
> found by Juliette Urrutia

Teach it

1. Write this on the board

Is there a verb?

Verb Proof: .

I__, you __, he __s

Ex:

(I saw, you saw, he saws)
We <u>saw</u> the cat.

In the yard.

PRACTICE THE CONVERSATION:

A: Read me the first sentence, please.

B: *I saw the cat.*

A: Perfect. Is there a verb?

B: Yes. Saw.

A: Prove that *saw* is a verb, please?

B: I saw, you saw, he saws?

A: That's right. Saw is a verb. It worked in at least one of those three blanks. Read me the second sentence, please.

B: *In the yard.*

A: Is there a verb in that sentence?

B: Hmm . . .

A: Let's try the proof on all of the words.

B: Okay, but . . .

A: I'll help. I in, you in, he ins. That's not a verb, right?

B: Right.

A: I the, you the, he thes. Nope. What about yard? Want to try that one?

B: I yard, you yard, he yards. No. It's not a verb.

A: That's right. That sentence has no verb. It can't possibly be a sentence. Great job.

2. **Explain:**

   This is one way to see if a sentence is really a fragment.

   How do you know if it's really a fragment? Here is one way to know. All sentences have at least one verb. So we look for a verb. If there's no verb, it can't be a sentence. If there's no verb, it's absolutely a fragment, just a part of a sentence.

   And how do we prove a verb? We use this **verb proof**:

   I blank, you blank, he blanks.

   We put the same word in all three blanks and listen. If at least one of the three words makes sense, then we have a verb. Who will try this out with me? (Enact the conversation.)

3. **Say:** *Open to your grammar chart and find the sentence wringer. Let's jot down the* **verb proof** *on the chart.*

   Note: Students may find more than one verb, and some fragments do have verbs, so finding a verb doesn't always mean it's a sentence. It's just one thing to check when scrutinizing the construction of a sentence.

Model it

4. Project the journal entry and read it.

5. Ask volunteers to read a sentence and find (and underline) the verb. Then have them and try out the **verb proof**.

Practice it

6. **Say:** *Look into your journal and find a sentence to try out. Underline the **verb** and get ready to have this conversation with a partner, proving you have a verb. Write the proof over each one.*

February 14

Lucy My Dog!

(I have, you have, he haves)

If you don't already know, I **have** an awesome dog named Lucy. When we first **saw** Lucy

(I saw, you saw, he saws)

(I was, you was, he was)

at the pound she had 5 hours to live and she **was** super skinny. I really liked her and took

(I called, you called, he called)

so many pictures. I kept thinking to myself I cannot let this dog go. We **called** for a helper

(I decided, you decided, he decided) (I signed, you signed, he signed)

and we **decided** we would take her. We **signed** a bunch of papers and she got spayed so

she was missing a lot of hair on her stomach. We got in the car and I sat in the passenger

seat so I held the dog. The dog was shaking, I'm sure she was scared. She was wrapped

(I think, you think, he thinks)

in a blanket and she didn't do much. I **think** she didn't know where she was, where she

was going, and who we are. So it must have been freaky to her. When we got back to the

house we let her walk around for a little bit. I could already tell she liked me. Already 8

months later and she is doing great. She can walk and run. She has all her stomach hair

back and my room is her castle. If you walk in my room she will growl. If I say stop she

will stop. She sleeps with me, right next to me every night. She always follows only me.

She is the dog I have always wanted. I take her on walks, buy her new toys, get her a new

dog tag every few months or so, clip her nails, give her a bath, brush her, play with her,

etc. . . . My point is that I love her! She is a Chihuahua by the way.

—Layne Dentinger
Grade 8

71

JOINING SENTENCES LEGALLY

" It was the smallest hesitation in time, but Silver knew what she had to do. **"**

—From *Tanglewreck* by Jeanette Winterson,
found by Anael Ashkenazi

Teach it

1. Write this on the board

> **Three ways to join sentences legally**
>
> > And (or other conjunction)
> > ;
> > . B
>
> Ex:
>
> > We had dinner it was good.
>
> **Three ways to fix this:**
>
> > We had dinner <u>and</u> it was good.
> > We had dinner<u>;</u> it was good.
> > We had dinner<u>.</u> It was good.

PRACTICE THE CONVERSATION:

A: Will you please read the example sentence?

B: *We had dinner it was good.*

A: How many statements did you hear?

B: Two.

A: How are they joined?

B: Right now, with nothing.

A: What is one way we could fix this?

B: By adding a word like *and.*

A: Let's hear that.

B: *We had dinner, and it was good.*

A: Okay, great. What's another way to fix it?

B: With a semicolon.

A: Read it that way please.

B: *We had dinner; it was good.*

A: Okay, and the third way?

B: To break it into two sentences. *We had dinner. It was good.*

A: So if you were the author of this, which way would you choose?

B: I'd have to go with the semicolon.

A: Great.

2. **Explain:**

   When we have two or more sentences, we have to look at what joins them. There are three ways to connect sentences together correctly. What are they?

   And, or another conjunction*. Do you know FANBOYS (for-and-nor-but-or-yet-so)? Any one of these conjunctions would work.*

   A semicolon*. Whatever is on either side of this semicolon should be a sentence.*

   *Go ahead and break them into two separate sentences. This isn't technically **joining the sentences** into one sentence, but it is one option.*

3. **Ask:** *Who will try this out with me?* (Enact the conversation.)

4. **Say:** *Open to your grammar chart, and let's find the sentence wringer. Let's jot down these three ways to **join sentences**.*

   Note: Of course, there is another use for a semicolon. We use semicolons instead of commas for items in a series, when the items are long phrases that contain commas already. But this basic use appears on high-stakes tests, and the secondary use isn't commonly tested.

Model it

5. Project the journal entry and read it.

6. Ask volunteers to find places where two sentences are joined. Ask them to identify which choice the writer used.

Practice it

7. **Say:** *In your journal today, try to use these three different ways to **join sentences**, underlining each one.*

February 26

I Had a Weird Dream

So I've heard that dreams are based on some of the last things you remember, **but**

last night my dream came from nowhere. Last night in my bed I slept easier with the

sound of Rhett and Link (two awesome YouTubers I listen to every week day night).

I slept on my dad's spare Temper-Pedic pillow**; it** was easier to sleep than ever! As I

dozed off into the world of dreams, I awoke and saw a world of computer animations.

The genre of animation was something like World of Warcraft. I saw my friends as

mythical creatures (mostly dwarfs, elfs, and knights, etc.) Seeing everyone in battle

against demon-like goblins, I drew my sword and wildly chopped off heads and limbs

of the goblins to save my friends (Annabell and her sister Star, William, Ben, Asher,

Anael, Claire, Lindsay, Talia, Kennedy, and Preston). This encouraged me to get World

of Warcraft.

—Evan Katzman
Grade 6

72

JOINING SENTENCES ILLEGALLY

“ My rules were too ingrained. She was safer this way. ”

—From *I Am Not a Serial Killer* by Dan Wells, found by Ethan Weingart

Teach it

1. Write this on the board

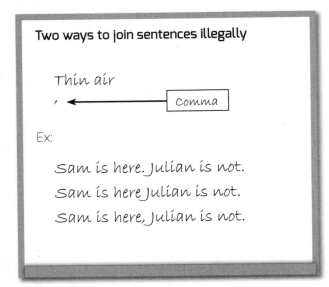

Two ways to join sentences illegally

Thin air

, ← Comma

Ex:

Sam is here. Julian is not.

Sam is here Julian is not.

Sam is here, Julian is not.

PRACTICE THE CONVERSATION:

A: Will you please read the two sentences in the example?

B: *Sam is here. Julian is not.*

A: What's one wrong way to join them?

B: With thin air.

A: And how would that sound?

B: Sam is here Julian is not.

A: Nothing is there but thin air?

B: Right.

A: And that is so . . .

B: Wrong.

A: Right. What's another wrong way to join those sentences?

B: With a comma.

A: Exactly. Can you join two sentences with a comma?

B: Never, never, never.

A: Perfect.

2. **Explain:**

*When we have two or more sentences, we have to look at what joins them. Sometimes people **join sentences incorrectly**, using strategies considered wrong, substandard, and illegal in the grammar world. What are these two ways?*

- *Just running them together with nothing but thin air between them.*
- *Slapping a comma between the two sentences. We call this a comma splice.*

Both of these ways result in what are called run-on sentences.

3. **Ask:** *Who will try this out with me?* (Enact the conversation.)

   (Draw a huge X across the examples.)

4. **Say:** *Open to your grammar chart, and let's find the sentence wringer. Let's jot down these two ways **not to join sentences**.*

Model it

5. Project the journal entry and read it.

6. Ask volunteers to find where two or more sentences are joined. Ask them to identify which correct choice the writer used (see Lesson 71).

Practice it

7. **Say:** *In your journal today, try to notice if you use either of these* <u>**illegal choices when joining sentences**</u>.

February 21

I have had many weird dreams, but few nightmares. One that I could remember for the

longest time was when I was about 5. It was from a Scooby Doo movie, IRL though. So

this was my nightmare.

   I was going down the frozen section in a store on Shaggy's shoulders. Then the

monsters from the movies started chasing us. Next thing I can remember was that me,

my dad, and some other people were in a cage in the fruits and vegetables department.

We were trying to unlock it with these shapes that reminded me of Dora for some

reason. I knew it was a dream, and I was trying to open my eyes, but I wasn't able to.

Finally, I get them open. I guess all nightmares seem scary, but when you look back,

they seem kind of pathetic.

—Madeleine Restaino
Grade 6

73

SENTENCE WRINGER PRACTICE

" Why did I need to speak to her at all? I know why. Because I'm an idiot! And she **"** doesn't believe it. Any of it!

—From *The Killing Woods* by Lucy Christopher, found by Kennedy Cantu

Teach it

1. Write this on the board

Sentence wringer

1. Statement? (The Psst! Test)
2. Verb in it?
(I ___, you ___, he ___s)
3. If there is more than one sentence, how are they joined?
and
;

Ex:

We went home.

PRACTICE THE CONVERSATION:

A: Will you please read me the sentence?

B: *We went home.*

A: Does it make a statement?

B: It does.

A: Can you prove that?

B: Psst! David!

David: What?

B: We went home.

A: Did you tell him something?

B: I sure did.

A: Okay. Next . . . does it have a verb?

B: It does. *Home.*

A: Can you prove it?

B: I home, you home, he homes. That's not a verb. Um . . . *went.*

A: Prove it?

B: I went, you went, he wents.

A: It's a verb; it worked in two of those. What's last? Is it more than one statement?

B: Nope, just one.

A: Then it's a correct sentence. Good.

2. **Explain:**

> *Now that you know the three parts of the sentence wringer, we can put them together to check any sentence, from capital to period.*

> - *If the sentence doesn't pass the first two questions, it's definitely a fragment and needs to be fixed.*

> - *If it doesn't pass the third, it's a run-on sentence and needs to be fixed.*

Look at the example sentence. We can check all three parts of the __sentence wringer__ on this sentence to make sure it's not a __fragment__ or a __run-on sentence__.

3. **Ask:** *Who will try out a __sentence wringer__ with me?* (Enact the conversation; make sure to cast someone in the role of David today.)

4. **Say:** *Open to your grammar chart and find __sentence wringer__. Let's make sure we have all three parts of the sentence wringer on the chart.*

Model it

5. Project the journal entry and read it.

6. Ask volunteers to read any sentence from the journal entry. Run the sentence through the **wringer** to see whether it's a fragment, a sentence, or a run-on sentence.

Practice it

7. **Say:** *While writing in your journal today, think about the **sentence wringer**.*

January 29

So I was watching the "State of the Union" speech and I realized three things:

1. I don't know what "State of the Union" is.

2. The speech is super boring.

3. Why do royal, presidential people get a formal name-calling-thing?

I want to elaborate on #3. So, the formal name-calling-thing. . . . I don't understand

why you have to be so fancy to be announced. I mean think, when have you ever been

to a restaurant and heard: "Please rise for the arrival of Maggie Davis and family." Or if

you go to a store and hear: "Now walking in is Maggie Davis!" I just don't get it. Every

once in a while it would be nice. "Hear ye, hear ye, Maggie is finished with her journal!"

—Maggie Davis
Grade 7

74

PARAGRAPH OVERHAUL

66 And where did you get your dog? 99

—From *School's Out—Forever*, by James Patterson,
found by Alicia Narvaez

Teach it

1. Write this on the board

> ### Sentence wringer
>
> 1. Statement? (The Psst! Test)
>
> 2. Verb? (I __, you __, he __s)
>
> 3. If there is more than one sentence, how are they joined?
> and
> ;
> .

**PRACTICE THE CONVERSATION:
WRINGING OUT SENTENCE 1**

A: Read the sentence please.
B: *I played a soft song.*
A: Does it make a statement?
B: Psst! David!
David: What?
B: I played a soft song.
A: Did you tell him something?
B: Yes.
A: Is there a verb?
B: Played. I played, you played, he played.
A: And how many are there?
B: Just one.
A: Great. It's a good sentence. Let's copy it down in the second part of the form because it's already fixed.

2. **Explain:**

Sometimes, when you're reading something, it's difficult to notice when sentences are incorrectly written. It's much easier to notice the construction of a sentence when it's by itself.

For that reason, I like use what I call a **paragraph overhaul** *to check my sentences. Do you know what it means to overhaul an engine that isn't working?*

That's right. You take the engine apart so that you have a pile of parts. Then you check each part, fix or replace the broken parts, and then you put it back together.

**PRACTICE THE CONVERSATION:
WRINGING OUT SENTENCE 2**

A: Read the sentence please.
B: *On my piano.*
A: Does it make a statement?
B: Psst! David!
David: What?
B: On my piano.
A: Did you tell him something?
B: No.
A: Is there a verb?
B: Um . . . I on, you on . . . no . . . I piano, you piano . . . no . . . I my, you my . . . nope. No verb.
A: Then it can't be a sentence, can it?
B: No, I don't believe it can.
A: How do you want to fix it?
B: Can't we add it to the sentence before it?
A: Sure we could. Let's do.

That's exactly what we're going to do with this paragraph.

Look at the **_paragraph overhaul_** practice sheet I gave you. Klarissa wrote a well-written paragraph, but we messed up the sentences for practice.

Here's what you do with the form:

Step 1. List the sentences, just as they are.

So copy the sentences in a list, without changing a thing.

From capital to period, what's sentence number 1?

I played a soft song.

Let's copy that down next to number one.

Sentence number 2?

On my piano.

Number 3?

It's hard playing with two hands.

And number 4?

It gets easier you have to practice.

PRACTICE THE CONVERSATION: WRINGING OUT SENTENCE 3

A: Read the sentence please.

B: _It's hard playing with two hands._

A: Does it make a statement?

B: Psst! David!

David: What?

B: It's hard playing with two hands.

A: Did you tell him something?

B: Yes.

A: Is there a verb?

B: Playing.

A: Prove that?

B: I playing, you playing . . . no . . .

A: Look at _it's_. What does that mean?

B: _It is._ Hey, _is_ is a verb.

A: Prove it?

B: I is, you is, he is! It fits on one of them!

A: Then it's a verb. And how many statements are there?

B: Just one.

A: Great. It's a good sentence. Let's copy it down because it's not broken.

(Continued)

(Continued)

Step 2. Fix them.

Second, we put the sentences through the wringer, one by one. (Enact the conversations.)

Step 3. Reshape the fixed sentences into the shape of a paragraph.

In the third space, write the sentence in the form of a paragraph.

Note: See extra paragraph overhauls in the appendices so you can continue to practice this with students. There's also a blank located there, so you can create paragraph overhauls from your own students' writing. Ask them to intentionally write some fragments and run-ons, or if they don't know how, you can let them know that you'll mess the writing up for them. Encourage them to practice this on their own drafts.

PRACTICE THE CONVERSATION: WRINGING OUT SENTENCE 4

A: Read the sentence please.

B: *It gets easier you have to practice.*

A: Does it make a statement?

B: Psst! David!

David: What?

B: It gets easier you have to practice.

A: Did you tell him something?

B: Yes.

A: Is there a verb?

B: Gets. I gets, you gets, he gets.

A: And how many statements are there?

B: Two.

A: What's the first one?

B: It gets easier.

A: The second one?

B: You have to practice. Psst! David!

David: What?

B: You have to practice. Yep, it makes a statement. I have, you have, he haves. There's a verb.

A: Excellent. So how are these two joined right now? What is between them?

B: Thin air.

A: And that's not right. How can we fix it? Let's add a comma.

B: No way.

A: Can you join two sentences with a comma?

B: Never, never, never.

A: Okay then. How can we join two sentences?

B: With a conjunction like *and*. With a semicolon. Or just break them up into two sentences.

A: And which would you like to do? What's your choice here?

B: Let's add *but* in between them.

A: Perfect. Let's write that sentence now.

Paragraph Overhaul

the Soft Song
by Klarissa Martinez

I played a soft song. On my piano.
It's hard playing with two hands. It gets
easier you have to practice.

List the sentences, just as they are →

1. _____
2. _____
3. _____
4. _____

Fix them and list →

1. _____
2. _____
3. _____
4. _____

Re-shape them into a paragraph.

_____
_____
_____
_____

75

AAAWWWUBIFICATION

" The lone passenger's fingers gripped the armrest as the wheels of the plane **"** bumped against the ground.

—From *The Sword Thief* by Peter Lerangis, found by Grayson Kyle

Teach it

1. Write this on the board

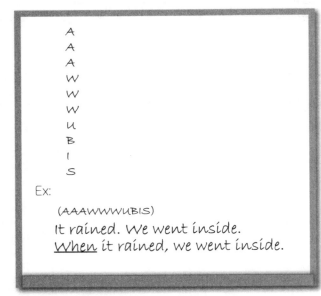

A
A
A
W
W
W
U
B
I
S

Ex:

(AAAWWWUBIS)

It rained. We went inside.
<u>When</u> it rained, we went inside.

PRACTICE THE CONVERSATION:

A: Will you read the first sentences?

B: *It rained. We went inside.*

A: Okay. Now will you read the bottom sentence?

B: *When it rained, we went inside.*

A: Great. Which word is the AAAWWWUBIS?

B: *When.*

A: Yes. If you took it off, what would you have?

B: Two sentences, joined with a comma.

A: Can you join two sentences with a comma?

B: Never, never, never.

A: But after the **AAAWWWUB-ified** sentence, it's okay to put a comma?

B: It is. Because they are not two complete sentences anymore. It's one complete sentence and one that has been **AAAWWWUB-ified** into a fragment.

A: Great.

2. **Explain:**

    Rather than joining two sentences together exactly as they're written, writers sometimes see a better way to combine them. One of the most useful ways to join sentences is to **AAAWWWUB-ify** *them.*

    (Have everyone pronounce Ah-woo-biss! a time or two.)

    AAAWWWUBIS *is an acronym for these words.* (Write them on the board, and have students copy them into their notes.):

After	Where	If
Although	While	Since
As	Until	
When	Because	

    If you add an **AAAWWWUBIS** *to a sentence, it will become a fragment. It would fail the Psst! test. You have to combine* **two complete sentences** *for an* **AAAWWWUBIS** *to work.*

    Look at the example sentence:

    *   *The underline means I intentionally made a grammatical choice here.*
    *   *The proof above the word shows that I know why I made the choice; I know about* **AAAWWWUBIfication**.

3. **Ask:** *Who will try out the* **AAAWWWUB-ified** *sentence with me?* (Enact the conversation.)

4. **Say:** *Open to your grammar chart and find* **AAAWWWUBIS**. *Let's jot down an example on the chart.*

    Note: AAAWWWUBIS originated in Jeff Anderson's book *Mechanically Inclined* (2005).

Model it

5. Project the journal entry and read it.

6. Ask volunteers to read the sentences with **AAAWWWUBIS** aloud. Ask them to use the proof to show that they know the rule.

Practice it

7. **Say:** *In your journal today, try to use at least five of the **AAAWWWUBIS** words, underlining each use.*

November 18

I Want a Turtle

I will have a leash for my turtle.

It will be named Garfunkle Dobbins Tuppins Bobbins.

I will smell it every day.
(if)
<u>If</u> it smells funny, I'll wash it.

I will listen to it. Every day.
(if)
<u>If</u> its heart isn't beating, it is dead.
(if)
<u>If</u> it is dead, I will cry.
(if)
<u>If</u> I cry, I will be teased.
(if)
<u>If</u> I am teased, I will get angry.
(if)
<u>If</u> I get angry, people will feel my wrath.
(if)
<u>If</u> they feel my wrath, they will wish they hadn't teased me.
(if)
<u>If</u> they wished they hadn't teased me, they will apologize.
(if)
<u>If</u> they apologize, I will feel better.
(if)
<u>If</u> I feel better, I will get another turtle.
(if)
<u>If</u> I get a turtle . . .

That's a big if.

—Preston Oliver
Grade 6

PART VI

PITCHFORKING

Word Count: 350

Maggie Davis

Language Arts

March 17

The City Life; the Best Life

Nothing beats the city. Not the cows in the fields, not the lush green country side, and *definitely* not the bugs in every nook and cranny of my house. If you were looking for me you would look one place and I would be there: the big city. It's *much* better to be in New York City, Las Vegas, or Miami than to be in the rural parts of Texas, Kansas, or Nebraska.

I am four, the city was the only thing I know. I don't know about the thousands of miles of nothing but fields, cattle, and wildflowers. It's the same schedule every day; wake up, school, Whataburger, Kim Possible, playtime, dinner, shower, and then bed. There is not enough time in the day for a little four year old to go drive for an hour just to look at grass and livestock. The city is home, the city is amazing, the city is perfect. Nothing is better than it.

I am seven and Sophie just moved to a small town that I hadn't heard of. Bergheim. I am at her little white house running around her property and what happens? I fall and sprain my ankle. I think that the city is safer and :lefinitely better.

I am ten and I just had the most amazingly fun sleepover at Sophie's house. We played with her new puppies Juliette and Java, hopped around in the puddles on her

After I wrote my essay on the test, I spent some time proofreading. I noticed pitchforking I had inserted in my writing without noticing. I guess it became instinctive and second nature after years of doing it.

—Jonah Katzman, eighth grader

A pitchfork has one handle and multiple prongs or tines. In "pitchforking" students learn to take one individual part of any sentence they write and split it into multiples. This may produce compound sentences, compound predicates, compound objects of a preposition, and compound adjectives or clauses. I never tell them this ahead of time, though; I say, "Hey . . . this is a pitchfork!"

And they know what to do with the parts. On the reading tests, summaries of informational paragraphs often lead to pitchforking to create the basic structure of the passage. Students who recognize this have an easier time navigating the passage and questions.

76

PITCHFORKING ACTIONS

> ❝ I rarely left the house, spent quite a lot of time in bed, read the same book over and over, ❞ ate infrequently, and devoted quite a bit of my abundant free time to thinking about death.

—From *The Fault in Our Stars* by John Green, found by Talia Delambre

Teach it

1. Write this on the board

Pitchforking actions

Plain sentence:

I stood in the middle of the field.

Pitchforked action:

I <u>stood</u> in the middle of the field, <u>stamping</u> my feet and <u>shivering</u> in the cold, <u>waiting</u> for something to happen.

—Ben Brody

PRACTICE THE CONVERSATION:

A: Read the first sentence please.

B: *I stood in the middle of the field.*

A: Good. Now let's see how this writer pitchforked an action in the next sentence. Read it, please.

B: *I stood in the middle of the field, stamping my feet and shivering in the cold, waiting for something to happen.*

A: Hmm . . . how is that a pitchfork? Can you explain?

B: Well, the writer took the word *stood* and added three other actions.

A: How is that like a pitchfork?

B: It started out as one and branched out into three more actions. Just like the shape of a pitchfork.

A: Good!

2. **Explain:**

Pitchforking means taking one thing—in this case an action—and branching it out to describe several actions.

It's a way to write better, richer, more sophisticated sentences and to give the reader more of a mental image of what's happening.

Look at the example sentence. The underline means I intentionally made a grammatical choice here. The drawing above the sentence signals what my choice was: I used pitchforking.

3. **Ask:** *Who will try out this pitchforking idea with me?* (Enact the conversation.)

4. **Say:** *Open to your grammar chart and find **pitchforking actions**. Let's jot down an example on the chart.*

Model it

5. Project the journal entry and read it.

6. Ask volunteers to read the sentences with the **pitchforked actions** aloud. Ask them to explain what pitchforking is: that it splits one thing into several things.

Practice it

7. **Say:** *In your own journal, try to use at least three __pitchforked actions__, underlining each use. Write the proof over each one.*

April 3

Think You Really Know Me? Well, You're Wrong . . .

Most people think they know me, but really they don't even know the half of who I am

or what I have been through, or what I have **done, seen, heard.** The only people who

really know me **and accept me for who I am** are my boy and girl best friends, my sister

(non blood related) and my family. No one else has seen who I really am. Many people

think I am the quiet shy girl. Or they don't even know I exist. If you knew the real me,

you probably would find it hard to believe. Especially if you think I'm a quiet shy girl. I

have been through some tough situations too. **I have been suicidal, I have cut myself,**

I've been bullied, used, hated, invisible. You think I'm just that quiet girl. But behind my

quiet voice and my fear of talking, I am a very outgoing, funny, crazy, silly kind of person.

You don't know half my story. You have no idea of who I really am.

—Alyssa Rico
Grade 8

77

PITCHFORKING NOUNS

> " The rest of us—me, Tobias, Caleb, Peter, Christina, Uriah, and Cara—set out with " our meager possessions along the railroad tracks.
>
> —From *Allegiant*, by Veronica Roth, found by Maggie Davis

Teach it

1. Write this on the board

Pitchforking nouns

Plain sentence:

A soccer player has lots of choices.

Pitchforked nouns:

A soccer player can choose what soccer is to him: is it <u>a hobby</u>? <u>a job</u>? or most important, <u>a passion</u>?

—Jake Torres

PRACTICE THE CONVERSATION:

A: Read the plain sentence, please.

B: *A soccer player has lots of choices.*

A: Okay. Let's hear what the writer decided to pitchfork. Will you read the pitchforked sentence?

B: *A soccer player can choose what soccer is to him: is it a hobby? a job? or most important, a passion?*

A: Can you explain how that's a pitchfork?

B: Sure. One thing branched out into three things. *What soccer is* branched out into a *hobby,* a *job,* and a *passion.*

A: What part of speech are all of those?

B: They're nouns.

A: Good!

2. **Explain:**

   Pitchforking means taking one thing—in this case a noun—and branching it out into several nouns.

   It's a way to write better, richer, more sophisticated sentences and to give the reader a more detailed mental image.

   Look at the example sentence. The underline means I intentionally made a grammatical choice here. The drawing above the sentence signals what my choice was: I used pitchforking.

3. **Ask:** *Who will try out this pitchforking idea with me?* (Enact the conversation.)

4. **Say:** *Open to your grammar chart and find **pitchforking nouns**. Let's jot down an example on the chart.*

Model it

5. Project the journal entry and read it.

6. Ask volunteers to read the sentences with the **pitchforked nouns** aloud. Ask them to explain what pitchforking is, that it splits one thing into several things.

Practice it

7. **Say:** *In your journal today, try to use at least three **pitchforked nouns**, underlining each use. Write the proof over each one.*

February 7

Why I Want to Be a Bird

I want to be a bird **(like a pigeon, a mockingbird, a grackle)** because you can fly and

poop on peoples' cars, **bikes, or strollers**. If you have good aiming, then maybe even

their heads! Just think about how fun it would be to drop your waste on somebody's

property. And you get to sit **in a tree, on a roof or a telephone line**, minding your own

business chirping your lungs out to annoy people. There are so many fun things to do

when you're a bird.

—Carleigh Dentinger
Grade 6

78

PITCHFORKING USING BA-DA-BING

> " I was sitting in a taxi, wondering if I had overdressed for the evening, when I "
> looked out the window and saw Mom rooting through a Dumpster.

—From *The Glass Castle* by Jeannette Walls, found by Alicia Narvaez

Author's note: For additional information on ba-da-bings, visit www.bernabeiwritingtools.blogspot.com.

Teach it

1. Write this on the board

Pitchforking ba-da-bings

Plain sentence:

This weekend I watched *The Lego Movie* for the third time.

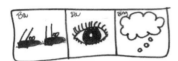

Pitchforked ba-da-bing:

Seated at the center of the many rows of seats, munching popcorn, I watched the familiar film designed almost entirely with Lego bricks. In the dark tombs, there were orderly rows of lights to my side and one great screen bright before me. My brain was satisfied because instead of strange people and violence, this movie was filled with orderly bricks.

—Michael Squire

PRACTICE THE CONVERSATION:

A: Will you read the plain sentence, please?

B: *This weekend I watched The Lego Movie for the third time.*

A: Okay. Now, do you know what a ba-da-bing sentence is?

B: Yes, I do. See those three icons in a row? Feet, eye, thought bubble?

A: Why yes.

B: You write a sentence that tells what your feet were doing, what your eye saw, and what you thought, all at that moment. That's a ba-da-bing.

A: So how would you pitchfork that?

B: You'd tell more than one thing for each icon. Several things you were doing physically, several things you saw, and several things you thought.

A: Good explanation! Now will you read the pitchforked ba-da-bing?

B: *Seated at the center of the many rows of seats, munching popcorn, I watched the familiar film designed almost entirely with Lego bricks. In the dark room, there were orderly rows of lights to my side and one great screen bright before me. My brain was satisfied because instead of strange people and violence, this movie was filled with orderly bricks.*

A: Wonderful. Does it matter that it's broken up into more than one sentence?

B: I don't think so. It's good writing.

A: It sure is.

2. **Explain:**

Pitchforking means taking one thing and branching it out into several things—in this case, by using ba-da-bing. It's a way to write better, richer, more sophisticated sentences and to give the reader a more detailed mental image.

A ba-da-bing sentence is guided by the three icons and tells . . .

- *what a person's body was doing*
- *what they saw*
- *what they thought*

Look at the example sentence. The underline means I intentionally made a grammatical choice here. The drawings above the sentence signal what my choice was: I used pitchforking, combined with ba-da-bings.

3. **Ask:** *Who will try out this **pitchforked ba-da-bing** with me?* (Enact the conversation.)

4. **Say:** *Open to your grammar chart and find **pitchforked ba-da-bings**. Let's jot down an example.*

Model it

5. Project the journal entry and read it.

6. Ask volunteers to read the sentences with the **pitchforked ba-da-bings** aloud. Ask them to explain what pitchforking is: that it splits one thing into several things.

Practice it

7. **Say:** *In your journal today, try to use at least three **pitchforked ba-da-bings,** underlining each use. Write the proof over each one.*

October 10

Memories (are lost)

Imagine you woke up in a hospital, with no recollection of anything, the only thing you

know is that you're doomed. On a hospital bed **you get up, go in the hallway and you see**

flashing lights, papers scattered, doors closed or wide open, everything that gives you

the chills, but it seems familiar.

You decide to walk around, same as before, but then you find something, something

that might give you some answers, maybe. It's a door glowing with sunlight down the

hall. This is not concerning for some reason. Closer and closer you approach. You here?

These might be answered by a single door hinge. Finally you're there. Ten feet away, your

steps start to turn to baby steps and they echo the normal steps. You take a breath . . .

To be continued on October 12.

Evan Katzman
Grade 6

79

PITCHFORKING USING EXCLAMATIONS

> " Everywhere I looked I saw mountains of rare goods piled high. Bales of silk and " tobacco! Chests of tea! A parrot! A monkey!

—From *The True Confessions of Charlotte Doyle* by Avi, found by Nina De La Torre

Teach it

1. Write this on the board

Pitchforking exclamations

Plain sentence:

It is going to rain.

Pitchforked with exclamations:

Guys! Guys! Look! Look! It's going to rain! Everybody take cover! Oh my gosh!

—William Kavy

PRACTICE THE CONVERSATION:

A: Please read the plain sentence.

B: *It is going to rain.*

A: Good. Now think about exclamations. How would you say this same sentence if you were excited? Will you read the second sentence?

B: *Guys! Guys! Look! Look! It's going to rain! Everybody take cover! Oh my gosh!*

A: Where are the exclamations?

B: Before and after the original sentence.

A: Is that fair? Can you do that?

B: Sure. It works!

A: It does. Good job.

2. **Explain:**

Pitchforking means taking one thing and branching it into several things—in this case, by using exclamations. It's a way to write better, richer, more sophisticated sentences and to give the reader a more detailed mental image.

Look at the example sentence:

- *The underline means I intentionally made a grammatical choice here.*
- *The drawing above the sentence signals what my choice was: I used pitchforking.*

3. **Ask:** *Who will try out this pitchforked sentence with me?* (Enact the conversation.)

4. **Say:** *Open to your grammar chart and find **pitchforking exclamations**. Let's jot down an example on the chart.*

Model it

5. Project the journal entry and read it.

6. Ask volunteers to read the sentences with the **pitchforked exclamations** aloud. Ask them to explain what pitchforking is, that it splits one thing into several things.

Practice it

7. **Say:** *In your journal today, try to use at least three __pitchforked exclamations__, underlining each use. Write the proof over each one.*

August 30

One time when I was eight, my mom had bought a plant that had peppers. I didn't know what pepper it was but I thought to myself, wouldn't it be cool to try it? So I went to my mom and said, "Mom, I'd like to try one of those peppers."

September 3

My mom said, "Why not?"

"If you try one with me then I will try one," I said.

"Fine," my mom said with a sigh.

So we both took one of the tiny peppers and put it in our mouths. Both me and my mom's faces turned as red as a strawberry! **The peppers were hotter than the sun! My mouth was about to explode!**

"I need water! Water!" I yelled.

I got water but that did not work at all. So I tried getting some more water but that didn't work.

Ring, ring! Ring, ring! Oh, no! The phone had just rung.

"Milk! I need milk!" I screamed. I jugged down the milk so fast I thought that I was faster than a cheetah!!! That did the trick. I think back and say to myself, why did I eat that pepper? **It's crazy how hot that pepper was!**

Annabell Lang
Grade 6

80 PITCHFORKING USING DESCRIPTIONS

> " An old, dusty pillowcase, dyed black, still flapped off the house's front porch, " warning neighbors to stay away from the diseased house.

—From *Scarlet*, by Marissa Meyer, found by Kaylee Gurr

Teach it

1. Write this on the board

Pitchforking descriptions

Plain sentence:

It would be better.

Pitchforked description:

Well, how cool would it be if XOS-7 had a Megastone? It would be <u>cool</u>, <u>stronger</u>, and <u>more powerful</u>.

—Alex Melchor

PRACTICE THE CONVERSATION:

A: Read the plain sentence please.

B: *It would be better.*

A: Good. Hm. We don't know what *it* is, do we? Or how it might *be better*. Let's hear.

B: *Well, how cool would it be if XOS-7 had a Megastone? It would be cool, stronger, and more powerful.*

A: Where is the pitchforked description?

B: It's at the end. *Cool, stronger, and more powerful.*

A: How is that a pitchfork?

B: Well, it started as one thing, *better*. And it branched out into three different descriptions. One word branched out into three. Get it? It's a pitchfork.

A: I see. Great job.

---

2. **Explain:**

   Pitchforking means taking one thing and branching it into several things—in this case, by using descriptions.

   It's a way to write better, richer, more sophisticated sentences and to give the reader a more detailed mental image.

   Look at the example sentence:

   - *The underline means I intentionally made a grammatical choice here.*
   - *The drawing above the sentence signals what my choice was: I used pitchforking.*

3. **Ask:** *Who will try out the pitchforked sentence with me?* (Enact the conversation.)

4. **Say:** *Open to your grammar chart and find **pitchforking descriptions**. Let's jot down an example on the chart.*

Model it

5. Project the journal entry and read it.

6. Ask volunteers to read the sentences with the **pitchforked descriptions** aloud. Ask them to explain what pitchforking is: that it splits one thing into several things.

Practice it

7. **Say:** *In your journal today, try to use at least three **pitchforked descriptions**, underlining each use. Write the proof over each one.*

December 18

Is correctness important? Why? When?

Well now, if you're in your English exam and you have to write an essay about how you

would populate the moon, then grammar correction and punctuation being perfect is

key to getting a good grade. But it isn't as important. It's the meaning of the sentences

and how powerful and meaningful and even how thoughtful it is. One example of a **good**

and powerful sentence that isn't filled with correct grammar and punctuation is: "As I

turned the corner, I saw my mom, it was the first time in my life, I just thought to myself,

this is sunting Iv'e wanted to bee ablue tu doo all mi lyfe." Even though that sentence

is chockful of inaccuracies, it's a **ba-da-bing sentence filled with power and emotion**,

which is acceptable in a case like this. But if you're going to write a sentence that is

just **plain and humdrum** without any **meaning, emotion and power**, such as: "When I

was five, I saw a dog." That sentence may have good grammar and punctuation, but it's

humdrum and meaningless. But with the other sentence, it's **meaningful and emotional**,

making it a good sentence even though the grammar and punctuation are awful.

Dan Meishar
Grade 8

---

81 PITCHFORKING USING SOUNDS

> " A few moments passed; Harry heard the door close but remained bent double, " listening; the only sounds he could hear were the blank picture on the wall sniggering again and the wastepaper basket in the corner coughing up the owl droppings.

—From *Harry Potter and the Order of the Phoenix* by J. K Rowling, found by Sara Toms

Teach it

1. Write this on the board

Pitchforking sounds

Plain sentence:

I was standing in the hallway by the corner of the classroom.

Pitchforked sounds:

Standing by the corner of the classroom, I could hear the usual, routine hallway sounds: the <u>slamming of one locker</u>, which can only be done in a loud way; the <u>click of a pencil</u>, almost like a mouse-click; the <u>squeaking of too-small shoes</u>; the <u>crinkling of paper</u>; <u>high voices of children</u> feeling lost, asking for help; and the <u>commanding voice of a teacher</u> counting down from five.

—Phillip Kaplan

PRACTICE THE CONVERSATION:

A: Will you read the plain sentence, please?

B: *I was standing in the hallway by the corner of the classroom.*

A: Okay. Now let's hear the same sentence, with pitchforked sounds.

B: *Standing by the corner of the classroom, I could hear the usual, routine hallway sounds: the slamming of one locker, which can only be done in a loud way; the click of a pencil, almost like a mouse-click; the squeaking of too-small shoes; high voices of children feeling lost, asking for help; and the commanding voice of a teacher counting down from five.*

A: Wow. How many sounds were listed there?

B: Let's see. The locker, pencil, shoes, voices. Lots.

A: Great sentence, isn't it? Do you notice anything unusual about the punctuation?

B: Yes. There's a colon, and the pitchforked sounds have semicolons between them.

A: Why do you think this writer used those? To join different sentences?

B: No. To separate the items in the series.

A: I thought we used commas for that.

B: We do. But look at this set of items. The sounds are so detailed that they already have commas in each one of them. So instead of using *more* commas, the writer switched to semicolons. It makes it clearer to see what goes with what.

A: Great explanation!

B: Thanks. You know I'm just reading this, don't you?

A: Reading what?

2. **Explain:**

Pitchforking means taking one thing and branching it into several things—in this case, by describing sounds. It's a way to write better, richer, more sophisticated sentences and to give the reader a more detailed mental image.

Look at the example sentence:

- *The underline means I intentionally made a grammatical choice here.*
- *The drawing above the sentence signals what my choice was: I used pitchforking.*

3. **Ask:** *Who will try out this pitchforked sentence with me?* (Enact the conversation.)

4. **Say:** *Open to your grammar chart and find **pitchforking sounds**. Let's jot down a short example on the chart.*

Model it

5. Project the journal entry and read it.

6. Ask a volunteer to read the sentence with the **pitchforked sounds** aloud. Ask him or her to explain what pitchforking is: that it splits one thing into several things.

Practice it

7. **Say:** *In your journal today, try to use a few **<u>pitchforked sounds</u>**, underlining each use. Write the proof over each one.*

December 7

This will be my 15th journal entry. What is it that I have already written in this journal? I

don't remember. I will reread what I have written in this journal at the end of the year. I

hear <u>**pens clicking**</u>, <u>**paper turning**</u>, <u>**feet tapping**</u>, <u>**chairs squeaking**</u>, <u>**pens being tapped on**</u>

<u>**the desk**</u>. Is this a sign of boredom? This is all I can write about today.

—Justin Johns
Grade 9

PITCHFORKING USING SMELLS/TASTES

> 66 Every morning, just after two o'clock, she fell asleep again to the smell of [her 99 Papa]. It was a mixture of dead cigarettes, decades of paint, and human skin.
>
> —From *The Book Thief* by Markus Zusak, found by Tori Shiver

Teach it

1. Write this on the board

Pitchforking smells/tastes

Examples:

At the marketplace, I could smell <u>pineapples, limes, and cigarette smoke</u> in the air, and the unique smell of Israel.

—Dan Meishar

I woke up smelling <u>pancakes, syrup and heaven</u>.

—Kaylee Gurr

PRACTICE THE CONVERSATION:

A: Read the first sentence, please.

B: *At the marketplace, I could smell pineapples, limes, and cigarette smoke in the air, and the unique smell of Israel.*

A: How many smells did the writer name?

B: Um . . . four.

A: What do you think the unpitchforked sentence would have said?

B: Probably something like *At the marketplace, I could smell lots of things.*

A: Probably right. This sentence is so much more detailed, isn't it? Will you read the second sentence? Let's see what this writer pitchforked.

B: *I woke up smelling pancakes, syrup and heaven.*

A: What do you notice about this pitchfork?

B: Well, one thing is that the first two smells are literal, and the third smell is a feeling.

A: Do you think that works in this sentence?

B: I do. I like it.

A: I do too.

2. **Explain:**

   Pitchforking means taking one thing and branching it into several things—in this case, descriptions of smells and tastes. It's a way to write better, richer, more sophisticated sentences and to give the reader a more sensory experience.

   Look at the example sentences:

   - *The underline means I intentionally made a grammatical choice here.*
   - *The drawing above the sentence signals what my choice was: I used pitchforking.*

3. **Ask:** *Who will try out this pitchforked sentence with me?* (Enact the conversation.)

4. **Say:** *Open to your grammar chart and find **pitchforking smells/tastes**. Let's jot down an example on the chart.*

Model it

5. Project the journal entry and read it.

6. Ask volunteers to read the sentences with the **pitchforked smells/tastes** aloud. Ask them to explain what pitchforking is: that it splits one thing into several things.

Practice it

7. **Say:** *In your journal today, try to use at least three **pitchforked smells/tastes**, underlining each use. Write the proof over each one.*

April 10

Journal, you know how medicine boxes always say "now made with real fruit"

or "new fruit flavor!"? Well journal, that's a bunch of bull. I think that whoever

makes the medicine has never tasted fruit. Whenever something says **cherry,**

grape, or lemon, they really mean **liquid cardboard, more sour than ever, and**

AAH!! get this out of my mouth! I'm supposed to believe that there's actually

fruit in the medicine if I can't pronounce anything in the ingredients?!

Oh well

More tomorrow

BYE!

P.S. medicine smells like **plastic, alcohol, and hospitalish**

—Maggie Davis
Grade 7

83 PITCHFORKING USING CONTRASTS

> " Some books should be tasted, some devoured, but only a few should be chewed " and digested thoroughly.
>
> —From *Inkheart* by Cornelia Funke, found by Christian Westbrook

Teach it

1. Write this on the board

Pitchforking contrasts

Plain sentence:

I decided what to buy.

Pitchforked contrasts:

Next, as I looked at all of the products they were selling, like <u>t-shirts or hats</u>, I'd check to see whether it was <u>high-quality or shoddy</u>, and decide whether it was actually <u>worth the price they were selling it for, or if I should haggle with the store owner so I could get the price lowered.</u>

—Dan Meishar

PRACTICE THE CONVERSATION:

A: Please read the plain sentence.

B: *I decided what to buy.*

A: Good. Now let's see what contrasts this writer added. Read the pitchforked sentence please.

B: *Next, as I looked at all of the products they were selling, like t-shirts or hats, I'd check to see whether it was high-quality or shoddy, and decide whether it was actually worth the price they were selling it for, or if I should haggle with the store owner so I could get the price lowered.*

A: Wow. So where is the first contrast?

B: *T-shirts or hats.*

A: The second contrast?

B: *High-quality or shoddy.*

A: And the third?

B: *Worth the price they were selling it for, or if I should haggle with the store owner so I could get the price lowered.*

A: Those three contrasts are different lengths. Is that okay?

B: *It looks like it works just fine.*

A: And so it does!

2. **Explain:**

   Pitchforking means taking one thing and branching it into several things—in this case, contrasting things. It's a way to write better, richer, more sophisticated sentences and to give the reader a more detailed mental image.

   One way to add details is to think about contrasting details, details that show opposites in some way.

   Look at the example sentence:

   - *The underline means I intentionally made a grammatical choice here.*
   - *The drawing above the sentence signals what my choice was: I used pitchforking.*

3. **Ask:** *Who will try out this pitchfork with me?* (Enact the conversation.)

4. **Say:** *Open to your grammar chart and find **pitchforking contrasts**. Let's jot down an example on the chart.*

Model it

5. Project the journal entry and read it.

6. Ask volunteers to read the sentences with the **pitchforked contrasts** aloud.

7. Ask them to explain what pitchforking is: that it splits one thing into several things.

Practice it

8. **Say:** *In your journal today, see if you can add **pitchforked contrasts**, underlining each use. Write the proof over each one.*

January 30

Yesterday, I sat and thought how even though some things might be going wrong

in my life, it's important to be grateful. Maybe I don't have a large house with

maids and chef, but I do have a shelter over my head and food to eat. Maybe I

wasn't able to go to that party last weekend, but I got to make better memories

with my family. Maybe I had a bad night and couldn't sleep well, but I'm glad that

I do have a bed to sleep on.

There's a lot to be grateful for in this world. The moon, stars, clouds, sun,

trees, friends, family, everything. To me **it isn't about wanting more, but about**

being grateful for what I do have in life.

—Tori Shiver
Grade 8

84

PITCHFORKING USING PARTICIPIAL PHRASES

> " Mark finally turned a corner and saw the shack across a small clearing. He " moved to make a final sprint for it, just as a horde of fleeing residents swarmed in from the other side, frantic and wild, scattering in all directions, heading for every door in sight.
>
> —From *The Kill Order*, by James Dashner, found by Evan Katzman

Teach it

1. Write this on the board

Pitchforking participle

Participle = verb that ends in -ing or -ed, used as description
Participial phrases have a few more words added.

Examples:

She has a <u>twisted</u>, <u>disturbing</u> sense of humor.

The French fries, <u>cooked in rancid grease</u>, then <u>hurled into a carton</u>, <u>stuffed into a dirty bag</u>, were now heading towards my son's hungry mouth.

PRACTICE THE CONVERSATION:

A: Will you please read the first example sentence?

B: *She has a twisted, disturbing sense of humor.*

A: Good. Where are the participles?

B: *Twisted* and *disturbing.*

A: Good. So how many participles are there?

B: Two.

A: And what do these words end with?

B: One ends with *–ed* and the other with *–ing.*

A: Exactly! That's what makes them participles. Now will you please read the second sentence?

B: *The French fries, cooked in rancid grease, then hurled into a carton, stuffed into a dirty bag, were now heading towards my son's hungry mouth.*

A: Eww. How many participles are there?

B: Three.

A: What is one?

B: *Cooked.*

A: Good! And what is *in rancid grease?*

B: It's the rest of the phrase. It's what turns the participle into a participial phrase.

A: Excellent! How many participial phrases are there here?

B: Three. They are pitchforked.

A: Nice work.

2. **Explain:**

Pitchforking means taking one thing and branching it into several things—in this case, by using participle phrases.

It's a way to write better, richer, more sophisticated sentences and to give the reader a more detailed mental image.

***A participle is a verb used as an adjective.** It will almost always have an –ing or an –ed ending.*

Look at the example sentence:

- *The underline means I intentionally made a grammatical choice here.*
- *The drawing above the sentence signals what my choice was: I used pitchforking.*

3. **Ask:** *Who will try out this pitchfork with me?* (Enact the conversation.)

4. **Say:** *Open to your grammar chart and find **pitchforking participles**. Let's jot down what participles are and write an example on the chart.*

Model it

5. Project the journal entry and read it.

6. Ask volunteers to read the sentences with the **pitchforked participles** aloud. Ask them to explain what participles are and also what pitchforking is: that it splits one thing into several things.

Practice it

7. **Say:** *In your journal today, try to use at least three **<u>pitchforked participles</u>**, underlining each use. Write the proof over each one.*

January 28

Phil's Laugh

Phil has the funniest laughter ever. The funniest moment I've ever seen was on a Friday.

I was having a conversation with Mrs. Black and we were all talking to each other. I said

to Mrs. Black, ". . . Man purse . . ." and Mrs. Black replied, "Did you say man pastrami?"

and Phil was **<u>standing up</u>**, **<u>chugging water</u>**, and Phil heard it and spit out his water. His

face got red, and he spit water everywhere. He set his water down and started to lean

on the desk, **<u>cracking up</u>**. About 30 seconds later, he started walking to the napkins and

just fell on the floor, **<u>kicking his feet on the floor</u>**, and **<u>banging his fist on the ground,</u>**

<u>coughing and choking on the ground</u>, **<u>rolling around</u>**. I'm laughing so hard. He grabs

the paper towels and as he comes back, somebody says something and he falls on the

desk, **<u>leaning while on his knees</u>** and **<u>doing a laugh with a red face</u>**. Phil has the best

laugh ever.

—Layne Dentinger
Grade 8

85

PITCHFORKING USING ABSOLUTES

❝ I stumbled, arms flailing, reaching for anything to stop my fall. ❞

—From *The Shifter* by Janice Hardy, found by Alicia Narvaez

Teach it

1. Write this on the board

Pitchforking absolutes

Absolute = noun + ing verb, used as description

Examples:

<u>Hair flying, laughter streaming, hearts pounding,</u> the girls raced down the hill. She opened the door, her <u>thoughts racing</u> and <u>hands trembling</u>.

PRACTICE THE CONVERSATION:

A: Will you explain to me . . . what is an absolute?

B: It's a noun plus an –ing verb.

A: Ok! Let's hear the example sentence.

B: *Hair flying, laughter streaming, hearts pounding, the girls raced down the hill.*

A: What part is the actual sentence?

B: *The girls raced down the hill.*

A: That's right. And why is it pitchforked? How many absolutes are there?

B: Three.

A: Good.

2. **Explain:**

Pitchforking means taking one thing and branching it into several things—in this case, by adding an absolute. It's a way to write better, richer, more sophisticated sentences and to give the reader a stronger mental image.

Absolutes *are a two-word trick:* **the first word is a noun; the second word is a participle**. *Together,* **they form a two-word adjective** *that is called an absolute.*

Look at the example sentence:

- *The underline means I intentionally made a grammatical choice here.*
- *The drawing above the sentence signals what my choice was: I used pitchforking.*

3. **Ask:** *Who will try out a pitchforked absolute with me?* (Enact the conversation.)

4. **Say:** *Open to your grammar chart and find* **pitchforking absolutes**. *Let's jot down an example on the chart, as well as a note about what an absolute is.*

Model it

5. Project the journal entry and read it.

6. Ask volunteers to read the sentences with the **pitchforked absolutes** aloud. Ask them to explain what pitchforking is, that it splits one thing into several things.

Practice it

7. **Say:** *In your own journal, try to work at least three __pitchforked absolutes__, underlining each use. Write the proof over each one.*

April 8

Lights flashing, buzzers beating, crowd chanting, momentum swinging, players screaming, that's the kind of amazing excitement and noises at basketball games.

And now, after the clutch shooting of Napier and Boatright for UConn, the Huskies are national champions. **Confetti flying, players crying,** and **fans high-fiving,** was the scene after the game. Kentucky's fans, players, and staff probably weren't as happy. The game was fantastic. Now, the only problem is, college basketball is over. But we still have the NBA, with its audience-luring players and money-guzzling players and owners. The NBA is smooth and fluid, unlike college. Shots dropping are always an occurrence at NBA games. But that's what makes college ball better: the mistakes. **Players intercepting** or **shots airballing** are more common in college. I love both. Basketball is so awesome no matter what. Especially when you see **players dunking** and **rims shattering**. Basketball rocks.

—Phillip Kaplan
Grade 8

PART VII

PARTS OF SPEECH

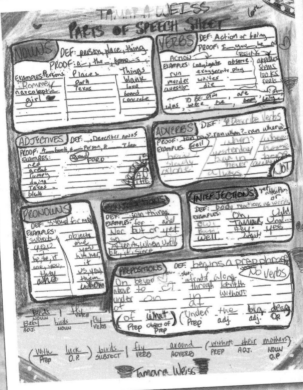

Sentences have to have a subject and a verb. A verb is a word that is an action. I guess a subject is usually a noun, but I don't know. You can't say "he food" or "eat food." But you can say "he ate food."

—Lee Kaplan

Do students need to know the parts of speech? I'm not sure that they do. But I do know that this knowledge proves useful at various times and that students like conquering the parts of speech. So I like to review what they know, using a one-page Parts of Speech sheet. Then we bust any myths necessary and fill in the gaps. Within just a couple of days' time, students have a tool to use whenever they need it.

When might they need it? When they're trying to use a new vocabulary word, for one thing. Or it might be when they don't remember whether to use a subject or object pronoun. After they complete the sheet, they usually reflect that they have gained useful insights about the logic behind words. Of course, they don't say it exactly that way. It often comes out more like, "A word can be lots of different things. So yeah."

People aren't just one thing. We play different roles in different situations. You're someone's child, someone's student, someone's teacher, someone's grandchild or cousin, someone's customer, someone's audience. You wear different hats at different times.

Words are like us. They can play different roles, depending on what job they're performing in a sentence. Take the word *sleep*. It can be a verb (I sleep, you sleep, he sleeps) or a noun (a sleep, the sleep, some sleep) or even an adjective (a sleepy book, a sleepy person, a sleepy idea, a sleep disorder). Words don't have their own singular identities; they do jobs. When we figure out what job a word is doing, we know what part of speech it is right then.

Jonah asked me the other day, "Is *protagonize* a word?" It must be. We reasoned out some possible meanings: (1) to cause a minor character to become the main character and (2) the opposite of antagonize. If students are comfortable with the parts of speech, you can practically see their logic developing before your eyes.

86 NOUNS

> 66 Decent kids, decent grades, decent athletes. Decent is good. Especially in the 99 Midwest.

> —From *Right Behind You*, by Gail Giles, found by Alyssa Rico

Teach it

1. Write this on the board

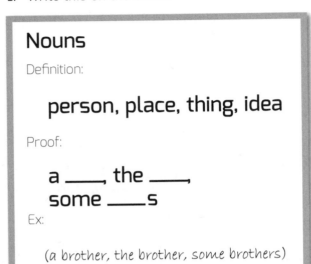

Nouns

Definition:

person, place, thing, idea

Proof:

a ___, the ___, some ___s

Ex:

(a brother, the brother, some brothers)
My brother swims well.

PRACTICE THE CONVERSATION:

A: Will you read the sentence, please?

B: *My brother swims well.*

A: Good. Is there a noun in this sentence?

B: *Brother* is a noun.

A: Hmm, I'm not so sure.

B: It is!

A: I don't think so. Can you prove it?

B: A brother, the brother, some brothers.

A: You're right! *Brother* is a noun. And you can use this proof any time you want to check to see if a word is a noun.

2. **Explain:**

Let's review **nouns**. What's the definition of a **noun**?

That's right, a **noun** names a person, place, or thing—or idea.

Next, how can you prove something is a **noun**? Use this proof: a ___, the ___, some ___s. Put the word into all three of the blanks, and if it makes sense **in even just one of them**, it's a **noun**.

Look at the example sentence:

- The underline means I intentionally made a grammatical choice here.
- The proof above the word shows that I know why I made the choice; I know how to prove it's a **noun**.

3. **Ask:** Who will try out our **noun** proof with me? (Enact the conversation.)

4. **Say:** Let's add the noun notes to your Parts of Speech sheet. We know a short definition and proof, so let's write those first.

Next, let's add some examples to the sheet. In the first column, let's add some persons (for example, Mary, principal, mother, etc.). In the second column, let's add some places (for example, home, forest, France, etc.). In the third column, let's add some things (for example, pen, shoe, beauty, freedom, frustration).

Model it

5. Project the journal entry and read it.

6. Ask volunteers to read the sentences with the **nouns**. Ask them to use the proof.

Practice it

7. **Say:** *In your journal today, try to use at least five **nouns**, underlining each use. Write the proof over each one.*

October 2

Turning random dictionary words into insults!

(a toad, the toad, some toads)
You are such an energetic **toad**! A brunette nostril, and especially an

(a fox terrier, the fox terrier, some fox terriers)   *(a jail, the jail, some jails)*
indomitable **fox terrier**! Not to mention, a top dollar **jail,** and a referent

(a consumer, the consumer, some consumers)   *(a hammer, the hammer, some hammers)*
and an . . . an . . . audacious **consumer**! A thargic **hammer**! A fleming

(an armchair, the armchair, some armchairs)
armchair! And not to forget, a professional muffler and a pepperoni

(a manuscript, the manuscript, some manuscripts)   *(a kindergartner, the kindergartner, some kindergartners)*
manuscript! And last but not least, a sassy **kindergartner**! Wait! There's more,

(a futon, the futon, some futons)
you four-wheeler cookbook! You morbid lefty! You're such an indefensible **futon.**

(a diaper, the diaper, some diapers)
you colonial **diaper**! And an incredible europium!

—Miriam Stein
Grade 6

87

VERBS

> " The manservant rolled on to his back, caught them by the collars of their donkey **"** jackets, and flipped them into Dublin harbor.

—From *Artemis Fowl* by Eoin Colfer, found by E. J. Easterly

Teach it

1. Write this on the board

Verbs

Definition:

action or being

Proof:

I ____, you ____, he ____s

Ex:

(I swims, you swims, he swims)
My brother <u>swims</u> well.

PRACTICE THE CONVERSATION:

A: Will you please read the sentence?

B: *My brother swims well.*

A: Do you see a verb?

B: I do! *Swims* is a verb.

A: No, I'm afraid not.

B: I think it is.

A: Can you prove it?

B: I swims, you swims, he swims?

A: It sounds weird in the first two, doesn't it? But in the third one, it works. So you're right! *Swims* is definitely a verb.

2. **Explain:**

    We're going to review **verbs**. *What's the definition of a* **verb**?

    Yes, a verb shows **action** *or* **being.**

    How can you prove something is a **verb**? *Use this proof: I ___, you ___, he ___ s. Put the word into all three of the blanks and listen to it.* **If it makes sense in even just one of them, it's a** **verb.**

    Look at the example sentence:

    - *The underline means I intentionally made a grammatical choice here.*

    - *The proof above the word shows that I know why I made the choice; I know how to prove it's a* **verb.**

3. **Ask:** *Who will try out our* **verb** *proof with me?* (Enact the conversation.)

4. **Say:** *Let's add notes to your Parts of Speech sheet.*

    We know a short **definition** *and* **proof**, *so let's write those first.*

    Next, let's add some examples to the sheet. Start with the bottom. Do you know the forms of the verb **to be**? *Write these:*

am	was	been
are	were	being
is	be	

To be is the most commonly used verb in the English language. Now let's add, to the blanks above, some one-syllable **action verbs** (fry, act, dash, scowl), some two-syllable verbs (announce, restore), and some three-syllable (verify, activate).

Model it

5. Project the journal entry and read it.

6. Ask volunteers to read the sentences with the **verbs**. Ask them to use the proof.

Practice it

7. **Say:** *In your journal today, try to use at least five **verbs**, underlining each use. Write the proof over each one.*

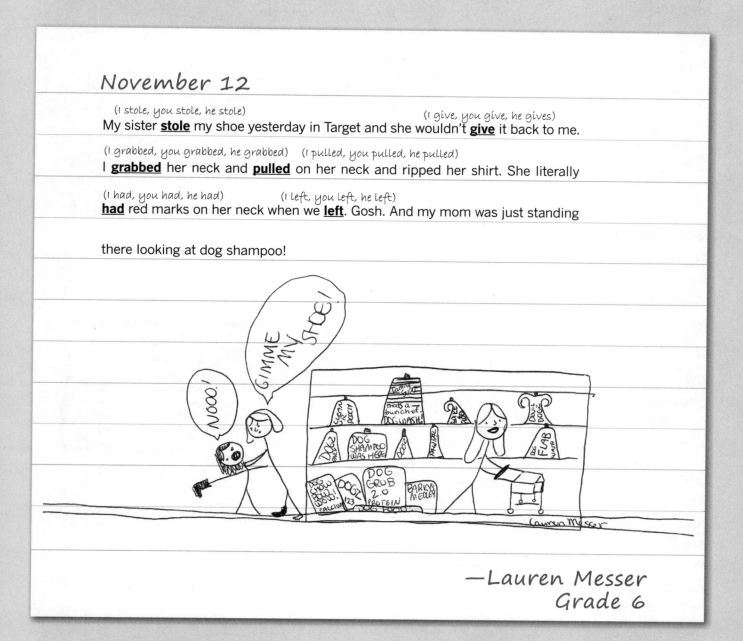

November 12

(I stole, you stole, he stole)   (I give, you give, he gives)

My sister **stole** my shoe yesterday in Target and she wouldn't **give** it back to me.

(I grabbed, you grabbed, he grabbed)   (I pulled, you pulled, he pulled)

I **grabbed** her neck and **pulled** on her neck and ripped her shirt. She literally

(I had, you had, he had)   (I left, you left, he left)

had red marks on her neck when we **left**. Gosh. And my mom was just standing

there looking at dog shampoo!

—Lauren Messer
Grade 6

88

ADJECTIVES

> **"** The strangest figures we saw were the Slovaks, who are more barbarian than **"** the rest, with their big cowboy hats, great baggy dirty-white trousers, white linen shirts, and enormous heavy leather belts, nearly a foot wide, all studded over with brass nails. They wore high boots, with their trousers tucked into them, and had long black hair and heavy black moustaches. They are very picturesque, but do not look prepossessing.

—From *Dracula* by Bram Stoker, found by Jonah Katzman

Teach it

1. Write this on the board

Adjectives

Definition:

   describe nouns

Proof:

   a _____ book, a _____ person,
   a _____ idea.

Ex:

   (a weird book, a weird person, a weird idea)

   Phillip drew a __weird__ chicken.

PRACTICE THE CONVERSATION:

A: Read the sentence please.

B: *Phillip drew a weird chicken.*

A: Good. Which word is an adjective?

B: *Weird.*

A: I don't think so.

B: A weird book, a weird person, a weird idea.

A: Ah! It's definitely an adjective!

2. **Explain:**

   *Let's review **adjectives**. What's the definition of an **adjectives**?*

   That's right, a describing word.

   *How can you prove that a word is an **adjectives**?*

   *Use this proof: a ___ book, a ___ person, a ___ idea. Try the word in all three of the blanks and listen to it. If it makes sense, in even one of those, you have an **adjectives**.*

   Look at the example sentence:

   - *The underline means I intentionally made a grammatical choice here.*
   - *The proof above the word shows that I know why I made the choice; I know how to prove it's an **adjective**.*

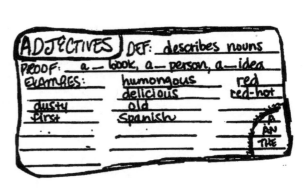

3. **Ask:** *Who will try out our **adjectives** proof with me? (Enact the conversation.)*

4. **Say:** *Let's add adjective notes on the Parts of Speech sheet.*

   *We know a short **definition** and **proof**, so let's write those first.*

   *Next, let's add some **examples** to the sheet. Let's get some common and proper adjectives and a hyphenated one.*

   *Notice the tiny little corner with room for three words? There are three adjectives that are so commonly used that they have their own name. Anyone know what these are? They're called **articles.** Fill in **a, an,** and **the.***

Model it

5. Project the journal entry and read it.

6. Ask volunteers to read the sentences with the **adjectives**. Ask them to use the proof.

Practice it

7. **Say:** *In your journal today, try to use at least five **adjectives**, underlining each use. Write the proof over each one.*

January 30

Yesterday I watched a documentary on bears and when they attack; not just on hiking

(a city book, a city person, a city idea)   *(a bear book, a bear person, a bear idea)*
trails but also on **city** grounds. It said there have been 9 reported **bear** attacks that people

(a human book, a human person, a human idea)
survived from, 3 of them being near-death experiences. They come into **human** cities in

(a human book, a human person, a human idea)   *(an easier book, an easier person, an easier idea)*
search of **human** garbage. Like most animals, bears have **easier** access to garbage and

(a junk book, a junk person, a junk idea)
like humans, love the taste of **junk** food. Bears come into human neighborhoods and

(a calorie book, a calorie person, a calorie idea)
scavenge for the food to provide their daily **calorie** routine. But the closer and the more

humans live side by side with bears, the more common the attacks become. Unlike

(an Alaskan book, an Alaskan person, an Alaskan idea)
the bears from Kodiak Island. Kodiak bears can weigh 500 lbs. more than the **Alaskan**

grizzly. They can reach up to 9–10 feet, about the

(a scarce book, a scarce person, a scarce idea)
size of a polar bear. They have a **scarce** food supply

because of the lack of human establishments. They

hunt whatever they can, including and especially

humans.

—Jonah Katzman
Grade 8

89

ADVERBS

> **" "** They went under a tall stone arch with two malevolent gargoyle faces glaring down contemptuously at them, and then into an alley with high walls on either side. The dimensions of the buildings, the gaping windows, arches, and doorways, were huge, as if they'd been built for incredibly tall buildings.

—From *Tunnels*, by Roderick Gordon and Brian Williams,
found by Shaine Carpenter

Teach it

1. Write this on the board

Adverbs

Definition:

adds to verbs

Proof:

**runs how? ___ runs where? ___
runs when? ___**

Ex:

(runs when? always)

Michael <u>sometimes</u> speaks

(runs how? clearly)

<u>harshly</u> to his friends.

PRACTICE THE CONVERSATION:

A: Will you please read the sentence?

B: *Michael sometimes speaks harshly.*

A: There are two adverbs labeled here. What's the first one?

B: *Sometimes.*

A: That's not an adverb.

B: I think it is.

A: Can you prove it?

B: Runs when? Sometimes.

A: Oh! It is an adverb!

B: And there's another one. Harshly.

A: Can you prove that's an adverb?

B: Runs how? Harshly.

A: Great job! How about *to his friends*? That tells where. Runs where? *To his friends.* Isn't it an adverb?

B: No. *To his friends* is three words. Adverb proofs can have only **one word.**

A: Excellent!

2. **Explain:**

   *We're going to review **adverbs**. What's the definition of an **adverb**?*

   Yes, adverbs modify, or add on to, verbs.

   *How can you prove something is an **adverb**?*

   Use this proof: ran how? ___ ran where? ___ ran when? ___.

   *Try the word in all three of the blanks and listen to it. If it makes sense in even just one of them, it's an **adverb**. It can't be a group of words or a phrase—just **one word**.*

   Look at the example sentence:

   • *The underline means I intentionally made a grammatical choice here.*

   • *The proof above the word shows that I know why I made the choice; I know how to prove it's an **adverb**.*

3. **Ask:** *Who will try out our **adverb** proof with me?* (Enact the conversation.)

4. **Say:** *Let's add notes on **adverbs** to the Parts of Speech sheet. We know a short **definition** and **proof,** so let's write those first.*

Next, let's add some **examples** to the sheet.

• In the first column, let's write words that would answer "ran how?"

• In the second column, let's think up some words that would answer "ran where?"

• In the last column, let's write some words that would answer "ran when?"

Notice the little spot in the bottom corner? There, let's write the most commonly used adverb in the English language. Do you know what it is? **Not.** Think about it. It answers all three adverb proof questions. How did you run the marathon? I did not run the marathon. When did you run? I did not run. Where did you run? I did not run. Interesting, isn't it?

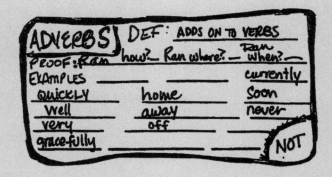

Model it

5. Project the journal entry and read it.

6. Ask volunteers to read the sentences with the **<u>adverbs</u>**. Ask them to use the proof.

Practice it

7. **Say:** In your journal today, try to use at least five **<u>adverbs</u>**, underlining each use. Write the proof over each one.

November 13

That night we went to Medieval Times. It was beyond cool!

(runs where? there) (runs when? early)
We got **<u>there early</u>** to look at the exhibits they had. It was really funny to hear the

(runs how? loud) (runs how? basically)
people talk so **<u>loud</u>** and in the old timey English. They **<u>basically</u>** screamed every

word! We looked around, bought some things. I bought Phil and Jake gifts for

Chanukah. I really should've got them both wooden swords and let them have

fun but my mom didn't think it was a good idea. We got my grandma a necklace

that's a heart with a ruby in it. I want to write a poem with it, which I might do

after I finish telling about the rest of my time there . . .

A little while after we got there, we bought these non-alcoholic piña coladas.

(runs how? actually)
They were **actually** good. We walked around drinking them and saw the prettiest

(runs when? mostly)
horses. There were some brown but **mostly** white. They were just BEAUTIFUL!

They looked as if they were glowing!! By the way, the whole time we were

wearing yellow and red crowns.

A little while later, we were called by crown color to our seats. Our place was

first row in the center. They were AMAZING seats! You could see everything.

Our waitress was amazing. She was so funny! To start off she asked what we

wanted to drink.

They started the show with introducing the "king" and "princess." They gave

us soup with bread. It was some tomato bisque thing. I dipped my bread in it

and it was actually really good. I forgot to mention, there was no silverware for

the whole meal! Super fun!!

The show continued and they served this HUGE piece of chicken! It was the

thigh and breast, and it was really good!

—Tori Shiver
Grade 8

Notes

90

PRONOUNS

> **❝** He held his left wrist toward her, embedded with his ID chip, but Cinder waved a **❞**
> gloved hand at him. "No, thank you. It will be my honor."
>
> —From *Cinder* by Marissa Meyer, found by Genesis Thomas

Teach it

1. Write this on the board

Pronouns

Definition:

stand for nouns

Ex:

(subj. pronoun)   (obj. pronoun)

<u>We</u> don't care about <u>them</u> very much.

PRACTICE THE CONVERSATION:

A: Read the example sentence, please.

B: *We don't care about them very much.*

A: Great. We have two pronouns. What are they?

B: *We* and *them.*

A: Yes. Let's hear what happens if you switch those words. Read that, please?

B: *Them don't care about we very much.*

A: Sounds crazy?

B: Sounds crazy.

A: Your ear knows the difference between subjects and objects. Which one of those pronouns is used as a subject?

B: *We.*

A: Right. And which is used as an object?

B: *Them.*

A: Exactly. So if you wanted to switch them correctly, how would it sound?

B: *They don't care about us very much.*

A: Good work!

2. **Explain:**

*We're going to review **pronouns**. What is a **pronoun**?*

It stands for a noun.

*Some pronouns serve as **subjects** and some serve as **objects**.*

People confuse them often, and misuse of these simple words is a serious literacy marker.

Look at the example sentence:

- *The underline means I intentionally made a grammatical choice here. The proof above the word shows that I know why I made the choice: I know what a **pronoun** is.*

- *The proof also shows that I know which pronouns should be used as **subjects** and which should be used as **objects**.*

Note: Many students learn the difference between a subject and an object for the first time during this lesson. They learn it through the Practice Conversation, plus the use of the chart. I see kids going "ohhhh" as they write them down on their grammar chart. That's why we use the chart.

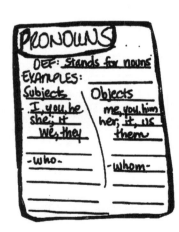

3. **Ask:** *Who will try out our **pronoun** sentence with me?* (Enact the conversation.)

4. **Say:** *Let's add notes on pronouns to the Parts of Speech sheet.*

---

*We know a short **definition**, so let's write that first.*

*Next, let's add some examples to the sheet. There are two columns. Let's write **subjects** at the top of one and **objects** at the top of the other. Let's fill in with pronouns.*

Model it

5. Project the journal entry and read it.

6. Ask volunteers to read the sentences with the **pronouns**. Ask them to explain whether the pronouns are subject or object pronouns.

Practice it

7. **Say:** *In your journal today, try to use at least five **pronouns**, underlining each use. Write the proof over each one, labeling it as a subject or object.*

February 21

(subj. pronoun)
I have had many weird dreams, but few nightmares. One that I could remember

(subj. pronoun)
for the longest time was when I was about 5. **It** was from a Scooby Doo movie,

IRL though. So this was my nightmare.

I was going down the frozen section in a store on Shaggy's shoulders. Then

(obj. pronoun)
the monsters from the movies started chasing **us.** Next thing I can remember

was that me, my dad, and some other people were in a cage in the fruits and

vegetables department.

(subj. pronoun)   (obj. pronoun)
We were trying to unlock it with these shapes; that reminds **me** of Dora for

some reason. I knew it was a dream, and I was trying to open my eyes, but I

wasn't able to. Finally, I get them open. I guess all nightmares seem scary, but

(subj. pronoun)   (subj. pronoun)
when **you** look back, **they** seem kind of pathetic.

—Madeleine Restaino
Grade 6

91

PREPOSITIONS

Teach it

1. Write this on the board

Prepositions

Definition:

> starts a prepositional phrase

Ex:

> to, at, with, of, on, around, for, off, over, under, beside, from, near, because of

Ex:

> (prep.)
> Ben broke his leg (at the
> (object of the prep.)
> concert).

PRACTICE THE CONVERSATION:

A: Will you read the sentence, please?

B: Sure. *Ben broke his leg at the concert.*

A: Do you see a prepositional phrase?

B: I do. *At the concert.*

A: Can you prove to me that this is a prepositional phrase?

B: Yes. *At* is on the list of prepositions, and you can say *at what? At the concert.*

A: Good. Is there a verb in that prepositional phrase?

B: No. There's never a verb in a prepositional phrase.

A: What part of speech is the word *concert?*

B: It's a noun.

A: Prove that?

B: A concert, the concert, some concerts.

A: Good. So an object of a preposition is going to be a noun?

B: Yes, or a pronoun.

A: Nicely done.

2. **Explain:**

*We're going to review **prepositions**. Does anyone know the one and only job a **preposition** has?*

Yes! It starts a prepositional phrase.

*So how can you prove a **preposition** starts a phrase?*

*You say the **preposition**. Then you say the word **what**—for example,*

to what?	**on** what?
with what?	**around** what?
of what?	**at** what?

If there is an answer and if the answer is a noun, *then you have a prepositional phrase.*

*There is never a **verb** in a prepositional phrase.*

Look at the example sentence:

• *The underline means I intentionally made a grammatical choice here.*

• *The proof above the word shows that I know why I made the choice; I know how to prove it's a **preposition**.*

3. **Ask:** *Who will try out our **preposition** proof with me?* (Enact the conversation.)

4. **Say:** *Let's make our notes about **prepositions** on the Parts of Speech sheet.*

   *We know a short **definition**, so let's write that first.*

   *Next, let's write some examples of prepositions on the sheet. In the strange circle on the right, we'll fill it in with a big hint about prepositional phrases: **NO VERBS**. If there's a verb after a preposition, it's something else (like a clause or an infinitive), but it's not a prepositional phrase.*

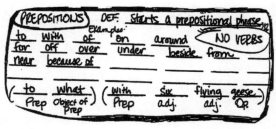

   *A prepositional phrase **can** contain many other words between the start (preposition) and the finish (object of the preposition [OP]), but the start and finish will always be a preposition and an OP. Let's note an example on the bottom (see example below).*

Model it

5. Project the journal entry and read it.

6. Ask volunteers to read the sentences with the **prepositional phrases**. Ask them to use the proof— *to what?*—and to name the object of the preposition.

Practice it

7. **Say:** *In your journal today, try to use at least five **prepositional phrases**, underlining each use. Write the proof (to what?) over each one, labeling the prepositions and the object of the preposition.*

December 5

(prep., object of prep.)

The next day, Moodiseeus was worried. He stood **on** the **balcony** of his marble

(prep., object of prep.)   (prep., object of prep.)

palace. He looked **over** the **field** in front of his great Empire. He looked **upon** his

(prep., object of prep.)

garden and roads leading **to** different **lands** when he noticed something.

December 6

It was an army, an army of Meese! But this wasn't Moodiseeus' army of Meese,

it was an army of Moosisi!

"Sound the alarm!" yelled Moodiseeus. "Battle stations!"

(prep., object of prep.)

The battle waged on, a battle **between** the **Meese and the Moosisi**. It was a

civil war, Moose turning on Moose.

December 9

It was every moose for himself. Moodiseeus watched his army of Meese die.

They were losing. Moodiseeus was worried. But he had an idea . . .

He called his Meese to retreat.

A day. That's how long it took to build a second Trojan horse. Well, not exactly

a horse. It was a Moose. It took them a day but they finished the Trojan Moose.

They painted it white as a sign of "surrender." He loaded all of his soldiers into

the moose and wheeled it out to his enemies.

"We surrender," he lied.

—Ben Brody
Grade 6

CONJUNCTIONS

" They were coming with small dreams or large dreams or none at all. "

—From *The Martian Chronicles* by Ray Bradbury, found by Lee Kaplan

Teach it

1. Write this on the board

Conjunctions

Definition:

    join things

Fanboys

    (coordinating conjunctions)

Ex:

                           (FANBOY)

Mrs. Smith shut the door, <u>but</u> we could still hear the chainsaw in the hall.

AAAWWWUBIS

    (subordinating conjunctions)

Ex:

(AAAWWWUBIS)

<u>Though</u> Mrs. Smith shut the door, we could still hear the chainsaw in the hall.

PRACTICE THE CONVERSATION:

A: Will you read the top example sentence?

B: *Mrs. Smith shut the door, but we could still hear the chainsaw in the hall.*

A: Great. Did you hear a conjunction?

B: I sure did. *But.*

A: And what does *but* join?

B: It joins two different sentences.

A: Can you join two sentences with a conjunction?

B: You sure can.

A: Can you name those conjunctions? Can you name the FANBOYS?

B: For, and, nor, but, or, yet, so.

A: Great. Now let's look at the other kind of conjunction. Will you read the bottom sentence?

B: *Though Mrs. Smith shut the door, we could still hear the chainsaw in the hall.*

A: Do you see an AAAWWWUBIS?

B: I sure do. It's *though.*

A: That's another way to combine two sentences. Do you see a difference?

B: I do. The FANBOYS let the two sentences stay two sentences, but AAAWWWUBIS turn them into one.

A: Right. Another way to say that is that the first sentence is a compound sentence and that the second sentence is a complex sentence.

2. **Explain:**

*We're going to review **conjunctions**. What is a **conjunction**?*

*Right! **Conjunctions** join things together.*

*The most common coordinating **conjunctions** can be remembered by their acronym, FANBOYS:*

    For

    And

    Nor

    But

    Or

    Yet

    So

Look at the example sentence. The underline means I intentionally made a grammatical choice here. The proof above the word shows that I know why I made the choice; I know how to label a coordinating conjunction.

3. **Ask:** *Who will try out a* **conjunction** *with me? (Enact the conversation.)*

4. **Say:** *Let's add notes on* **conjunctions** *to the Parts of Speech sheet.*

   We know a short definition and proof, so let's write those first.

   Next, let's add the FANBOYS on the top lines. These are the most common **coordinating conjunctions***.*

   There's another kind of conjunction, and these are nicknamed **AAAWWWUBIS.** *If you put an* **AAAWWWUBIS** *on a sentence, it turns it into a fragment. To make it complete, it has to have another sentence with it. These* **AAAWWWUBIS** *are also called* **subordinating conjunctions***. Watch how one can turn a whole sentence into a fragment (write on board):*

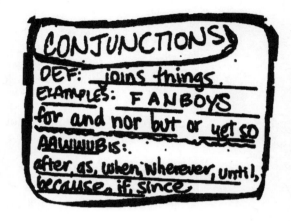

   It rained.   When it rained.   Because it rained.   If it rained.

   See? The AAAWWWUBIS in front of a sentence turn it into something less than a sentence; it **subordinates** *the sentence.*

   Let's add some of these to the Parts of Speech sheet, too. You know the definition. Let's write the AAAWWWUBIS examples on the bottom lines.

Model it

5. Project the journal entry and read it.

6. Ask volunteers to read the sentences with the **conjunctions**.

Practice it

7. **Say:** *In your journal today, try to use at least five* **conjunctions***, underlining each use. Write the proof over each one, labeling them FANBOY or AAAWWWUBIS.*

January 21

New Journal

Today I am starting my new journal! I am bummed because I was so far in my

(FANBOYS)   (AAAWWWBIS)

old journal, **and** knowing that I have to start a new journal makes me sad. **If** I

find my old journal I will most likely keep this as a spare. But I don't think my

old journal will ever come around again. It's almost like I want to put signs up

everywhere saying, "Wanted, Writing Journal." I really can't seem to find it. It's

(FANBOYS)

like it ran away from home. The office said they would keep a lookout for it **and**

that if they found it they would give it to me straight away. I was so close to

(FANBOYS)

finishing my old journal **and** had a lot of writings in that journal. The front office

(FANBOYS)

of the school said that they share the playground with the JCC **so** the JCC could

(FANBOYS)

have found it **and** instead of returning it to the school office, they might have

taken it to the JCC lost and found with a lot of other stuff. Another thing that

might have happened is that they might have thrown it away. I'm hoping that if

(FANBOYS)   (FANBOYS)

someone does have it **or** finds it they return it. Now that I'm done with this **and**

I am in trouble with the JCC and school, I have to take down my signs and that

will take forever . . .

—Layne Dentinger
Grade 8

Notes

93

INTERJECTIONS

> " "Well," said he, "my mate, Bill, would be called the captain, as like as not." "
>
> —From *Treasure Island* by Robert Louis Stevenson, found by Michael Squire

Teach it

1. Write this on the board

Interjections

Definition:

    get attention or show excitement

Ex:

    (interjection)

    <u>Uh oh!</u> I don't know what

                 (interjection)

    happened, <u>honey</u>.

PRACTICE THE CONVERSATION:

A: Read the sentence, please.

B: *Uh oh! I don't know what happened, honey.*

A: Do you see a couple of interjections?

B: I do. *Uh oh!* and *honey.*

A: Will you read the sentence without them?

B: *I don't know what happened.*

A: How are the sentences different?

B: Well, with interjections, it sounds like an actual person talking.

A: That's true, isn't it?

B: Without the interjections, it sounds more formal.

A: Which one is better?

B: It depends on what you're writing, I guess.

A: Excellent.

2. **Explain:**

Interjections are like noises we make before we say something. They are attention words, or spelled-out reactions.

*In talking, we use them often. If you want to make your writing more full of what sounds like human voice in real conversation, then hey! Don't neglect **Interjections**.*

Look at the example sentence:

- *The underline means I intentionally made a grammatical choice here.*

- *The proof above the word shows that I know why I made the choice; I can identify an **Interjection**.*

3. **Ask:** *Who will try out the sentence with me?* (Enact the conversation.)

4. **Say:** *Let's add notes about **interjections** to your Parts of Speech sheet.*

We know a short definition so let's write that first.

Next, let's add some examples to the sheet. (See below.)

Model it

5. Project the journal entry and read it.

6. Ask volunteers to read the sentences with the **interjections**. Ask them to explain what interjections do.

Practice it

7. **Say:** *In your journal today, try to use at least five **interjections**, underlining each use. Write the proof over each one.*

October 28

(interjection)
Hello again! Today is Tuesday and boy (or girl, whoever is reading this), it is going to be

                 (interjection)   (interjection)   (interjection)
a great day! I said Great! day! and **um . . . well**? **ah** (sigh) **Lost it! Drat . . . well**, see you

              (interjection)   (interjection)   (interjection)   (interjection)   (interjection)
later. But wait!!! There's more! **oh–oh** – **almost** . . . **hold on** . . . **almost** . . . **hold on** . . .

(interjection) (interjection) (interjection)   (interjection)
almost . . . **got it**! **Nooooo**!!!! Lost it again! **Drat**. . . .

—Grayson Kyle
Grade 6

94

SENTENCE PATTERNS

" I wiped at my eyes with the back of my hand. "

—From *Smashed* by Lisa Luedeke, found by Kaylee Gurr

Teach it

1. Write this on the board

Sentence patterns

Ex:

Noun—verb—direct object.

Diane had visions.

Ex:

Adjective—noun—verb.

Happy kids played.

Ex:

(Prep. phrase) pronoun—verb—adverb (prep. phrase).

In the mornings, we eat together in the kitchen.

---

2. **Explain:**

    *Now that we've covered the parts of speech, let's put them together. Let's look at some typical **sentence patterns**.*

    These aren't the only patterns, but they are a good beginning.

3. **Ask:** *Who will read these with me?* (Enact the conversation.)

PRACTICE THE CONVERSATION:

A: Will you read the first sentence?

B: Sure. *Diane had visions.*

A: Good. What are the parts of that sentence?

B: *Diane* is a noun, used as the subject; *had* is a verb; and *visions* is a noun, used as a direct object.

A: One of those is wrong, I'm afraid.

B: Hmm. I don't think so. A Diane, the Diane, some Dianes, check. I had, you had, he had, check. A vision, the vision, some visions, check.

A: Wow. Let's do the last sentence.

B: *In the mornings, we eat together in the kitchen.*

A: When you're looking at it to identify the parts of speech, which one do you look for first?

B: The verb.

A: You do?

B: Yep. Everything springs out from there.

A: I usually look for the prepositional phrases first. If you put parentheses around those, you can see what's left.

B: What's the right way?

A: There isn't a right way. It's whatever works best for you. So where's the verb?

B: *Eat.* I eat, you eat, he eats.

A: Good. What else to you notice?

B: *We* is a pronoun. *Together.* Hmm. . . . Ran how? Together. It's an adverb.

A.: Nice. What does that leave?

B: *In the mornings* is a prepositional phrase.

A: Can you prove that?

B: *In* is right here on the preposition list, and you say, *in what? In the mornings.* There's no verb. It's a prepositional phrase. *In what?* In the kitchen. Same thing.

A: Nice work.

B: Don't you mean magnificent?

A: Yes. Yes, I do.

---

4. **Say:** *Let's make notes of examples at the bottom of your Parts of Speech sheet. (See example below.)*

Note: *If students haven't been introduced to direct objects, you might want to teach them that lesson first.*

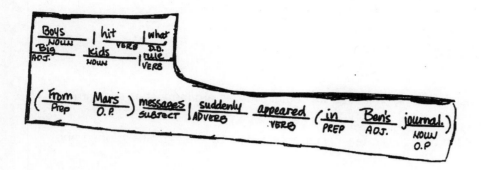

Model it

5. Project the journal entry and read it.

6. Ask volunteers to choose a sentence and identify the parts of speech in it.

Practice it

7. **Say:** *In your journal today, give it a shot. See if you can choose a sentence and identify every part of speech.*

November 15

Friday the 13th

We turned the corner, sprinting as fast as we could. I turned around just as the zombie version of Miss Golden (the music teacher) grabbed Talia by the leg. She tripped and Miss Golden pulled her back towards her vomit-green body. **I heard her scream.** I ran faster, leading the entire school (only 83 kids) down the street. We were heading towards my neighborhood.

2 hours earlier, **I walked to school.** We were late, my brother (Ethan), sister (Claire), and me. It was 5 minutes before school started. **I ran up the black stairs to the upper part of the school.** I clutched my "Vote for Lindsay" poster as I neared my locker. I overheard the kids in the hall talking, but I'm not dumb, so I could figure out what they were talking about by the snippets I heard.

8 o'clock, zombies escape, teachers, or *dinner* are some of the words I heard. That could only mean one thing. At 8:00 the teachers and all the adults will turn into zombies and eat us. But I was one step ahead. I had a plan.

2 Years Later

I was sitting on the couch at home in the living room. The old crew was there with me.

It was the Friday the 13th again, 2 years since the zombies first came.

The TV reporter spoke worriedly. I sat up. "Breaking news! A new plague has started."

Pictures started popping up of fires and people screaming. And in every single one of

them was Grandma.

"Oh no," said Talia, rubbing her temples. "Here we go again."

Except this time was different because I started to shake and shiver. My hand was a

sickly green.

"The morphing," breathed Ben. A new era had begun.

The End

—Lindsay Weingart
Grade 6

PART VIII

BEYOND VERBS

April 10

Dear Tim,

Please return the book on theft and robbery that you took from **me** *(indirect object)* when you came over.

—An angered friend,

John

Dear John,

Your book on ungratitude was terrible; because I suffered the entire book, I will keep the books *(indirect object)* you lent **me**.

—A friend with indignation,

Tim

Dear Tim,

I never lent **you** *(indirect object)* those books. You took them. Return them right now. You're interrupting my reading *(indirect object)* of <u>A Book About Lying</u>. Don't tell **me** it's not true.

—A person questioning your friendship,

John

Listen to me, John,

You anger me like never before. It is extremely rude to send **me** *(indirect object)* a book titled *How to Eliminate Anger*. Besides, I read the first chapter and it is not helping. Send **me** *(indirect object)* something better.

—Your enemy,

Tim

—Michael Squire
Grade 8

You can live well for a long time without knowing the difference between a direct object and a predicate nominative. But students who are curious and motivated like to know how and why our language works, and they like to be right when they argue with each other. So it's good for them to know that someone who says, "This is she," on the phone is speaking correctly, but the same person makes a mistake when she says, "My boss promoted Jennifer and I." It all starts with the verbs.

If they're going to learn direct objects, it just makes sense that they should also be treated to indirect objects.

And verbals—? Verbs are changing hats to act as other parts of speech. People use them all the time without knowing what they are. In restaurants, we study menus, comparing the participles and participial phrases, possibly without a thought to their grammatical labels. ("Wait . . . is this grilled? Sautéed? Covered with mushrooms? Fried in lard? I just can't decide.")

In *Image Grammar,* Harry Noden (1999) offers the most kid-friendly introduction to grammatical constructions like participial phrases, teaching students to apply them as brushstrokes. I like to show students where they fit into the overall scheme of language on the grammar chart.

The lessons in this section aren't fluff, but if we run out of year before we get to the predicate adjectives and nominatives or to the indirect objects, I don't fret. Much.

However, if students are on the competitive tracks, these lessons will give them some polish, which may prove helpful when they want to know they are speaking (or writing) correctly.

95

DIRECT OBJECTS

" Jim didn't like the spiders, and the spiders didn't like Jim. "

—From *Huckleberry Finn* by Mark Twain,
found by Dan Meishar

Teach it

1. Write this on the board

> Direct objects
>
> action verb + what?
>
> Ex:
>   (d.o. = what?)
> My daughter writes <u>songs</u>.

PRACTICE THE CONVERSATION:

A: Read the sentence please.
B: *My daughter writes songs.*
A: Great. What's the verb in this sentence?
B: *Writes.*
A: Can you prove that?
B: Sure. I write, you write, he writes.
A: Yes! So how do we find the direct object?
B: We say the verb and *what*. So . . . writes what?
A: And?
B: *Songs* is the direct object.
A: Perfect.

2. **Explain:**

   *We're going to talk about **direct objects**. All sentences have subjects (either a noun or a pronoun) and verbs. Some sentences have direct objects, objects of the action.*

   *One way to find the direct object is to locate the verb, say it, and then say **what?***

   Confusing, right? Not when we try it out.

3. **Ask:** *Who will help find a **direct object** with me?* (Enact the conversation.)

   *Direct objects will only follow **action verbs**. Whenever you write a **direct object**, you can underline and label it.*

   - *The underline means I intentionally made a grammatical choice here.*
   - *The label above the word means that I know what this is; it's a **direct object**.*

4. **Say:** *Open to your grammar chart. Let's find **direct objects** and jot down the proof.*

   Note: If the verb is not an action verb, but a *being* verb, then what follows the verb won't be a direct object. It could be a predicate adjective or predicate nominative. **Direct objects** must follow an action verb. See Lesson 87, "Verbs," to review the difference between an action verb and a being verb.

Model it

5. Project the journal entry and read it.

6. Ask volunteers to read the sentences with the **direct objects** aloud. Ask them to use the proofs, starting with the verb proof and then asking *verb what?* to find the direct object.

Practice it

7. **Say:** *In your journal today, try to write five* **<u>direct objects</u>**, *underlining each use. Write the proof over each one.*

February 11

I have to say

(d.o. = what?)   *(d.o. = what?)*
I have to say that I've never liked **<u>reading books</u>,** but then I met my **<u>inspiration</u>.**

(d.o. = what?)   *(d.o. = what?)*
I saw a **<u>book</u>**, it looked so cool that I read **<u>it</u>** and then got so into it that I saw the

(d.o. = what?)
<u>movie</u>. I have to say it wasn't quiet inside but the movie was great. I have to say

I'm already on the 3rd scene and I've got to say it's going to be the best book I

will ever read . . . I have to say . . . in my life. I might even have to say that I might

(d.o. = what?)
like another **<u>book</u>** and I have to say that it's going to be more interesting.

—Klarissa Martinez
Grade 8

96

INDIRECT OBJECTS

> " I fear his shifting moods. They show me something unstable inside of him, and " instability is dangerous.
>
> —From *Divergent* by Veronica Roth, found by Ben Brody

Teach it

1. Write this on the board

> Indirect objects
>
> action verb + what? = direct object
> to whom? = indirect object
>
> Ex:
>
> (indirect object) (d.o.)
> My daughter sends <u>me</u> <u>text</u>
> <u>messages</u> from the subway.

PRACTICE THE CONVERSATION:

A: Please read the sentence.

B: *My daughter sends <u>me</u> text messages from the subway.*

A: Let's start with the verb. What is it?

B: Sends. I sends, you sends, he sends.

A: Good. So next, how do we find the direct object? Do you remember?

B: Sends *what?*

A: Great. So what's the direct object?

B: Text messages.

A: Yes! Now how do we find the indirect object?

B: Sends text messages *to whom?*

A: So what's the indirect object?

B: To me. *Me* is the indirect object.

A: Let's give this student a hand! (What's the indirect student of that?)

B: This student!

A: That's pretty darned good.

2. **Explain:**

   We're going to talk about __indirect objects__. All sentences have subjects (either a noun or a pronoun) and verbs.

   Some sentences have direct objects, objects of the action. And some of these have __indirect objects__.

   One way to find the direct object is to locate the verb, say it, and then say **what?** *If there's also an* __indirect object__, *you ask* **to whom?**

   Confusing, right? Not when we try it out.

3. **Ask:** *Who will help find an __indirect object__ with me?* (Enact the conversation.)

   Whenever you write an __indirect object__, you can underline and label it.

   The underline means I intentionally made a grammatical choice here. The label above the word means that I know what this is, an __indirect object__.

4. **Say:** *Open to your grammar chart. Let's find __indirect objects__ and jot down an example.*

   Note: If the verb is not an *action* verb but a *being* verb, then what follows the verb won't be a direct object. It could be a predicate adjective or predicate nominative. Direct objects must follow an action verb. And without a direct object, there can be no indirect object. See Lesson 87, "Verbs," to review the difference between an action verb and a being verb.

Model it

5. Project the journal entry and read it.

6. Ask volunteers to read the sentences with the **indirect objects** aloud. Ask them to use the proofs, starting with the verb proof and then asking *verb what?* to find the direct object.

Practice it

7. **Say:** *In your journal today, try to write five **indirect objects**, underlining each use. Write the proof over each.*

April 10

Dear Tim,

Please return the book on theft and robbery that you took from me when you came over.

—An angered friend,

John

Dear John,

Your book on ungratitude was terrible; because I suffered the entire book, I will keep the books
(indirect object)
you lent **me.**

—A friend with indignation,

Tim

Dear Tim,
(indirect object)
I never lent **you** those books. You took them. Return them right now. You're interrupting my reading
(indirect object)
of A Book About Lying. Don't tell **me** it's not true.

—A person questioning your friendship,

John

Listen to me, John,
(indirect object)
You anger me like never before. It is extremely rude to send **me** a book titled How to Eliminate
(indirect object)
Anger. Besides, I read the first chapter and it is not helping. Send **me** something better.

—Your enemy,

Tim

—Michael Squire
Grade 8

97

GERUNDS

" Again and again I made the water prove its value by slicing through it, kicking " hard, pushing off, and diving under.

—From *Right Behind You* by Gail Giles, found by Alyssa Rico

Teach it

1. Write this on the board

> ### Gerunds
>
> We use this verb form as a noun.
> <u>Running, doing, being, going, playing</u>
>
> Ex:
>
> (gerund)
> <u>Talking</u> got them in trouble again.

2. **Explain:**

    Verbals are verbs doing the job of some other part of speech. That is, they are not acting as verbs.

    One type of verbal is a **gerund**. *A* **gerund** *is a verb in its i-n-g form that is used as a noun.*

    Whenever you write a verb that has an i-n-g on the end that is acting as a noun, underline it and label it **gerund**.

    *   *The underline means I intentionally made a grammatical choice here.*
    *   *The label above the word means that I know what this is, a* **gerund**.

3. **Ask:** *Now, who will demonstrate a* **gerund** *with me?* (Enact the conversations.)

4. **Say:** *Open to your grammar chart. In the verbals section, let's find* **gerunds** *and jot down an example.*

Model it

5. Project the journal entry and read it.

6. Ask volunteers to read the sentences with the **gerunds** aloud. Ask them to explain what a **gerund** is.

Practice it

7. **Say:** *In your journal today, try to work at least five **gerunds**, underlining each use. Write the proof over each one.*

March 24

Divergent!

(gerund)
Best movie ever! The action, tension, **fighting**. It was awesome and when I say awesome

(gerund)
I may or may not mean the **fighting**. Tris killed people (I want to say who but I don't know

if you read the book so I'm not going to tell you) and hurt people. People killed people

and hurt them. I'm not saying it is right to do that or that when the Dauntless hurt and

kill people it is "brave" but I am saying I was sitting at the movie theater and saw the

(gerund)
action start in the movie Divergent and I thought this was amazing, that **watching** is

kind of fascinating . . . for me. I'm more of that fighting, violence, action girl who likes

(gerund)   (gerund)
fighting and **seeing** it on screen. They didn't film the part when someone (not naming)

get stabbed in the eye with a butter knife. Again, violence isn't right, but we do watch it

for entertainment. Have you ever thought about what faction you would pick if you had

(gerund)
to? **Surviving** would be difficult. I think I would be Dauntless, only if I was divergent like

Tris and could hide it. If I could not hide it, then I'd have to run away before they kill me.

—Anael Ashkenazi
Grade 6

98

PARTICIPIAL PHRASES

> 66 Colored lights played over the dance floor, turning it into a multicolored fairyland 99 of blues and acid greens, hot pinks and golds.
>
> —From *City of Bones* by Cassandra Clare, found by Christian Westbrook

Teach it

1. Write this on the board

Participials:

We use this verb form as an adjective.

Ex:

(participle)

<u>Grilled</u> steak, <u>steamed</u> vegetables, <u>fried</u> potatoes, and <u>mouthwatering</u> cheesecake made us full and happy.

Participial phrases

a participle with more words; the whole phrase serves as an adjective.

Ex:

(participial phrase)

<u>cooked</u> over an open fire <u>drizzled</u> with chocolate <u>pleasing</u> millions daily

---

PRACTICE THE CONVERSATION:

A: Read the first example sentence, please.

B: *Grilled steak, steamed vegetables, fried potatoes, and mouthwatering cheesecake made us full and happy.*

A: Sounds good. Do you see any participles?

B: I do indeed. *Grilled* is a participle.

A: How do you know? What's a participle?

B: It's a verb, grill, and it has the ending –ed.

A: Is it acting like a verb in this sentence?

B: Nope, it's acting like an adjective.

A: How can you tell?

B: It describes *steak*.

A: Exactly. Do all participles end in –ed?

B: No. They can also end with –ing.

A: Do you see one of those?

B: *Mouthwatering* is one.

A: Excellent.

2. **Explain:**

Verbals are verbs doing the job of some other part of speech. That is, they are not acting as verbs.

Participles *are one type of verbal. A **participle** is a verb, often with an –ed or –ing ending, that is used as an* **adjective.**

*If it has additional words, it's a **participial phrase**.*

*Whenever you write a **participle** or **participial phrase**, underline and label it.*

- *The underline means I intentionally made a grammatical choice here.*
- *The label above the word means that I know what this is, a **participle**.*

3. **Ask:** *Who will demonstrate a **participle** with me?* (Enact the conversation.)

4. **Say:** *Open to your grammar chart. In the verbals section, let's find **participles** and jot down an example.*

Model it

5. Project the journal entry and read it.

6. Ask volunteers to read the sentences with the **participles** aloud. Ask them to explain what a **participle** is.

Practice it

7. **Say:** *In your journal today, try to use at least five **participles** or **participial phrases**, underlining each use. Write the proof over each one.*

January 30

Two days ago, I went to the orthodontist. They tightened my braces, and put a chain on

them to pull my teeth close together. It's pretty much the most painful experience I've

had involving my teeth. And that's saying a lot, because I chipped my tooth at the nerve

(participial phrase)
playing football. I hate remembering that day. It was on the day of my Bar Mitzvah, so

in all of our pictures, my smile is pretty weird. That event is still stuck in my mind: I can

(participial phrase)   (participial phrase)
picture Lee **stretching his arm to stiff-arm me**; and there I am, **running into his elbow**,

(participial phrase)   (participial phrase)
falling to the ground laughing, **hearing him exclaiming**, **"Oh (expletive), your tooth is**

(participle)   (participial phrase)   (participial phrase)
broken!" and **running inside**, **checking the tooth**, and **noticing its nice little bumps**, where

(participial phrase)
the beautiful half of my tooth used to sit so nicely, **enabling my glorious smile to shine**

(participial phrase)
with absolute perfection, and **allowing me to eat normally**. And now, it's gone. Since then

(participle)
the tooth was **fixed**. It's a filling because the real tooth couldn't be found. I kept thinking

about how Lee was so upset and apologetic. Even though I was without half a tooth, I was

(participial phrase)
touched by his sorrow. That was a strange day. Later we had our Bar Mitzvah party, as

this happened after the morning ceremony and before the evening party. It's all back to

normal. I got my tooth fixed the next day. That was a really crazy day!

—Phillip Kaplan
Grade 8

99

INFINITIVES

" I just don't like to be injected with strange substances. **"**

—From *Allegiant* by Veronica Roth, found by Claire Weingart

Teach it

1. Write this on the board

> ## Infinitives
>
> We use this verb form as a noun.
> <u>to go</u>, <u>to be</u>, <u>to do</u>, <u>to see</u> . . .
>
> Ex:
>
> (infinitive)
> I really love <u>to go</u> to the games.

PRACTICE THE CONVERSATION:
A: Will you please read the sentence?
B: *I really love to go to the games.*
A: Yes. Now, where is the infinitive?
B: *To go.*
A: Yes. How do you know that's an infinitive?
B: It starts with *to* and has a verb.
A: That's it?
B: Yep.
A: Good.

2. **Explain:**

   Verbals are verbs doing the job of some other part of speech. That is, they are not acting as verbs.

   *One type of verbal is an **infinitive**. An infinitive is a verb with the word **to** in front of it, like the examples on the board. It's most often used as a noun, as a thing.*

   *So whenever you write an **infinitive**, underline it and label it above the word.*

   - *The underline means I intentionally made a grammatical choice here.*
   - *The label above the word means that I know what this is, an **infinitive**.*

3. **Ask:** *Now, who will demonstrate an **infinitive** with me?* (Enact the conversation.)

4. **Say:** *Open to your grammar chart. In the verbals section, let's find **infinitives** and jot down an example.*

Model it

5. Project the journal entry and read it.

6. Ask volunteers to read the sentences with the **infinitives** aloud. Ask them to explain what an infinitive is each time.

Practice it

7. **Say:** *In your own journal, try to use at least five __infinitives__, underlining each use. Write the proof over each one.*

January 27

On Friday we had no school because it was too icy. They're saying that it might also ice

over tomorrow and Wednesday. I don't know if we'll miss school, but it'll for sure be very

cold. My family up north said the weather with the wind chill got down to almost −50

degrees. I can't even imagine what that feels like. I bet you can't be outside for more

than 2 minutes! I hope that we miss school, but then we have *(infinitive)* **to make** it up so I have

mixed opinions on the matter. There are two make-up days, but after that we have *(infinitive)* **to go**

into our summer break. My family up north have missed so many days of school. In my

family, I have two teachers up north, one in Minneapolis, Minnesota, and one in Madison,

Wisconsin. The one in Minnesota is a music/choir teacher, and the one in Wisconsin is

like a 2nd grade teacher. I really want *(infinitive)* **to go** and see them, but it's so cold! I can imagine

my cousins and I wanting *(infinitive)* **to play** football, and getting frostbite. *(infinitive)* **To be** in that kind of cold

could theoretically be life-threatening.

—Ilan Sonsino
Grade 8

---

100 PREDICATE NOMINATIVES

"That's my cat," I said "And she's a goddess, not a demon."

—From *The Red Pyramid* by Rick Riordan, found by Tamara Weiss

Teach it

1. Write this on the board

> ### Predicate nominatives
>
> This noun = <u>that noun</u>.
> That noun = <u>this noun</u>.
>
> Ex:
>
> My mom is the world's
> (predicate nominative)
> greatest <u>teacher</u>.
>
> The world's greatest teacher is
> (predicate nominative)
> <u>my mom</u>.

2. **Explain:**

   *You're about to find out all about **predicate nominatives**.*

   *You know how verbs can be either action or being? Well, this deals only with the nonaction **being verbs**, which we also call **linking verbs.***

   To be** is the most common one, but variations of **to be** include **to seem, to appear, to feel, to look, to prove, to remain.

   *These are all **linking verbs**—nonaction verbs— **being verbs.***

   *Any time the verb in a sentence is a **linking verb**, it might be followed by a noun.*

   *If you think of that **linking verb** as an equal sign, what follows it is the **predicate nominative**. If you switch the **predicate nominative** and the subject, they should still make sense.*

   *Look at the example sentence. The underline means I intentionally made a grammatical choice here. The proof above the word shows that I can identify that this is a **predicate nominative**.*

3. **Ask:** *Who will explore **predicate nominatives** with me?* (Enact the conversation.)

4. **Say:** *Open to your grammar chart and find **predicate nominatives**. Let's jot down an example on*

PRACTICE THE CONVERSATION:

A: Will you please read the first example sentence?

B: *My mom is the world's greatest teacher.*

A: Perfect. What is the verb in this sentence?

B: *Is.*

A: Can you prove that?

B: I is, you is, he is.

A: It works in one of those, so yep! *is* is the verb. And the subject of the sentence is what?

B: My mom.

A: Yes! So what is a predicate nominative?

B: It's a noun that comes after a verb like *is*. It's not an action verb. It's a state-of-being verb, aka a linking verb. So a predicate nominative just means the name in the back of the sentence. It kind of renames the subject.

A: Good job. So could you switch the subject and the predicate nominative?

B: You could. Yes. You could! Just like two sides of an equation.

A: How is that different from a direct object and an action verb?

B: You can't switch those. The dog bites you, or you bite the dog. They mean two different things.

A: Eww.

B: But in a predicate nominative, you *are* the dog, and the dog is you. They mean the same thing when you reverse them.

A: Well that makes it simple.

B: One more thing.

A: Yes?

B: A predicate nominative is always a noun. If it's an adjective, it's something else.

A: What?

B: A predicate adjective. But that's another story.

---

the chart.

Note: Pronouns, of course, could take the place of any noun anywhere. They are not included here just for "introductional" oversimplification. When students are starting to learn a new concept, it's best to keep it simple and introduce the wrinkles afterward or, even better, as the students bring them up.

Model it

5. Project the journal entry and read it.

6. Ask volunteers to read the sentences with the **predicate nominatives**. Ask them to explain what a predicate nominative is.

Practice it

7. **Say:** *In your journal today, try to use at least five **predicate nominatives**, underlining each use. Write the proof over each one.*

February 26

The field trip yesterday was so much fun! One of my favorite parts was **the audience**. It *(predicate nominative)*

(predicate nominative)
was a great **event**, watching the little kids bob their heads up and down while the Russian

music was playing. A lot of the Russian music would speed up in the middle of the song.

(predicate nominative)
Part of the program was **music** from Spain. There also was African music. The African

(predicate nominative)
music was probably my favorite **type** of music. The main vocalist said he was cool because

of the hat he was wearing. He also said that when we get home, he could just imagine

hundreds of kids asking their moms for hats and then a bunch of them wearing one. The

(predicate nominative)
field trip will become a nice **memory**.

—Nina De La Torre
Grade 7

PREDICATE ADJECTIVES

> **“** Mother and Father's voices were muffled and hard to make out. Grandfather's **”** was not to be heard at all. Grandmother's was surprisingly slurred.
>
> —From *Boy in the Striped Pajamas* by John Boyne,
> found by Zachary Prescott

Teach it

1. Write this on the board

Predicate adjectives

Proof:

The noun is an <u>adjective</u>.

Ex:

(predicate adjective)
That tree looks <u>ancient</u>.

PRACTICE THE CONVERSATION:

A: Will you please read the sentence?

B: *That tree looks ancient.*

A: Good. What's the verb here?

B: *Looks.* I look, you look, he looks.

A: Yes. Is it an action verb? or a being verb?

B: Hmmm . . . the tree looks . . . well, the tree doesn't have eyes. It just means the tree seemed ancient. It was ancient. So it's a being verb.

A: Perfect reasoning. So what part of speech is *ancient*?

B: Adjective. An ancient book, an ancient person, an ancient idea.

A: Yep. So what else does that make ancient?

B: It's a predicate adjective.

A: It is!

2. **Explain:**

   *You're about to find out all about **predicate adjectives**.*

   You know how verbs can be either action or being?

   *Well, this deals only with the nonaction **being verbs**. Being verbs are also called **linking verbs**.*

   ***To be** is the most common linking, or being, verb but variations of **to be** include*

to seem	to look
to appear	to prove
to feel	to remain

   These are all linking verbs, nonaction verbs—being verbs.

   *When the verb in a sentence is a linking verb, it might be followed by an adjective. This is called a **predicate adjective**.*

   Look at the example sentence:

   - *The underline means I intentionally made a grammatical choice here.*
   - *The proof above the word shows that I can identify that this is a **predicate adjective**.*

3. **Ask:** *Who will explore **predicate adjectives** with me?* (Enact the conversation.)

4. **Say:** *Open to your grammar chart and find **predicate adjectives**. Let's jot down an example on the chart.*

Model it

5. Project the journal entry and read it.

6. Ask volunteers to read the sentences with the **predicate adjectives**. Ask them to explain what a **predicate adjective** is.

Practice it

7. **Say:** *In your journal today, try to use at least five **predicate adjectives**, underlining each use. Write the proof over each one.*

October 24

(predicate adjective)
This pen is **erasable**! I like these a lot! Well, anyway, I got a 100 on my geometry pop

(predicate adjective)
quiz. We have a test tomorrow and I feel **confident**. I'm switching pens to see if the

eraser will erase on this one. Yaaa . . . no. It doesn't work. The other pen is just not

(predicate adjective)
good. You can erase it with your finger and it is hard to write smoothly. I'm putting it

(predicate adjective)
back on Ms. Bernabei's desk. I don't like this pen either because it is **smeary**, but oh

well. At least it enhances the smoothness by letting out so much ink. I guess you can

(predicate adjective)
say this pen is **agile.** It is an asset to my writing. I'm gonna cull the other pens. I'll

desist from using them.

—Lee Kaplan
Grade 8

APPENDIX

KEEPERS 101 CHART—BLANK

Common errors
- They're Proof
- There Proof
- Their Proof
- You're Proof
- Your Proof
- We're Proof
- Were Proof
- Where Proof
- Already Proof
- All ready Proof
- All right Proof
- Used to Proof
- Me/I Proof
- S/V Agr Proof

Too Proof · Two Proof · To Proof · It's Proof · Its Proof · Who Proof · Whom Proof · Who's Proof · Whose Proof · Our Proof · Are Proof · Than Proof · Then Proof · A lot Proof

- Less Proof
- Fewer Proof
- Lie Proof
- Lay Proof
- Should've Proof
- Accept Proof
- Except Proof
- Loose Proof
- Lose Proof
- Affect Proof
- Effect Proof

Punctuation
- Apostrophes in contractions
- Apostrophes in possessions (Singular)
- Apostrophes in possessions (Plural)
- No apostrophes on plurals
- No apostrophes in verbs ending in "s"
- Quotations: question marks inside
- Quotations: ending in punctuation
- Hyphenated adjectives
- Punctuating dialogue: chicken dance
- Commas in a series
- Commas in a letter
- Commas in appositives
- Commas after beginning phrases/clauses
- Commas before ending phrases/clauses
- Commas with direct address
- Commas in a date
- Commas between city and state
- Colons

Parts of speech
- Nouns Proof
- Verbs proof
- Adjectives proof
- Adverbs proof
- Pronouns: sub | obj
- Prepositions
- Interjections
- Conjunctions FANBOYS AAAWWWUBIS

Sentence wringer
1. Statement?
2. Verb?
3. How many? Joined how? — no / yes

Spelling rules
- Silent E
- Words ending in Y
- Words ending in consonants
- I before E
- Ce/ci/ge/gi

Capitalization
- Proper nouns
- Proper adjectives
- Letter closing
- First words in sentences
- First words in quotations
- Religions
- Titles

Pitchforking
- actions
- nouns
- ba-da-bing
- exclamations
- descriptions
- sounds
- smells
- contrasts
- participial phrases
- absolutes

Verbals
- Participial phrases
- Infinitives
- Gerunds
- Direct objects
- Indirect objects
- Predicate nominatives
- Predicate adjectives

KEEPERS 101 CHART—FILLED OUT

Top header row (homophones/usage):

Word	Proof	handwritten
Too	Proof	so/also
Two	Proof	2
To	Proof	
It's	Proof	it is
Its	Proof	his
Who	Proof	he
Whom	Proof	him
Who's	Proof	who is
Whose	Proof	his
Our	Proof	your
Are	Proof	were
Then	Proof	now
Than	Proof	More
A lot	Proof	whole

Common errors

Word	Proof	handwritten
They're	Proof	they are
There	Proof	here
Their	Proof	our
You're	Proof	you are
Your	Proof	our
We're	Proof	we are
Were	Proof	are
Where	Proof	here
Already / yet	Proof	not ready
All right / all	Proof	wrong
All ready	Proof	not ready
Used to	Proof	
Me/I	Proof	me
S/V Agr.	Proof	we were / we was

Punctuation

- Commas in a series — cats, dogs, ...
- Commas in a letter — Dear Jake, ... Sincerely,
- Apostrophes in contractions — don't, didn't = do not
- Apostrophes in possessions (Singular) — dog's bowl
- Commas in appositives — Nina, my friend,
- Apostrophes in possessions (Plural) — dogs' bowls
- Commas after beginning phrases/clauses — Every day,
- No apostrophes on plurals — 3 dogs
- Commas before ending phrases/clauses
- No apostrophes in verbs ending in "s" — goes
- Commas with direct address — Mom,
- Quotations: question marks inside — "What?!"
- Commas in a date — Oct. 10, 2014
- Quotations: ending in punctuation — "Oh."
- Commas between city and state — San Antonio, Texas
- Hyphenated adjectives — red-hot
- Colons Like this: 1, 2, 3.
- Punctuating dialogue; chicken dance

Parts of speech

- **Nouns** — some ___
- **Verbs** — I ___, he ___s
- **Adjectives** — a book, a person, a idea
- **Adverbs** — ran when? where? how?
- **Pronouns** — sub / obj — I, she, he, her / we, thou, us, then
- **Preposition** — to what
- **Interjections** — no! oh...
- **Conjunctions** — FANBOYS; i AAAWWBUIS — After, as, while, until, because

Predicate nominatives — she is Nina
Predicate adjectives — she is nice
Direct objects
Indirect objects

Sentence winger

1. Statement? — Psst.
2. Verb?
3. How many? Joined how? — no / yes

Spelling rules

- Silent E — hope = hoping
- Words ending in Y — city = cities
- Words ending in consonants — hop = hopping
- I before E — thief, receive, weigh
- Ce/ci ge/gi — ace/age

Capitalization

- Proper nouns — Maggie
- Proper adjectives — Chinese food
- Letter closing — Sincerely,
- First words in sentences — B
- First words in quotation — "If..."
- Religions — Catholic
- Titles — Mrs.

Pitchforking

- actions
- nouns
- ba-da-bing
- exclamations — No! No! No!
- descriptions — big, red, fluffy
- sounds
- smells
- contrasts
- participial phrases — ing... ing...
- absolutes — N + ing

Verbals

- Participial phrases — tired of ing
- Infinitives — to be
- Gerunds — swimming

PARAGRAPH OVERHAUL—BLANK

Name _____

Paragraph Overhaul

_____
_____
_____
_____
_____

List the sentences, just as they are.

1. _____
2. _____
3. _____
4. _____

Fix them and list.

1. _____
2. _____
3. _____
4. _____

Reshape them into a paragraph.

_____
_____
_____
_____

Available for download from **www.resources.corwin.com/bernabeigrammar**

PARAGRAPH OVERHAUL–KLARISSA

Name _____

Paragraph Overhaul

The Soft Song
by Klarissa Martinez

I played a soft song. On my piano.

It's hard playing with two hands. It gets easier you have

to practice.

List the
sentences,
just as
they are.

1. _____
2. _____
3. _____
4. _____

Fix them
and list.

1. _____
2. _____
3. _____
4. _____

Reshape
them
into a
paragraph.

PARAGRAPH OVERHAUL—PHIL

Name _____

Paragraph Overhaul

*Hanging Out With Brian
by Phil Silberman*

I sat down on the sofa in Brian's den.

I opened a Monster I took a sip. I felt glad for caffeine.

And for seeing my friend again too.

List the sentences, just as they are.

1. _____
2. _____
3. _____
4. _____

Fix them and list.

1. _____
2. _____
3. _____
4. _____

Reshape them into a paragraph.

_____
_____
_____
_____
_____

PARAGRAPH OVERHAUL—TORI

Name _____

Paragraph Overhaul

Mother's Day Lunch
by Tori Shiver

As we walked to our table. I looked at other people's food. I saw potatoes and steaks. I saw fish platters. I decided I wanted fish. Not steak.

List the sentences, just as they are.

1. _____
2. _____
3. _____
4. _____

Fix them and list.

1. _____
2. _____
3. _____
4. _____

Reshape them into a paragraph.

_____
_____
_____
_____

PARTS OF SPEECH SHEET—BLANK

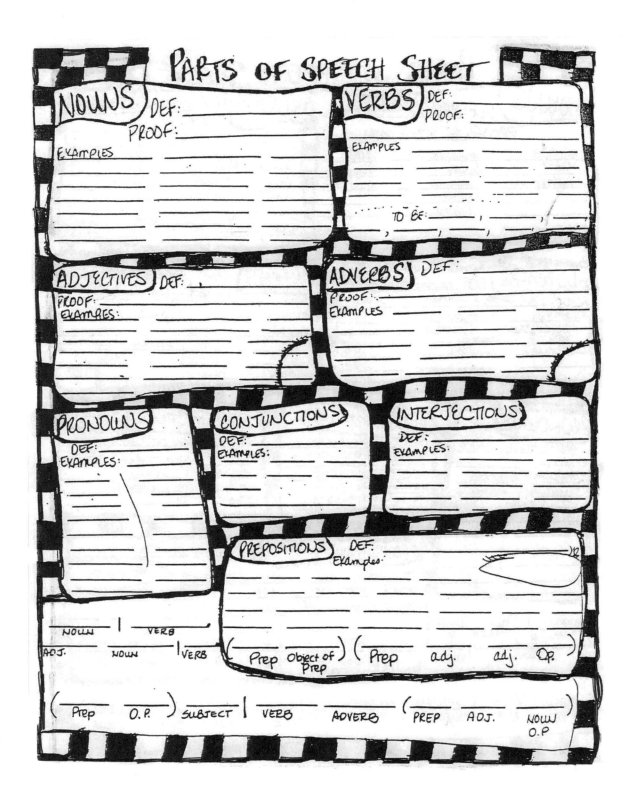

PARTS OF SPEECH SHEET—FILLED OUT

PARTS OF SPEECH SHEET

NOUNS
DEF: Persons, Places, things
PROOF: a —, the —, some —s.

EXAMPLES
Mary — home — pen
principal — forest — shoe
mother — France — beauty
Champion — The Hobbit
President Lincoln

VERBS
DEF: action or being
PROOF: I —, you —, he —s.

EXAMPLES
fry — announce
act — restore
dash

TO BE: am, are, is
was, were, be, been, being.

ADJECTIVES
DEF: describes nouns
PROOF: a — book, a — person, a — idea
EXAMPLES:
humongous — red
delicious — red-hot
dusty — old
first — Spanish

A
AN
THE

ADVERBS
DEF: ADDS ON TO VERBS
PROOF: Ran how? Ran where? Ran when?
EXAMPLES
quickly — home — currently
well — away — soon
very — off — never
gracefully

NOT

PRONOUNS
DEF: Stands for nouns
EXAMPLES:
Subject | Objects
I, you, he | me, you, him
she, it | her, it, us
we, they | them

— who — | — whom —

CONJUNCTIONS
DEF: joins things.
EXAMPLES: FANBOYS
for and nor but or yet so
AAWWWUBIS:
after, as, when, wherever, until,
because, if, since

INTERJECTIONS
attention words or
DEF: spelled-out body reactions
EXAMPLES: Hey! — Well,
Yep! — Golly! — Hey lady..
ACK! — Ouch... — yes,
Um...

PREPOSITIONS
DEF: starts a prepositional phrase
Examples:
to — with — of — on — around — NO VERBS
for — off — over — under — beside — from
near — because of

Boys | hit | what
NOUN | VERB | D.O.
Big | kids | rule
ADJ. | NOUN | VERB

(to | what) (with | six | flying | geese)
Prep | Object of Prep | Prep | adj. | adj. | O.P.

(From | Mars) messages | suddenly | appeared (in | Ben's | journal.)
Prep | O.P. | SUBJECT | ADVERB | VERB | PREP | ADJ. | NOUN O.P.

STATE TESTING

The standards and assessments landscape in the field of education is evolving as never before. Current state standards and planned assessments are both under intense scrutiny in many states, some involving legislative action. It will be imperative to check state websites on a regular basis for the latest information in this rapidly changing area.

For the State by State Standards and Assessments database, located on this book's companion website (**www.resources.corwin.com/bernabeigrammar**), all states were contacted via e-mail (some twice), and 32 states responded. In some cases, state standards are in the middle of being revised or rewritten, and assessment decisions must wait on these documents. In other states, assessments are currently being developed that will be used in spring 2015. As South Carolina candidly replied, "We do not know yet the tests that students in Grades 3–11 will be taking" (Dr. Susan Creighton, Office of Assessment).

Even though many states participated in field tests in the spring of 2014 from the two major consortia, SBAC (Smarter Balanced Assessment Consortium) and PARCC (Partnership for Assessment of Readiness for College and Careers), a few states are still deciding whether or not to go ahead with the SBAC and PARCC assessments for spring 2015.

To correlate the standards for English/Language Arts with this, the starting point was to match the lessons with the Common Core State Standards in Grades 3–11. Over 40 states still use these documents as the basis for their own state standards, although some states have included additions. Next, the lessons were correlated with several states that have modified the CCSS or have written their own standards. Grades 4 and 7 were used as a representative sample. Every lesson in this book connected with one or more of the language standards.

Finally, sample test questions were collected from state-released tests to show the many ways in which the grammar skills can be assessed. Clearly, the lessons provided in this book are right on target with both standards and assessments. *Grammar Keepers* will be an invaluable resource for English/Language Arts teachers everywhere.

—Judith Reimer

Access State Correlation Testing Charts at
www.resources.corwin.com/bernabeigrammar

A SAGE Company

Corwin is committed to improving education for all learners by publishing books and other professional development resources for those serving the field of PreK–12 education. By providing practical, hands-on materials, Corwin continues to carry out the promise of its motto: **"Helping Educators Do Their Work Better."**

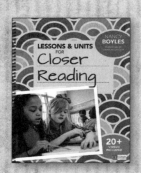

BECAUSE ALL TEACHERS ARE LEADERS

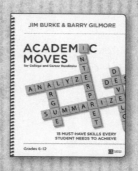